Best Hikes Near
CHARLOTTE

JENNIFER PHARR DAVIS

FALCONGUIDES

GUILFORD, CONNECTICUT
HELENA, MONTANA

AN IMPRINT OF GLOBE PEQUOT PRESS

To my husband—always.

To buy books in quantity for corporate use
or incentives, call **(800) 962–0973**
or e-mail **premiums@GlobePequot.com**.

FALCONGUIDES®

FalconGuides is an imprint of Globe Pequot Press.
Falcon, FalconGuides, and Outfit Your Mind are registered trademarks of Morris Book Publishing, LLC.

Maps: Design Maps Inc. © Morris Book Publishing LLC
TOPO! Explorer software and SuperQuad source maps courtesy of National Geographic Maps. For information about TOPO! Explorer, TOPO!, and Nat Geo Maps products, go to www.topo.com or www.natgeomaps.com.
Interior photos: Jennifer Pharr Davis
Text design: Sheryl P. Kober
Project editor: Julie Marsh
Layout: Melissa Evarts

Library of Congress Cataloging-in-Publication Data

Davis, Jennifer Pharr.
  Best hikes near Charlotte / Jennifer Pharr Davis.
    p. cm.
  Includes index.
  ISBN 978-0-7627-7148-6
  1. Hiking–North Carolina–Charlotte Region–Guidebooks. 2. Trails–North Carolina–Charlotte Region–Guidebooks. 3. Charlotte (N.C.)–Guidebooks. I. Title.
  GV199.42.N662C54 211
  917.56'76—dc23
                                                                    2011024256
Printed in the United States of America
10 9 8 7 6 5 4 3 2 1

Contents

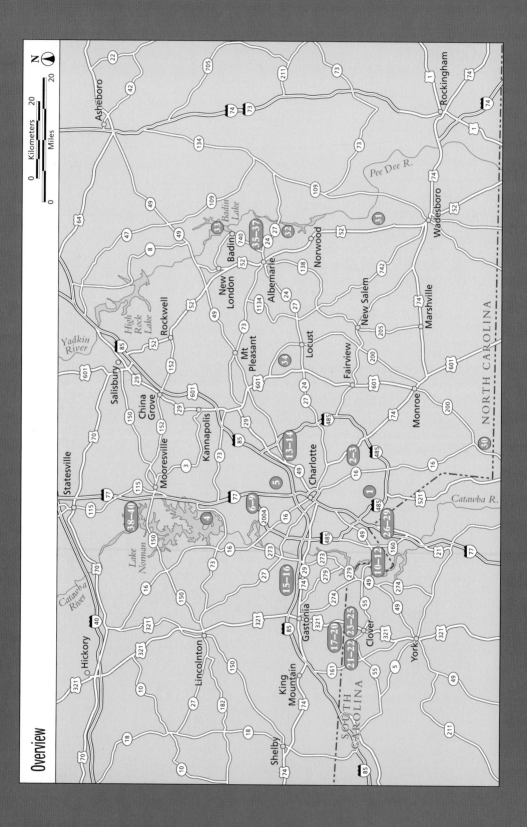

Overview

Acknowledgments

I am grateful to the many park and preserve employees in the Charlotte area who dedicate themselves to protecting the region's wilderness and educating others concerning its significance. These people have very demanding jobs, and they do a great job managing the parks and keeping people safe—from themselves. Despite their hectic schedules and demanding work environments, the men and women who govern the trails mentioned in this book took the time to help with hike selection, descriptions, and the final approval of this guidebook. They did this because they care about getting people to experience the outdoors.

I also want to give a special nod to the private organizations in Charlotte that help to preserve and protect the wonderful trails near the city. In particular, the Carolina Thread Trail, Catawba Lands Conservancy, and the Trust for Public Land work very hard to create hiking trails and promote those paths within the community. These organizations also work very hard to create a long-term vision that strives to protect potential hiking trail corridors that can be developed in the future.

Also, I want to thank the trail maintainers and volunteers who help to keep these paths accessible to the general public. Without their generous donation of time, many of Charlotte's trails would not exist or would become impassible. If you ever see a volunteer trail crew working on the path, please thank them or, better yet, join them.

I wish to recognize my grandparents, Jones and Polly Pharr. My visits to their farm outside of Charlotte comprise some of my best childhood memories. Daily excursions on old gold-mining trails and walks at dusk to search for deer grazing in the open fields fostered within me a love for hiking in the piedmont region of North Carolina. I also want to thank my father, who kept me company on many hiking trips to Charlotte and who continually supports my passion for the outdoors.

Most of all, I want to thank my husband, whose love, encouragement, and trust allows me to pursue my dreams and the trails. I am looking forward to seeing where our path leads.

Introduction

My earliest childhood memories of hiking come from my grandparents' farm outside of Charlotte. I will never forget the joy and anticipation I felt upon spotting deer at dusk with my grandmother or spending hours searching under shrubs and bushes for "hoppy toads" to take to my grandfather. My grandfather was an avid outdoorsman, and he tried his hardest to teach me the skills of marksmanship and successful casting. However, I never cared much for shooting or hooking an animal—I just wanted to find them and pet them. I'll never forget seeing my first wild turkey, or shrieking and running away when I found a black snake in the woods.

As I grew older I supplemented my search for animals with a more selfish pursuit. My grandparents would tell me stories of central North Carolina's gold rush and then take me on hikes to abandoned mines on the outskirts of their property. I used to dream of finding a huge gold nugget, one that was too big to carry, and I scoured every quartz rock and stream to try to find my prize. (It was entertaining to

A trail sign points to all the highlights at Reed Gold Mine
(hike 34).

explore the trails near Charlotte as an adult and still want to examine every glossy white rock I passed for a vein of gold running through it—some dreams never die.) My grandparents never discouraged my pursuit—they simply asked me not to fall into any old mine shafts . . . and to share a part of the proceeds if I found anything.

Often my grandmother and grandfather would come into the woods with me. On these long strolls together, they taught me the difference between hardwood and pine trees. Then, back at the house, they explained that they used pine chips to help start fires in their fireplace and then used aged wood such as oak and maple to keep the flames alive. They conveyed that the forest and the animals were both gifts and a resource, and it was our job to care for them.

I am forever grateful for my grandparents instilling a love for the outdoors in me. They taught me that the great outdoors was a safe place to play and that most of life's major lessons could be learned on a walk in the woods. That love exploded in my adult life. It has become my passion and profession to pass on those lessons that my grandparents taught me to a society that is obsessed with cell phones, computers, and traveling at 65 miles per hour.

A wooden boardwalk travels through the wetlands at Four-Mile Creek Greenway (hike 1).

The intricacies woven into the Charlotte landscape have the ability to turn a short stroll in the woods into a memory that will last forever. Looking back at my childhood escapades, I never considered my adventures to be "hiking trips," yet each separate occasion took me several miles into the woods. I still consider Charlotte hiking to be far more than just exercise. My time in the woods can be better classified as an adventure, a history lesson, a scavenger hunt, or a peaceful retreat.

Charlotte-area hiking is unique in that almost every trail travels on, by, or near a significant historical site. Whether it is a 200-year-old homestead, abandoned mine shaft, Revolutionary battlefield, or a Native American trading route, the trails help communicate our history as a people by revealing insights into our past.

The piedmont region is also significant due to its diverse ecological environment. Situated halfway between the mountains and coast of North Carolina, the Charlotte-area forests are a collision of pine and hardwood trees. These trees show the effects of hurricanes and tornadoes that periodically ravage the piedmont, but also display the adaptive powers of Mother Nature as the strewn and fallen trees have created the ideal environment for many woodland birds, as well as provided cover for larger animals such as deer, bobcats, and coyote. The multiple lakes and rivers in the region also provide homes for migrating winter waterfowl and afford lodging to beavers and river otters throughout the year.

And although many Charlotte residents like to travel to the beach or to the mountains for vacation, they are surrounded with enough trails to keep them happy and hiking throughout the rest of the year. The city of Charlotte and Mecklenburg County have an excellent collection of nature preserves. These preserves are varied in terrain and attractions and—no matter what side of the city you live on—there is a good chance that you can drive to a nature preserve in fifteen minutes.

Charlotte is also fortunate to have several state parks within an hour's drive of the city. Crowders Mountain, Kings Mountain, Lake Norman, and Morrow Mountain not only offer day-hiking trails, but they also contain campgrounds and recreational opportunities that can keep you occupied and engaged for days at a time.

There is also a smattering of other places to hike and learn near the Queen City, including a national military park, national wildlife refuge, national forest, the U.S. National Whitewater Center, and a state historic site. Add the regional parks and greenways to the mix, and you will become overwhelmed with all the outdoor walking options. (Luckily this guidebook keeps them straight for you!)

The hiking terrain surrounding Charlotte can range from flat-shoreline strolls to a strenuous mountain ascent, but it is most often categorized by the rolling hills found between the extremes. However, whether a hike is categorized as "easy" or "strenuous," arriving prepared at the trailhead can mean the difference between an "enjoyable" or "less enjoyable" excursion.

Springtime's new growth and wildflowers along with the fall's colorful foliage make transitional times the preferred seasons to hike in the piedmont region. This is also a great time to look for wildlife. Animals often are out and about during the spring and fall months, looking for food before or after a long, cold winter. The weather during these two seasons is phenomenal. During the spring and fall, the average daytime lows are in the 50s F with highs in the 80s, but no matter how perfect the day appears when you leave the house, always, always, hike with extra food, water, and clothing.

If you hike year-round, be especially thoughtful when arranging your summer treks. Try to schedule your summer hikes on trails that are well shaded with leaf cover, and if possible, schedule your hike for the early morning or evening to avoid the midday heat. Several of the hikes in this guidebook border a lake that is open to recreational swimming in the summer—consider incorporating a quick dip into your summer hiking route to keep your body temperature regulated. Most important, no matter the distance or difficulty of the hike, be sure to bring lots of water and a bottle of sunscreen.

Something that always enhances your time on the trail is knowledge. Consider bringing a birding or wildflower identification book with you to learn more about the forest. Or better yet, consider joining a local club or group that can help you learn about the surrounding plants and animals. Many of these hikes are located near a nature center, where a ranger or informational display may provide new information.

If you are comfortable hiking and enjoy the routes near Charlotte, then consider taking a friend or family member with you on the trail. Exposing someone

Dragonfly Pond is beautiful even when partially frozen (hike 14).

to the natural resources in the area is one of the best ways to increase awareness and encourage people to become active and invested in the outdoors. On the other hand, if you do not feel comfortable hiking alone and are looking for a hiking partner or group, there are several groups in Charlotte that will take you under their wing and include you on group outings, such as the Carolina Bergs. They have been hiking the trails near Charlotte for nearly forty years.

Finally, consider that there are many ways to enjoy the trails. You can hike by yourself or with a group, you can hike fast or slow, you can take pictures or identify plants, you can take lots of rest stops or soldier on. As long as you are obeying the rules of the governing trail bodies, respecting others, staying within your physical limits, and leaving the trail in the same (or better) shape than how you found it, you should have an amazing experience in the woods.

For me, the task of compiling this guidebook provided the opportunity to return to my childhood wonderland. Despite the 9,000 miles I have hiked outside of Charlotte and the six continents through which I have trekked, the woodlands of central North Carolina—the vegetation, the animals, the historic significance of the area—remind me of why I originally fell in love with hiking and have restored my childhood awe once again.

The Itusi Trail travels through the middle of a dense lycopodium thicket (hike 40).

Charlotte is technically classified as a Humid Subtropical Climate Zone, and for a hiker that translates into year-round hiking! With cool winters, inviting springs, hot summers, and colorful falls, the trails in Charlotte can be enjoyed in any season.

On average Charlotte receives approximately 44 inches of rain per year. Unlike several regions where there is a defined "wet" and "dry" season, the precipitation in Charlotte is equally dispersed throughout the year and the majority of days fall within the sunny and warm category. For the most part hiking can be pursued and enjoyed during the occasional rainstorm, but hikers should be weary of being caught in one of the infrequent but nonetheless potential ice or snow storms that occur in winter and the more common thunderstorms that arrive in the warmer months.

Typically Charlotte only receives 4 to 5 inches of snow per year but can more often be subjected to a wintery mix, which results in icy patches and heavy tree limbs falling on the trails. Because of the mild winter weather in Charlotte, hikers sometimes take for granted encroaching cold fronts and changing weather patterns, which then become threatening to an underdressed hiker. It is important to hike with warm layers and wind protection in the winter, as hypothermia can be a threat to the unprepared hiker. In Charlotte average lows in the winter stay in the 30s F with daytime highs typically reaching the 50s or low 60s F.

During the summer hikers will need to consider the heat and humidity that

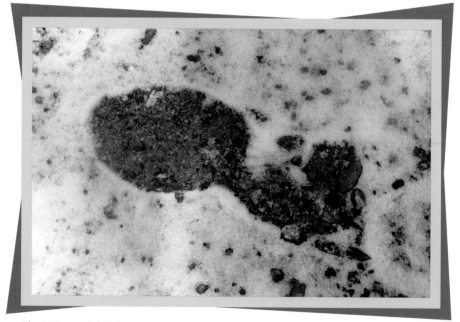

A boot print was left in the snow.

often engulf the Queen City. With highs that can easily reach the 100s, midday hiking in the warmer months can be a dangerous pursuit. Heat exhaustion, heat-stroke, and dehydration are strong possibilities in the Charlotte region.

FLORA AND FAUNA

Charlotte has a wide variety of plants and animals that can be found on the trails. The forests in this region are predominantly categorized as bottomland hard-wood forests, mixed pine and hardwood forests, and upland pine forests. A bottomland hardwood forest is classified as a predominant mix of deciduous trees that live in an alluvial plain, typically near water. Upland pine forests are found at an elevation that rises above the alluvial plain and consists of coniferous trees. Most of the woods around Charlotte, regardless of their location, are a mix of pine and hardwood trees.

Before settlers arrived in the piedmont region, the forests here were predominantly comprised of hardwood trees. However, there was also a lot of open farming and grazing land, and as many of these open spaces reforested, the fast-growing pines that dominate the nearby coastal region crept into the piedmont region and in many instances took over. Today, the most common trees in the forests near Charlotte include oak, hickory, maple, sourwood, sycamore, sweet gum, and beech, along with longleaf, shortleaf, loblolly, and Virginia pine.

A wild ginger plant emerges from under the leaf cover.

The wildflowers in the region are copious. They start poking their shoots through the cold earth in late February, and several species remain well into November. There are several non-native wildflowers found on trails near Charlotte, resulting from nearby urban flower beds. Native wildflowers include wild indigo, cardinal flowers, sunflowers, goldenrod, and asters.

Animals are abundant within the woods surrounding Charlotte. However, human threats such as urban sprawl and hunting have herded much of the wildlife into state parks and preserves. This increases the hiker's odds of enjoying animal encounters.

It is common in the Charlotte area to observe deer, wild turkeys, foxes, beavers, chipmunks, and squirrels. If you are hiking in the early or late hours of the day, it is also possible to spot raccoons, opossums, skunks, bobcats, and coyotes.

And no matter how cute these critters may appear, remember that it is never appropriate to approach or to feed a wild animal—after all, these animals are "wild" and can pose a threat to humans. Furthermore, there is a good chance that our tasty trail snacks might be harmful to the digestive system of a wild animal.

The piedmont of North Carolina also plays home to a wide variety of reptiles and birds. Many lizards, turtles, frogs, and toads roam the forest undergrowth, as do snakes, both poisonous and nonpoisonous. (Most of the snakes in the area are nonpoisonous and nonaggressive, but if bitten by a snake, seek medical attention immediately.) The birds of the region include endangered eagles, hawks, rap-

A Canada goose visits the Cross-Country Course (hike 3).

tors, and many smaller songbirds. Along the rivers and lakes, it is common to spot heron, ducks, and geese.

Also on a very important note, be sure to carry bug spray on all the hikes, especially on trails near water, as the moisture and warm weather combine to support insect breeding grounds, which flourish during the spring and early summer months.

WILDERNESS RESTRICTIONS/REGULATIONS

The following government and private organizations manage most of the public lands described in this guide, and they can provide further information on these hikes and other trails in their service areas. Please note that none of the hikes included in this book allow dogs to roam off-leash.

- **North Carolina State Parks,** Department of Parks and Recreation, 1615 MSC, Raleigh 27699; (919) 713-4181; www.ncparks.gov; parkinfo@ncmail. net. A complete listing of state parks is available on the website, along with park brochures and maps.

- **Mecklenburg County Park and Recreation Department,** 5841 Brookshire Blvd., Charlotte 28216; (704) 336-3854; www.charmeck.org/departments/park+and+rec/home.htm. A full directory of Charlotte parks, greenways, and nature preserves is available on the website, along with facility maps and information.

- **National Forests in North Carolina,** 160 Zillicoa St., Suite A, Asheville 28801; (828) 257-4200; www.fs.usda.gov/nfsnc; mailroom_r8_north_carolina_@fs.fed.us. This organization manages the Uwharrie National Forest, which includes Badin Lake and the Uwharrie Recreation Trail.

- **NC Historic Sites,** Dobbs Building, 430 N. Salisbury St., Suite 2050, Raleigh 27603; www.nchistoricsites.org; ncsites@ncder.gov. This website gives information and shares the historic significance of Reed Gold Mine.

- **National Park Service Southeast Region,** 100 Alabama St. SW, 1924 Building, Atlanta, GA 30303; (404) 507-5603; www.nps.org. This body is responsible for governing national parks in the Southeast, including Kings Mountain National Military Park.

National Recreation Trails in this area include Uwharrie Recreation Trail in Uwharrie National Forest and the Kings Mountain National Recreation Trail, which makes a large loop through Kings Mountain State Park and Kings Mountain National Military Park in South Carolina. More information on the Uwharrie Recreation Trail can be found at www.fs.usda.gov/nfsnc. To find out more about the Kings Mountain National Recreation Trail, visit either www.scprt.com or www.ncparks.gov.

For the purposes of this guide, the best hikes near Charlotte are confined to a 1½-hour drive from downtown Charlotte. The majority of hikes are located in the outskirts of Mecklenburg County as well as the neighboring counties of York, Gaston, Iredell, and Cabarrus. The most distant hikes are in the Uwharrie Mountains of Stanley and Moore County.

Charlotte is a maze of connecting highways, interstates, and ongoing road construction. The main arteries used to access the best hikes near Charlotte outside the city limits are I-85 (north–south) and I-77 (north–south) as well as US 74 (west), NC 24/27 (east), and NC 49 (east and west). Furthermore, the I-485 bypass can serve as a tool to create faster and more direct routes to several of the hike trailheads. It is somewhat confusing that I-485 is labeled "inner" and "outer." Just remember, inner means clockwise, and outer means counterclockwise.

If you use major roads, US highways, or state highways to access your hike, be warned: Charlotte roads often change names along their routes. It is smart to look at a map before driving to your trailhead. The roads in downtown Charlotte and the surrounding area form an abstract grid system that can sometimes help you find your way. However, if at any point you feel lost, it is recommended that you stop and ask for directions.

The Charlotte Area Transit System (CATS) offers bus and light-rail services throughout the greater Charlotte metropolitan area, with service to suburban cities including North Highlands, Roseville, Folsom, Rancho Cordova, and Elk Grove. For more information: Call Center: (704) 336-7433 (RIDE); customer service e-mail: telltransit@charlottenc.gov; website www.ridetransit.org.

A hairy seed pod rests on a wooden log at Pee Dee National Wildlife Refuge (hike 31).

How to Use This Guide

Take a close enough look and you'll find that this guide contains just about everything you'll ever need to choose, plan for, enjoy, and survive a hike near Charlotte. Stuffed with useful Queen City information, *Best Hikes Near Charlotte* features forty mapped and cued hikes. Here's an outline of the book's major components:

Each section begins with an **introduction to the region,** in which you're given a sweeping look at the lay of the land. Each hike then starts with a short **summary** of the hike's highlights. These quick overviews give you a taste of the hiking adventures to follow. You'll learn about the trail terrain and what surprises each route has to offer. Many chapters also include a kid-friendly recommendation that provides parents with a quick reference for keeping their youngster engaged.

Following the overview you'll find the **hike specs:** quick, nitty-gritty details of the hike. Most are self-explanatory, but here are some details on others:

Distance: The total distance of the recommended route—one-way for loop hikes, the round-trip on an out-and-back or lollipop hike, point-to-point for a shuttle. Options are additional.

Hiking time: The average time it will take to cover the route. It is based on the total distance, elevation gain, and condition and difficulty of the trail. Your fitness level will also affect your time.

Mossy rocks and fallen leaves adorn a trickling creek (hike 10).

Difficulty: Each hike has been assigned a level of difficulty. The rating system was developed from several sources and personal experience. These levels are meant to be a guideline only and may prove easier or harder for different people depending on ability and physical fitness.

- **Easy** hikes are generally short and flat and can be completed within a short period of time.

- **Moderate** hikes involve increased distance and relatively mild changes in elevation, and may take several hours to complete.

- **More challenging** hikes feature some steep stretches, greater distances, and generally could take a full morning or afternoon to finish.

Trail surface: General information about what to expect underfoot.

Best season(s): General information on the best time of year to hike.

Other trail users: Indicates whether you'll be sharing the trail with horseback riders, mountain bikers, inline skaters, etc.

Canine compatibility: Know the trail regulations before you take your dog hiking with you. Dogs are not allowed off-leash on any of the hiking trails in this book.

Land status: National forest, county open space, national park wilderness, etc.

Fees and permits: Whether you need to carry any money with you for park entrance fees and permits.

Maps: This is a list of other maps to supplement the maps in this book. USGS maps are the best source for accurate topographical information, but the local park map may show more recent trails. Use both.

Trail contacts: This is the location, phone number, and website for the local land manager(s) in charge of all the trails within the selected hike. Before you head out, get trail access information, or contact the land manager after your visit if you see problems with trail erosion, damage, or misuse.

Special considerations: This section calls your attention to specific trail hazards, like hunting seasons or a lack of water.

The **Finding the trailhead** section gives you dependable driving directions to where you'll want to park. **The Hike** is the meat of the chapter. Detailed and honest, it's a carefully researched impression of the trail. It also often includes lots of area history, both natural and human. Under **Miles and Directions,** mileage cues identify all turns and trail name changes, as well as points of interest. **Options** are also given for many hikes to make your journey shorter or longer depending on the amount of time you have. The **Hike Information** section provides information on local events and attractions, restaurants, hiking tours, and hiking organizations.

Don't feel restricted to the routes and trails that are mapped herein. Be adventurous and use this guide as a platform to discover new routes for yourself. One of the simplest ways to begin this is to just turn the map upside down and hike any route in reverse. The change in perspective is often fantastic, and the hike should feel quite different. With this in mind, it'll be like getting two distinctly different hikes on each map. For your own purposes, you may wish to copy the route directions onto a small sheet of paper to help you while hiking, or photocopy the map and cue sheet to take with you. Otherwise, just slip the whole book in your backpack and take it all with you. Enjoy your time in the outdoors and remember to pack out what you pack in.

HOW TO USE THE MAPS

Overview map: This map shows the location of each hike in the area by hike number.

Route map: This is your primary guide to each hike. It shows all of the accessible roads and trails, points of interest, water, landmarks, and geographical features. The selected route is highlighted, and directional arrows point the way. Remember though, it's best to grab a park map or bring a USGS topo map for additional and more detailed information.

A green spring vine climbs up the smooth trunk of a beech tree.

Trail Finder

Hike No.	Hike Name	Best Hikes for Children	Best Hikes for Views	Best Hikes for Water Lovers	Best Hikes for Wildlife	Best Hikes for Historians	Best Hikes for After Work
1	Lower McAlpine Creek, McMullen Creek, and Four-Mile Creek Greenway						●
2	McAlpine Creek Greenway: Nature Trail						●
3	McAlpine Creek Greenway: Cross-Country Course						●
4	Jetton Park Trai	●					●
5	RibbonWalk Urban Forest						●
6	Latta Plantation Nature Preserve: Mountain Island Lake			●			
7	Latta Plantation Nature Preserve: Raptor Trail				●		
8	Latta Plantation Nature Preserve: Latta Loops	●					
9	Latta Plantation Nature Preserve: Buzzard Rock			●			
10	McDowell Nature Preserve: Woodland Forest Trail				●		
11	McDowell Nature Preserve: Cove Loop			●			
12	McDowell Nature Preserve: Lake Wylie Trail			●			
13	Reedy Creek Park and Nature Preserve: Robinson Rockhouse Ruins					●	
14	Reedy Creek Park and Nature Preserve: Preserve Loop						●
15	U.S. National Whitewater Center: Lake Trail			●			
16	U.S. National Whitewater Center: North Trails						●
17	Crowders Mountain State Park: Kings Pinnacle		●				
18	Crowders Mountain State Park: Fern and Lake Trails	●					
19	Crowders Mountain State Park: Crowders Mountain Ridge Trail		●				
20	Crowders Mountain State Park: Summit Trail		●				

Trail Finder

Hike No.	Hike Name	Best Hikes for Children	Best Hikes for Views	Best Hikes for Water Lovers	Best Hikes for Wildlife	Best Hikes for Historians	Best Hikes for After Work
21	Kings Mountain National Military Park: Browns Mountain		●				
22	Kings Mountain National Military Park: Battlefield Trail					●	
23	Kings Mountain State Park: Living History Farm	●				●	
24	Kings Mountain State Park: Clarks Creek Trail			●			
25	Kings Mountain State Park: Buzzards Roost		●				
26	Anne Springs Close Greenway: Lake Haigler				●		
27	Anne Springs Close Greenway: South Loop						●
28	Anne Springs Close Greenway: Webb Grist Mill					●	
29	Anne Springs Close Greenway: History Walk	●				●	
30	Cane Creek Park						●
31	Pee Dee National Wildlife Refuge				●		
32	Uwharrie National Forest: Uwharrie Recreation Trail South				●		
33	Uwharrie National Forest: Badin Lake			●			
34	Reed Gold Mine State Historic Site: Reed Mine Hike	●				●	
35	Morrow Mountain State Park: Fall Mountain			●			
36	Morrow Mountain State Park: Hattaway Mountain				●		
37	Morrow Mountain State Park: Sugarloaf Mountain and Morrow Mountain		●				
38	Lake Norman State Park: Lake Shore Trail			●			
39	Lake Norman State Park: Itusi Trail—Laurel Loop				●		
40	Lake Norman State Park: Itusi Trail—Hawk Loop, Norwood Creek Loop, and Hicks Creek Loop				●		

Map Legend

Transportation

- Freeway/Interstate Highway (85)
- U.S. Highway (601)
- State Highway (49)
- Other Road (544)
- Unpaved Road
- Railroad
- State Line

Trails

- Selected Route
- Trail or Fire Road
- Direction of Travel

Water Features

- Body of Water
- River or Creek
- Marsh/Swamp

Land Management

- Local & State Parks/Preserve
- National Forests & Wilderness Areas

Symbols

- Boardwalk
- Boat Ramp
- Bridge
- Building/Point of Interest
- Campground
- Gate
- Observation Tower
- Mountain/Peak
- Parking
- Ranger Station
- Visitor/Information Center
- Picnic Area
- Restroom
- Scenic View
- Trailhead (20)
- Towns and Cities
- Tunnel

Central Region

Freshwater clams line the shore (hike 6).

The hikes nearest to Charlotte offer a wide variety of terrain, distances, and attractions. However, their biggest asset can be summed up in one word: location.

For individuals who truly love to hike, sometimes a weekend outing just isn't enough. The central hiking region near Charlotte offers sixteen hikes within thirty minutes of the city center. And although these hikes are close to town, some of them feel surprisingly rural, especially the routes found at Reedy Creek Park and Nature Preserve, McDowell Nature Preserve, and Latta Plantation Nature Preserve. These Charlotte-Mecklenburg nature preserves offer a substantial network of trails and can transport you to a forest or lakeside setting where the noise of traffic and the glare of city life disappear.

Another Charlotte-Mecklenburg nature preserve, RibbonWalk Urban Forest demonstrates how conserving a small piece of nature within an urban community can help revitalize and reinvent the surrounding neighborhoods. This small park allows families to come and fish and hike, as well as get an up-close view of a highly active beaver habitat. RibbonWalk Urban Forest also hosts some of the most magnificent beech trees in Mecklenburg County and the North Carolina piedmont.

Other hikes near Charlotte, such as the treks located on a greenway, are perfect for incorporating the entire family. The wide, level pathways found at McAlpine Creek Greenway, and Lower McAlpine Creek, McMullen Creek, and Four-Mile Creek Greenway, are perfect for pushing a stroller, a wheelchair, or hiking next to a tricycle or bike. The birding near these greenways can also be surprisingly good, especially near the wetlands at Four-Mile Creek Greenway.

Some of the hikes near the city can be turned into longer day trips when combined with activities near the trail. For example, a hike at Jetton Park could include tennis and picnicking, while an outing at the U.S. National Whitewater Center could also encompass paddling, zip-lining, and geocaching.

No matter what you are looking for in a hike, the good news is that you won't have to travel far to find it!

A path in Jetton Park divides a sweet scented pine forest from the shoreline of Lake Norman (hike 4).

Lower McAlpine Creek, McMullen Creek, and Four-Mile Creek Greenway

Usually hiking is differentiated from everyday walking by features such as mountains, forests, lakes, and dirt trails. A residential greenway has to be pretty amazing to be included in a hiking book. The Lower McAlpine Creek, McMullen Creek, and Four-Mile Creek Greenway hike does not pass any mountains or lakes, its trees are too sparse to be considered a forest, and it contains hardly any dirt tread. But it does include some beautiful wetlands and the most impressive stretch of wooden boardwalks in the region. This entire route is 5.8 miles long and can be completed in sections, as a shuttle, or as a long out-and-back hike. Whichever option you choose, you will be amazed at the natural treasures that are revealed behind residential neighborhoods and below the interstate overpass. The entire route travels beside creeks and over wetlands, where waterfowl and songbirds gather throughout the year. In addition, its proximity to downtown will have you coming back to this wooden, wet greenway time and time again.

Start: McMullen Creek Greenway parking lot off Pineville-Matthews Road

Distance: 5.8-mile shuttle

Hiking time: About 3 to 4 hours (one way)

Difficulty: Easy; level terrain

Trail surface: Gravel greenway, paved trail, wooden boardwalks

Best season(s): Fall, winter, spring

Other trail users: Bikers and in-line skaters

Canine compatibility: Leashed dogs permitted

Land status: County greenway

Fees and permits: None

Schedule: Open daily; sunrise to sunset

Maps: USGS Weddington; Greenway maps available for download at http://charmeck.org/meck lenburg/county/ParkandRec/Greenways/

Trail contacts: Mecklenburg County Park and Recreation Department; call 311 or (704) 336-7600; www.parkandrec.com

Finding the trailhead: From downtown Charlotte take I-77 South to exit 1B. Leave I-77 at exit 1B and follow I-485 East toward Pineville. After driving 1.4 miles merge onto I-485 South. Stay on I-485 South for 3.4 miles, and then exit onto Pineville-Matthews Road (NC 51 N). Travel Pineville-Matthews Road (east) toward Matthews for 1.2 miles, then turn right (south) into the Lower McMullen Creek Greenway parking area. It is a dirt lot located next to the creek and across the street from McMullen Creek Market. GPS: N35 05.212'/ W80 51.437'

THE HIKE

Ninety-nine percent of motorists who travel on I-485 near Pineville at 65 miles per hour have no knowledge of the wet wonderland that exists below their spinning wheels. Nor do they realize that nearly 6 miles of greenway is available to explore this birding and wildlife habitat. But if you take the time to slow down and enjoy this nature trail on foot, you will never speed past the NC 51 exit again without thinking of the mallards, blue herons, and red-shouldered hawks that live beneath the interstate.

The connecting Lower McAlpine Creek, McMullen Creek, and Four-Mile Creek Greenway isn't just a terrific place to view unique flora and fauna, it is a really fun place to hike. Remember when you were a child and you wished that the ground was a trampoline so that you could bounce wherever you needed to go? Well, unfortunately this greenway network is not comprised of springs and a jumping

> **🌿 Green Tip:**
> *Observe wildlife from a distance. Don't interfere with their lives—both of you will be better for it.*

A wooden observation deck stretches into the surrounding wetlands at Lower McAlpine Creek Greenway.

mat, but it does utilize a large network of wooden boardwalks, that—like a trampoline—are kinder on your joints than traditional asphalt. And the suspended slats also provide a wonderfully melodic *click, clomp, clack* with every step.

This hike begins at the McMullen Creek Greenway parking lot, off NC 51. However, you will need to decide before you start walking how far you want to go. If you want to hike the entire network of greenways, you will need to either plan a pickup at the end of the Four-Mile Creek Greenway, or you will need to do a very long out-and-back that totals 11.6 miles. If neither one of those options sounds feasible, then consider hiking a portion of this route. You can hike out and back on the McMullen Creek Greenway for a 4.2-mile hike, you can combine the McMullen Creek and Lower McAlpine Creek Greenways for an 8.0-mile hike, or you can park at one of the alternate trailheads to hike 3.6 miles (out and back) on the Four-Mile Creek Greenway.

Beginning your hike from the McMullen Creek trailhead, follow the gravel greenway south along the east shore of McMullen Creek. Within the first 200 yards, you will encounter a spur trail that leads over the creek on a bridge to a nearby neighborhood. The bridges are a really good place to step off the path and enjoy an overhead view of the creek. This is perhaps the place where you will spot a northern water snake or resident muskrat.

After 0.7 mile the trail meets its first wooden boardwalk. (As a note, wooden boardwalks can be slick during and after a rainstorm, so be careful!) From this point forward the greenway will be comprised of alternating boardwalk and paved trail. The first set of boardwalk follows an angular path through a narrow wetland. Soon you will hear the roar of I-485 nearby, and not long after, you will cross under it on the greenway.

The short section of trail to the south of the interstate is surprisingly quiet. Unlike other portions of the trail, there are no houses that closely border the path. Instead, tall sycamore trees rise up out of the marsh, and bluebirds and woodpeckers adorn the tree limbs. As a side note, you should also keep your eyes peeled for a tiny orange butterfly on this hike. The southern skipperling is usually found closer to the coast, but this specific flying insect was first spotted in Mecklenburg County on this stretch of greenways.

Once you cross back under the interstate, the trail again traces its course behind the fenced backyards of nearby houses. You are now officially on the Lower McAlpine Creek Greenway. This stretch of this hike is unique because the trail encounters two wooden observation platforms where you can peer into the wetlands for native plants such as pickerelweed, lizard's tail, and buttonbush. There are helpful information plaques stationed at each lookout designed to help you decipher exactly what you are looking for.

Past the observation decks, the path comes to a major intersection with the Four-Mile Creek Greenway. If you continue straight, you will arrive at the Johnston

Lower McAlpine Creek, McMullen Creek, and Four-Mile Creek Greenway

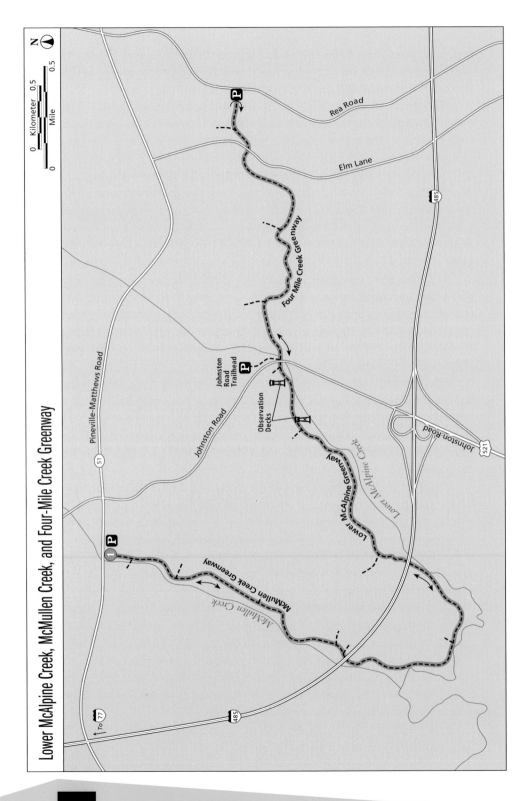

Road exit. To continue your hike, turn right and cross a bridge over Lower McAlpine Creek. The most beautiful stretches of boardwalk occur on this 1.8-mile greenway. One particularly long stretch of raised platform takes you over a wetland area that is filled with tall cattail plants. Frogs and crickets compete to fill the air with their serenades, and waterfowl are particularly common in this habitat.

When the greenway exits the wetlands and terminates at Rea Road, you will be reminded of just how close the greenway travels to stores, shops, and busy roads, but that will make you appreciate this convenient escape even more!

MILES AND DIRECTIONS

0.0   Start at the McMullen Creek Greenway trailhead off NC 51 and across the street from McMullen Street Market. The gravel greenway begins at the south end of the parking lot, next to McMullen Creek.

0.1   The greenway passes a spur trail on the right, which leads over the river to a residential neighborhood. This is the first of many residential access points. Because there are so many along the route, they will not all be listed here.

0.7   You will encounter your first wooden boardwalk on the hike. It is a lot of fun, and there is a lot more of it ahead!

1.4   The hike passes under I-485. It then begins to veer east amid a swamp of tall-standing sycamore trees.

2.8   Pass beneath the roar of the interstate one more time. The greenway now travels along the southeast side of a housing development.

3.6   Arrive at two wooden observation decks that extend into the wetland habitat. The first will be on your right, the second will be a little farther up the trail on your left.

4.0   The main greenway seems to continue straight, but this is the intersection with Four-Mile Creek. (***Option:*** By continuing north you will arrive at the Johnston Road trailhead.) To continue your hike, turn right (east) and cross McAlpine Creek on a bridge.

4.9   Pretty alert! This expansive wetland area is filled with cattails, frogs, and waterfowl. Take your time on the long stretch of boardwalk to look for wildlife and take in the scenery.

5.8   Conclude your hike at Rea Road. If you did not shuttle a car or schedule a pickup, then turn around and complete this gorgeous greenway all over again!

Local information: Charlotte Visitor Info Center, 330 S. Tryon St., Charlotte 28202; (704) 331-2700; www.visitcharlotte.com

Local events/attractions: Carolina Place Mall, 11025 Carolina Place Pkwy., Pineville 28134; (704) 543-9300; www.carolinaplace.com. Need a little retail therapy after your hike? Check out Carolina Place Mall—it even has an REI for all your hiking needs . . . and wants!

Good eats: Carolina Place Mall, 11025 Carolina Place Pkwy., Pineville 28134; (704) 543-9300; www.carolinaplace.com. There are plenty of eateries from which to choose at the mall and in the surrounding area. No matter what you are craving, you will find it here.

Organizations: The Carolina Thread Trail, Carolina Thread Trail Office, 105 W. Morehead St., Charlotte 28202; (704) 376-2556; www.carolinathreadtrail.org. "Weaving communities together" in and around Charlotte with walking paths.

Charlotte was given the nickname "the Queen City" because it was named after Princess Charlotte of Mecklenburg. Princess Charlotte married British King George III and became a queen, one year before the city of Charlotte was founded.

People aren't the only ones that live near the greenway. A set of mallards also calls this area home.

McAlpine Creek Greenway: Nature Trail

This route contours the straight and level McAlpine Greenway along the banks of the waterway. After passing under a railroad trestle and Monroe Road, the greenway will come within sight of the Sardis Road overpass. Before reaching this intersection, the path crosses McAlpine Creek and then winds through the forest on the northern bank. In the spring this path is lined with wildflowers, including the rare native larkspur. After hiking a little over a mile, the trail returns to the south shore of McAlpine Creek and traces the greenway back to the trailhead parking lot.

Start: McAlpine Creek Park parking lot
Distance: 4.1-mile balloon
Hiking time: About 2 to 2.5 hours
Difficulty: Moderate
Trail surface: Granular greenway and forested trail
Best season(s): Spring, fall
Other trail users: Bikers and joggers
Canine compatibility: Leashed dogs permitted
Land status: County greenway

Fees and permits: None
Schedule: Open daily; sunrise to sunset
Maps: USGS Mint Hill and Charlotte East; McAlpine Creek Greenway map available for download at http://charmeck .org/mecklenburg/county/ ParkandRec/Greenways/
Trail contacts: Mecklenburg County Park and Recreation Department; call 311 or (704) 336-7600; www.parkandrec.com

Finding the trailhead: From downtown Charlotte follow East US 74/Independence Boulevard. At the intersection with Village Springs Drive, turn right (south). Stay on Village Lake Drive to reach Monroe Road and then take a left (south). Once on Monroe Road look for McAlpine Creek Park on your left (east). The trailhead is located at the northeast corner of the parking lot, near the dog park. GPS: N35 09.042' / W80 44.625'

THE HIKE

This route is similar to the McAlpine Creek Cross-Country Course, except it has less elevation gain and fewer people. In fact, once you cross over McAlpine Creek to join the Cottonwood Nature Trail, you will most likely only pass a handful of people, if any. For some hikers, feeling remote and isolated within the city limits may seem eerie, but others will embrace the solitude found so close to downtown.

To start the hike, locate the dog park at the north end of the McAlpine Creek parking area. Walk toward the green field, often filled with playful pets, then turn right to cross a wide bridge that spans McAlpine Creek. On the east bank the greenway will span before you like a pedestrian interstate. Turn right and follow the greenway away from the fishing pond and athletic fields at McAlpine Park.

One of the best aspects of living in Charlotte is that you never have to drive far to find a place to walk. The city prides itself on its network of connecting greenways, and with more than 33 miles of completed paths and 173 miles of undeveloped or planned greenways, it is easy to see why. The route along McAlpine Creek

A train crosses over McAlpine Greenway.

is significant in that it was Charlotte's first implemented greenway. Completed in 1978, it has remained a favorite hiking destination among Charlotte residents for more than thirty years.

The first half of this hike does not necessarily give you a wilderness feel. However, the greenway does allow you to walk under a working railroad trestle, which suddenly becomes extra-fun when a mammoth freight train passes overhead. The path also provides plenty of benches along the banks of McAlpine Creek. These resting spots are strategically placed under the shade of mature sycamore trees. They provide a peaceful setting to enjoy a snack or look for a beaver or river otter playing on the banks of the creek.

And speaking of shade, don't expect it on the first half of your hike! The greenway is almost entirely exposed and should be avoided in the midday heat of summer. That said, after completing 2.0 miles on the greenway, you cross the creek on a bridge to find shade and solitude on the neighboring Cottonwood Nature Trail. The nature trail meanders through a beautiful hardwood forest of tulip poplar and oak trees. There is plenty of green underbrush lining the trail, and in the spring several different varieties of wildflowers dot the path. A rare form of native larkspur can also be found here in the spring. In fact, McAlpine Creek is the only place where the beautiful purple flower with five lobes and a long pointed cap has been identified in Mecklenburg County.

In searching off-trail for a glimpse of the aubergine-colored plant, however, be careful not to brush up against any three-leaved plants. Poison ivy not only grows alongside the path on the Cottonwood Nature Trail, it also climbs up tree trunks and weaves its way into the thick underbrush. The best way to avoid getting a rash is to stay on the path. This is also the eco-friendly option, as going off-trail can damage undergrowth, cause erosion, and harm the delicate larkspur. Remember, this is a rare plant, and you wouldn't want to go looking for it and then accidentally step on it!

At mile 2.7 you will be reminded of the surrounding neighborhoods and development when you skirt the perimeter of the tennis facility. Then, after a few more twists and turns in the forest, you will once again cross over McAlpine Creek on a small bridge to rejoin the greenway.

Turn left on the busy recreation path and retrace your route upstream toward McAlpine Park. When you reach the cross-country course and fishing pond, cross the waterway one more time to return to your car at the trailhead parking lot.

> **Green Tip:**
> *Keep to established trails as much as possible.*
> *If there aren't any, stay on surfaces that will be least affected,*
> *like rock, gravel, and dry grass.*

McAlpine Creek Greenway: Nature Trail

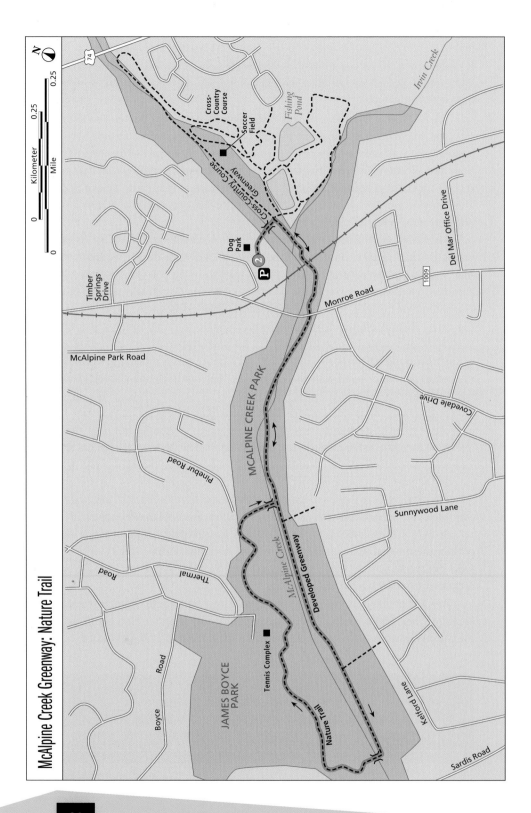

0.0   Park at the McAlpine Creek Park access area off Monroe Road, and start your hike by walking north toward the dog park.

0.1   South of the dog park, there is a bridge that spans McAlpine Creek. Cross the bridge to access the greenway.

0.3   Turn right and hike south along the granular path.

2.0   As you approach Sardis Road overpass, look to your right (west) for a bridge that spans McAlpine Creek. Cross the bridge to join the Cottonwood Nature Trail. (If you reach Sardis Road, you have gone too far.)

2.7   Skirt the south perimeter of a tennis facility to stay on the nature trail.

3.0   Veer right as two spur trails join the nature trail on the left.

3.1   Continue on the nature trail across McAlpine Creek to rejoin the greenway. Turn left (north) and hike upstream.

3.9   Across from the McAlpine fishing pond, turn left (west) and follow the bridge across the water to the dog park.

4.1   Conclude the hike at the McAlpine Park trailhead.

Discover More

If you enjoy the greenways that run throughout Charlotte, you are not alone. In fact, the greenways are so popular, and beneficial, that there is a plan to connect more of Charlotte with greenway paths—and then to connect those paths with towns in neighboring counties. The Carolina Thread Trail project is supported by the Catawba Lands Conservancy and the Trust for Public Lands. These two organizations are spearheading the effort to develop public walking corridors and build trails. The Carolina Thread Trail project believes that, if successful, the network of trails will positively benefit the economy, bring people together, and promote health and safety. The project is still in the early phases, but it hopes to make large strides in the near future. It will only become increasingly difficult to acquire public land in the future. If you want to find out more about the Carolina Thread Trail or attend an upcoming meeting, be sure to call the office or visit the website.

Local information: Charlotte Visitor Info Center, 330 S. Tryon St., Charlotte 28202; (704) 331-2700; www.visitcharlotte.com

Local events/attractions: Independence Square East Shopping Center, East Independence Boulevard, Charlotte 28227. Run errands before or after the hike at this shopping center.

Good eats: Bread Basket, 9315 Monroe Rd., Charlotte 28270; (704) 847-0062; www.breadbasket.com. Need a place to grab a muffin and some coffee before your hike? This is the place to go!

Organizations: The Catawba Lands Conservancy, 105 W. Morehead St., Suite B, Charlotte 28202; (704) 342-3330; www.catawbalands.org

Carolina Thread Trail, 105 W. Morehead St., Charlotte 28202; (704) 376-2556; www.carolinathreadtrail.org

> *If you want to identify the native larkspur and other regional wildflowers along the Cottonwood nature trail, consider taking a wildflower-identification book with you on your hike. You can learn more about native wildflowers at www.ncwildflower.org.*

McApline Creek is home to beavers and river otters.

McAlpine Creek Greenway: Cross-Country Course

Each fall hundreds of high school cross-country runners journey to McAlpine Creek Greenway to participate in the state championship. For the other 364 days a year, the course is open for pedestrians to enjoy at whatever pace they desire. The scenic loop follows the banks of McAlpine Creek before veering into a nearby patch of woods. When the route comes out of the forest, it explores the shoreline of two ponds that are home to ducks, herons, and Canada geese.

Start: McAlpine Creek Park parking lot
Distance: 3.5-mile loop
Hiking time: About 1.5 to 2 hours
Difficulty: Moderate
Trail surface: Granular greenway
Best season(s): Spring
Other trail users: Bikers and joggers
Canine compatibility: Leashed dogs permitted
Land status: County greenway
Fees and permits: None

Schedule: Open daily; sunrise to sunset
Maps: USGS Mint Hill and Charlotte East; McAlpine Creek Greenway map available for download at http://charmeck .org/mecklenburg/county/ ParkandRec/Greenways/
Trail contacts: Mecklenburg County Park and Recreation Department; call 311 or (704) 336-7600; www.parkandrec.com

Finding the trailhead: From downtown Charlotte follow East US 74/Independence Boulevard. At the intersection with Village Springs Drive, turn right (south). Stay on Village Lake Drive to reach Monroe Road and then take a left (south). Once on Monroe Road look for McAlpine Creek Park on your left (east). The trailhead is located at the northeast corner of the parking lot, near the dog park. GPS: N35 09.042'/W80 44.625'

Charlotte has a fabulous network of greenways weaving through the city. The greenway next to McAlpine Creek is especially appealing in that it is a dirt trail rather than a paved one. The northern portion of the greenway at McAlpine Creek has made a name for itself as the North Carolina state championship cross-country course. Even if you aren't on-site for the fall competition, you will still most likely see high school runners practicing on the course in the afternoon and on the weekend.

The good news is that you don't have to run this trail, unless you want to. It starts at the McAlpine Creek Park access off Monroe Road. From the parking lot hike north to locate the dog park and then veer east to cross McAlpine on a sturdy bridge made of steel and wood.

> 🌰 **Green Tip:**
> *If possible, carpool or take public transportation to the trailhead.*

The cross-country course travels near the shore of the fishing pond.

The bridge terminates at the granular greenway. Turn left and follow the path upstream. The next 0.5 mile of hiking is straight and flat. You will notice frequent signposts marking the trail. The numbers correspond with how far you have traveled on the cross-country course, so one way to make sure you are headed in the right direction is to track your distance traveled using the wooden markers.

The trail parallels the creek all the way to US 74. At this point a spur trail to the left leads across the creek and up to the road, but you will veer right and loop back through the trees. At the next trail intersection, cut back hard to the right and follow the path as it forms a small S shape. The trail can be a little confusing at this point as it twists and turns to add distance while staying in a relatively small area. You will trace the east sideline of a soccer field and then hike uphill on the only climb on the entire hike.

Once you conquer the small hill, the trail will quickly descend to the shore of a pond or marsh, depending on recent rainfall. No matter how high the water level is, geese, ducks, and herons love to visit this wetland habitat. Travel west along the water to reach the deeper and more defined fishing pond. There is a bridge between the two ponds that connects the path with the eastern portion of the hike. However, in order to stay true to the cross-country course, travel counterclockwise around the fishing pond to reach the exact same spot. Another short loop will take you through a bottomland hardwood forest that surrounds the wetlands. This is a great place to look for migrating birds and wildlife. The greenway even has information placards lining the trail with birding information. (I wonder if the cross-country runners stop to read these!)

Finally you will loop back around to the front of the fishing pond, at which point there is a relatively unglamorous metal gateway that arches above the cross-country course. This is the finish line for the cross-country championship, and whether you finished the hike in twenty minutes or two hours, it is still fun to walk underneath the marker with your hands held high and a smile on your face. After all, you just got in a great hike!

MILES AND DIRECTIONS

0.0 Park at the McAlpine Creek Park access off Monroe Road, and start your hike by walking north toward the dog park.

0.1 South of the dog park, there is a bridge that spans McAlpine Creek. Cross the bridge to access the greenway.

0.3 Turn left and hike north along the granular path.

0.8 At the US 74 access bridge, veer right and loop back (south) toward McAlpine Park on a dirt path.

McAlpine Creek Greenway: Cross-Country Course

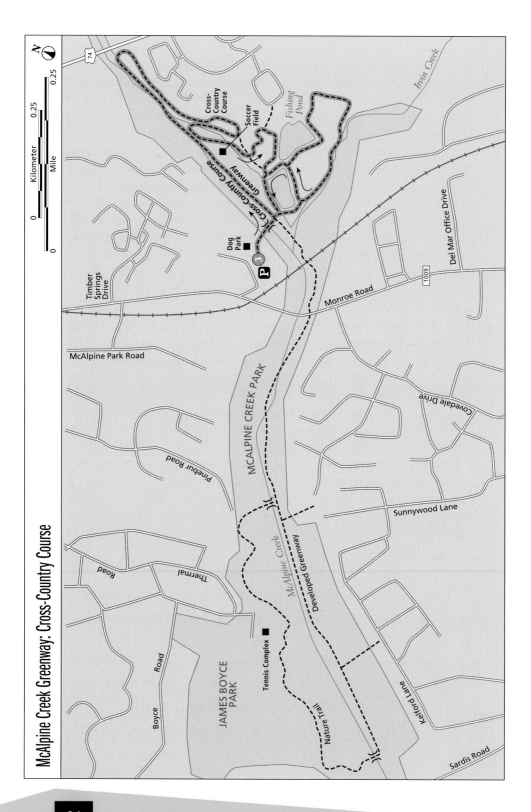

1.2   Arrive at a three-way intersection and cut back hard to the right (north). You will zigzag in the woods and then travel along the east boundary of a soccer field.

1.5   At a four-way intersection, continue straight (east) and uphill.

1.7   When you arrive at the top of the hill, several spur trails will veer off to connect with a nearby apartment complex. Stay on the trail by looking for the cross-country markers and following them south and downhill.

1.9   At the wetlands boundary turn right (west) and continue on the dirt path.

2.0   The trail comes to a three-way intersection. Continue straight and travel counterclockwise around the fishing pond to arrive at the same intersection.

2.4   A few dozen feet before completing your loop around the fishing pond, turn right and make a loop around the park's bottomland forest.

3.0   After hiking clockwise around the bottomland forest, retrace your steps counterclockwise around the fishing pond.

3.3   Throw your hands up in the air and cross under the metal beam that marks the finish line. You did it! Now backtrack over the nearby bridge to finish your hike.

3.5   Arrive back at your car.

HIKE INFORMATION

Local information: Charlotte Visitor Info Center, 330 S. Tryon St., Charlotte 28202; (704) 331-2700; www.visitcharlotte.com

Local events/attractions: Independence Square East Shopping Center, East Independence Blvd., Charlotte 28227. Run errands before or after the hike at this shopping center.

Good eats: Yen's Chinese Restaurant, 9101 Monroe Rd., Suite 110, Charlotte 28270; (704) 845-9444. Hiking and Chinese food are always a good combination.

Organizations: The Carolina Thread Trail, Carolina Thread Trail Office, 105 W. Morehead St., Charlotte 28202; (704) 376-2556; www.carolinathreadtrail.org. "Weaving communities together" in and around Charlotte with walking paths.

> *If you are interested in watching one of the inspiring cross-country races at McAlpine Creek, contact the Mecklenburg Parks and Recreation Department for a fall schedule (www.parkandrec.com). Likewise, if you don't want to be stampeded, you may want to do the same.*

You don't have to own a mansion on the shore of Lake Norman to enjoy a day at the lake. Jetton Park offers a sunning beach, picnic area, and scenic hiking trails where families can spend an afternoon or a full day enjoying the clear blue water of Lake Norman. The hiking trails at the park split their time between the scenic lakeshore and inland pine forest. The suggested route explores the shaded forest paths and then leaves the woods to contour the winding shoreline. The hike offers great views from the park's peninsula and even passes the public beach, where hikers can build a castle or dig their toes into the soft white sand. This outing is recommended for everyone, but especially for families with children.

Start: Jetton Park roadside parking, just past the park entrance and near the playground
Distance: 1.8-mile balloon
Hiking time: About 1 to 1.5 hours
Difficulty: Easy
Trail surface: Dirt trail and paved walkways
Best season(s): Spring, fall
Other trail users: Cyclists and in-line skaters
Canine compatibility: Leashed dogs permitted

Land status: County park
Fees and permits: Fees collected weekends and holidays
Schedule: Open daily; dawn to dusk
Maps: USGS Lake Norman
Trail contacts: Jetton Park on Lake Norman, 19000 Jetton Rd., Cornelius, 28013; (704) 336-3586; www.parkandrec.com

Finding the trailhead: From Charlotte take I-77 North to exit 28. At the end of the ramp, turn left (west) onto Catawba Avenue. Drive for a little over a mile and then turn right (north) onto Jetton Road. Continue straight for 0.5 mile and then turn left (west) into Jetton Park. The parking lot and trailhead are located just within the entrance of the park, 100 yards past the welcome stations. Look for the roadside parking to the left.

The trail starts in the pine forest to the east, beside the park playground. GPS: N35 28.492' / W80 54.006'

THE HIKE

Mecklenburg County offers a slew of family-friendly parks. However, Jetton Park is one of the few that can be considered a hiking destination. And the best part is that not only is Jetton Park a hiking destination, it also offers tennis courts, a sunning beach, picnic benches with grills, a scenic garden, and an indoor meeting space. Basically, it offers almost all the amenities of a country club (sans golf course). However, unlike an exclusive club, Jetton Park is open to the public and accessible at little to no cost—depending on what season and day you visit the park.

The hiking trails at the park offer a mix of paved pathways and dirt trails. And whereas you might encounter bikers or in-line skaters on the paved section of trail, the dirt tread is reserved solely for hikers. Because of the relatively level terrain on both surfaces, this is a great hike for young children, mothers pushing strollers, or older adults who don't want to worry about roots and rocks littering the path. The hike starts at the north end of the park. The parking for the trailhead is located off the main road, shortly after passing through the entrance and park welcome station.

At the beginning of this adventure, you will need to think of the route more as a corridor than a well-defined path. Follow a wide spur trail east toward a colorful

Events are held in this barn right on the trail at Lake Norman.

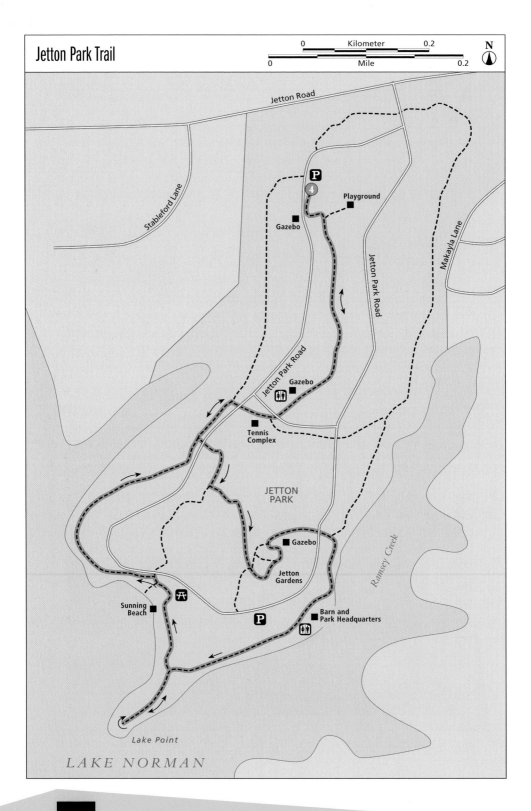

0   Kilometer   0.2

0   Mile   0.2

N

Jetton Road

Stableford Lane

P

4

Playground

Gazebo

Jetton Park Road

Makayla Lane

Jetton Park Road

Gazebo

Tennis
Complex

JETTON
PARK

Gazebo

Ramsey Creek

Jetton
Gardens

Sunning
Beach

P

Barn and
Park Headquarters

Lake Point

LAKE NORMAN

playground, which can be viewed through the tall pine trees lining the road. That's right, the first stop on this hike is the playground. There are two ways to utilize this impressive jungle gym. The first is to let your more enthusiastic companions expend some energy on the metal bars and twisted slides before continuing on a more focused and relaxed hike. The second option is to motivate your more reluctant fellow hikers by telling them that the hike not only starts but also ends at this playground, and if they are able to complete the entire walk (with a good attitude), they will be rewarded with some swing time at the conclusion of the hike. Either way, the playground presents a fun obstacle and a good way to turn this easy hike into a full-body workout.

To continue the hike, stay to the west of the playground and hike south. You will pass a gazebo on your right. This is one of three quaint gazebos that you will pass on this short hike. The path now veers through a planted grove of mature pine trees. These tall conifers with their straight limbs keep you protected from the hot sun. After hiking almost half a mile, you will leave the shade and exit the forest at a tennis court complex—play station number two! All right, so maybe you didn't stick a tennis racquet into your daypack, but it is still good to note that these courts are available on a first-come, first-served (served—get it?!) basis. Feel free to revisit these courts on a different trip to Jetton Park, or if you keep tennis racquets in your car, you can come back to play after completing your hike.

The route now skirts the tennis courts to the west. There is a paved sidewalk that travels counterclockwise around the courts and briefly crosses the main park road before veering back into the woods to the south of the tennis courts. The trail now once again travels through a forest of mostly pine trees, however, this patch of woods is not quite as well groomed as the previous section. On the opposite end of this forest, the path veers west toward the Jetton Park gardens. The gardens showcase many native species and also provide a popular resting spot for local birds. Keep your eyes peeled for a redheaded woodpecker or white-breasted nuthatch.

Past the gardens, cross the park road and turn right on the paved hiking trail. This trail now traces the outline of the Jetton Park peninsula. Follow it south through the egg-shaped entrance of a renovated barn, where private events are held, and past the park office and conveniently timed restroom facility. Beyond the park buildings, the paved trail continues along the lakeshore. When you arrive at

Green Tip:
Pack out your dog's waste or dispose of it in a trash can or a hole dug into the ground.

a trail junction, turn left and explore a short spur trail that leads out onto a small finger of the Jetton Park Peninsula. This short out-and-back offers the best views of the lake and also displays some smooth yet twisted driftwood along the trail.

Past the spur trail the paved walkway will next access the Jetton Park sunning beach. Although no swimming is allowed, this is still a great spot to stop and play in the warm white sand that borders the lake. Beyond the beach, the trail continues in the woods and passes several picnic sites, before returning to the tennis complex. Once you reach the tennis courts, cross the park road and retrace your steps to the playground to conclude your hike—and to release any remaining energy on the monkey bars!

MILES AND DIRECTIONS

0.0 Start at the roadside parking area, just past the park entrance, and hike east toward the barely visible playground.

0.1 Arrive at the playground and turn right (south). The playground will be on your left as you pass a gazebo on your right. Continue straight into a well-groomed pine forest.

0.4 Exit the pine forest at the Jetton Park Tennis Complex. Turn right (west) and bypass the tennis courts by following a paved walkway across the main park road.

0.5 Take your first available left (east) to travel back across the park road and continue your hike in the forest.

0.7 The path exits the forest and veers left (east) to visit the Jetton Park gardens.

0.8 After winding your way through the gardens, hike east across the park road and turn right (south) on the paved hiking trail to parallel the lakeshore.

0.9 Walk through the restored barn and then past the park offices and rest-room facilities. Continue on the paved hiking trail.

1.0 Turn left (south) to travel a short out-and-back on a narrow peninsula for great views of Lake Norman.

1.2 Pass the sunning beach to your left.

1.4 After passing several picnic areas, the tennis courts will become visible to your right. Leave the paved hiking trail and retrace your steps to the Jetton Park playground through the pine grove.

1.8 Conclude your hike at the park playground.

Local information: Lake Norman Tourism Information: Visit Lake Norman, 199900 W. Catawba Ave., Suite 102, Cornelius 28031; (704) 987-3300; www .visitlakenorman.org

Local events/attractions: Historic Rural Hill, 4431 Neck Rd., Huntersville 28078; (704) 875-3113; www.ruralhill.net. They're sharing and interpreting more than 250 years of piedmont history.

Good eats: Brooklyn Pizza, 19400 Jetton Rd., #201, Cornelius; (704) 896-2928; www.brooklynsouthpizzeria.com. Enjoy New York–style pizza in a family-friendly atmosphere.

Organizations: Lake Norman Ski Club, 643 Williamson Rd., Mooresville 28117; www.lakenormanskiclub.8m.com. Enjoy the lake on land and on the water!

If you like walking at Jetton Park, consider the trails at Lake Norman State Park, Lake Wylie, and Mountain Island Lake.

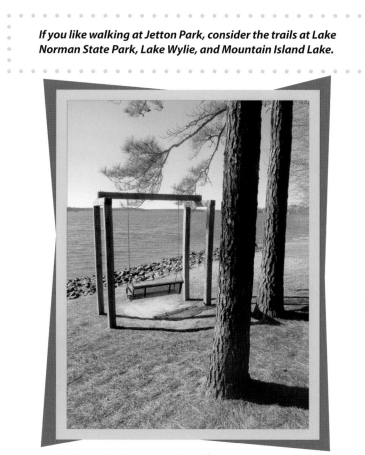

A swing overlooks the shore of Lake Norman.

RibbonWalk Urban Forest: Explorer Trail

This is one of the most unique hiking destinations near Charlotte, really near Charlotte. Located on Nevin Road off Stateville Avenue, this quaint nature preserve is surrounded by residential neighborhoods and shopping centers. That said, when you are hiking on the trails that weave through the park, you feel like you are in the middle of a forest, far away from the city. There are several highlights along this Explorer Trail, including a scenic covered bridge that leads to Hawk Meadow. However, the two most distinguishing aspects of RibbonWalk Urban Forest are the prized beech trees that tower above the forest canopy and are recognized within Mecklenburg County as Treasure Trees, and the highly active beaver habitat in the southern half of the preserve.

These intriguing features with fill adults and children with awe, and make you wonder how such an amazing natural environment can thrive so close to the city center.

Start: The trailhead kiosk at the entrance of RibbonWalk Urban Forest
Distance: 2.2-mile loop
Hiking time: About 1 to 1.5 hours
Difficulty: Easy
Trail surface: Mostly single-track dirt trail, with some road beds
Season(s): Fall, winter, spring
Other trail users: None
Canine compatibility: Leashed dogs permitted

Land status: Mecklenburg County nature preserve
Fees and permits: None
Schedule: Open daily; 7 a.m. to sunset
Maps: USGS Derita; RibbonWalk Urban Forest Trail Map, available at www.parkandrec.com
Trail contacts: RibbonWalk Urban Forest, 4601 Nevin Rd., Charlotte 28269; (704) 598-8857; www.park andrec.com

Finding the trailhead: From downtown Charlotte travel north on Statesville Avenue. Turn right (east) on Nevin Road. After driving 0.8 mile take the third right (southeast) to stay on Nevin Road. Travel another 0.4 mile and RibbonWalk Urban Forest will be on your left. Be on alert for the County Nature Preserve sign and the entrance as it is easy to miss. The hike starts at the information kiosk at the end of the entrance road, directly south of a locked gate. GPS: N35 17.651' / W80 49.194'

THE HIKE

RibbonWalk Urban Forest is one of the best places to hike near the downtown center of Charlotte. Note that RibbonWalk Urban Forest does not have any full-time staff on duty. There are Mecklenburg County park employees who visit the preserve on a daily basis to check on the trails and perform scheduled maintenance, but they may not be at the site when you are hiking. It is a good safety precaution to always hike the trails at this preserve with a friend.

The hike begins to the south of two unnamed lakes within the preserve. Begin your walk at the trailhead information kiosk and immediately head north and walk around the outskirts of a locked gate. The route now travels on a dirt road bed between a pond and a wetland bog. Though the best evidence of beaver activity comes at the end of this hike, there is a good chance that if you look closely, you will be able to see the gnawed stumps of trees lining the edge of this narrow land bridge. Also, if you look closely and walk quietly, there is a good chance that you will be able to spot resident turtles sunning themselves on a fallen tree or poking their heads out of the still, flat surface of the lake.

After passing between the two bodies of water, take a right on the Beech Walk Trail. Follow the red trail markers into the woods and skirt the southern shore of a small pond. This pond is referred to as the Woodland Pond, and it is rare to walk

The handiwork of beavers is evident near the wetlands at RibbonWalk Urban Forest.

beside it without hearing the serenade of croaking frogs fill the air. This wetland area is also a popular breeding area for mosquitoes in the late spring and early summer, so come prepared with bug spray.

Past the Woodland Pond the trail continues through a forest filled with different varieties of pine, as well as sourwood, sweet gum, and sycamore trees. You will pass a trail junction with the blue-blazed Hardwood Trail on your right. After hiking 0.7 mile you will arrive at an intersection with the Farmers Maze and Covered Bridge Trail. At press time, the first section of the Covered Bridge Trail was closed, so it was necessary to use the Farmers Maze to access the covered bridge and Hawk Meadow. The Farmers Maze is an interweaving web of trails that is not very extensive, but it can be confusing. To best navigate down to the covered bridge, turn right on the Farmers Maze path and then veer left at every opportunity. If you want to extend your hike and you're up for an adventure, feel free to explore the web of paths inside the maze.

By veering left, you will arrive at a quaint covered bridge that leads across a small stream to Hawk Meadow. Hawk Meadow is a beautiful open field surrounded by green pine trees. There is technically a trail that travels the outskirts of the meadow in a clockwise direction, but when the grass is high, the path is very difficult and uncomfortable to navigate. If this is the case, there is a parallel trail that is faint but travels within the confines of the forest to reach the backside of an old red barn that is located just inside the forest at the northwest corner of Hawk Meadow. Once you reach the barn, you can retrace your steps through the meadow, on the trail, or there is even a third path to the west that weaves its way back to the covered bridge across several small wooden platforms.

Back at the covered bridge, you will need to turn left, but then continually veer right to once again efficiently navigate the Farmers Maze. When you arrive back at the Beech Walk Trail, turn right and follow the path to an intersection with the Tricklin' Stream Trail. This intersection marks the beech tree grove (Treasure Tree Grove) that makes RibbonWalk Urban Forest so special. Beech trees are beautiful to begin with—their smooth bark looks like skin surrounding a strong muscular

Did you know that RibbonWalk was once a therapeutic horse farm? That is when most of the trails were built on the property. However, when the horse farm moved, there were plans to turn the RibbonWalk Urban Forest into a ninety-unit housing development and sewer-pumping station! Thankfully the financial banking of conservationist Mike North prevented the development and resulted in RibbonWalk becoming a county nature preserve.

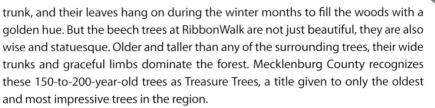

trunk, and their leaves hang on during the winter months to fill the woods with a golden hue. But the beech trees at RibbonWalk are not just beautiful, they are also wise and statuesque. Older and taller than any of the surrounding trees, their wide trunks and graceful limbs dominate the forest. Mecklenburg County recognizes these 150-to-200-year-old trees as Treasure Trees, a title given to only the oldest and most impressive trees in the region.

After gawking at the gorgeous beech trees, continue your hike on the green-blazed Tricklin' Stream Trail. The aptly named path now follows a small stream to the banks of the pond, near the entrance of the park. As the path continues to contour the north shore of the water, take your time to look for evidence of beavers near the edge of the pond. It shouldn't be hard to find trees ranging from an inch to 2 feet in diameter that the beavers have cut down with their sharp teeth. In the lake itself there is often a pile of these fallen trees that represent the beavers' home or lodge. If you are on the trail early in the morning or late in the afternoon, and if you take the time to sit quietly by the water, there is a good chance you will see a beaver swim across the pond or scout the shoreline for his next tree.

The Tricklin' Stream Trail terminates at the Beech Walk Trail. Turn right, passing between the lower pond and the wetland bog, and then take a left on the Hard-wood Trail to explore the south shore of the wetlands. There is once again heavy beaver evidence in this area. Just past the wetlands turn right and loop back to the RibbonWalk trailhead and parking area to conclude your hike.

MILES AND DIRECTIONS

0.0 Start at the trailhead information kiosk and parking area, located to the south of the park pond and wetlands, and to the west of an open field.

0.1 Walk past the locked gate and follow the old road bed past the preserve's lower pond and wetland area.

0.2 After reaching the north side of the wetland area, turn right onto the Beech Walk Trail.

0.3 Pass the Woodland Pond to your left. See if you can hear or see one of the many frogs that make this pond their home.

0.5 Pass the Hardwood Trail on your right and continue on the Beech Walk Trail.

0.7 Arrive at an intersection with the Farmers Maze and Covered Bridge Trail. Turn right to access the trails, and veer left to arrive at the covered bridge.

0.9 Cross the covered bridge and explore Hawk Meadow. If the grass in the meadow is too high for hiking, follow a faint trail inside the forest clock-wise, along the outskirts of the meadow.

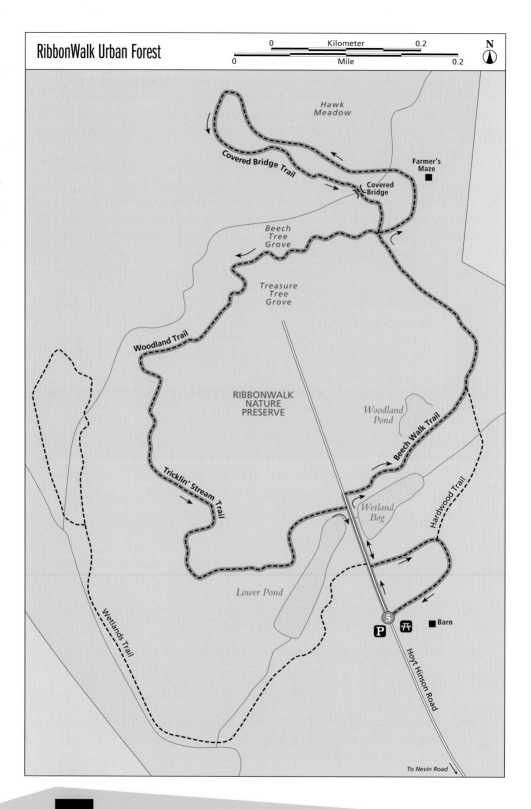

RibbonWalk Urban Forest

Kilometer
0   0.2
Mile
0   0.2

N

Hawk
Meadow

Covered Bridge Trail

Farmer's
Maze ■

Covered
Bridge

Beech
Tree
Grove

Treasure
Tree
Grove

Woodland Trail

RIBBONWALK
NATURE
PRESERVE

Woodland
Pond

Beech Walk Trail

Tricklin' Stream Trail

Hardwood Trail

Wetland
Bog

Wetlands Trail

Lower Pond

⑤
P 🏕 ■ Barn

Hoyt Hinson Road

To Nevin Road

1.1 Arrive at the backside of an old red barn and the northern boundary of Hawk Meadow. To the north you can see a housing development through the trees. Turn south and retrace your route, or explore a winding trail to your right—both lead back to the covered bridge.

1.3 Cross the covered bridge and return to the Beech Walk Trail via the Farmers Maze (remember to veer right if you don't want to explore the tangled web of intersecting trails).

1.4 Turn right on the Beech Walk Trail and start to keep your eyes peeled for the impressive beech trees that line the path.

1.5 At the intersection with the Tricklin' Creek Trail, you will be at the heart of the RibbonWalk beech grove. Take time to admire these gorgeous trees before continuing on the green-blazed Tricklin' Creek Trail.

1.8 Follow the north shore of a pond and look for the handiwork of the beavers near the edge of the water.

2.0 Intersect the Beech Walk Trail and turn right to travel between the pond and the wetlands. Past the water, take an immediate left on the Hardwood Trail.

2.1 After hiking beside the south boundary of the wetlands, turn right and continue on the Hardwood Trail.

2.2 After passing an open field to the south, conclude your hike at the trailhead kiosk and parking area.

HIKE INFORMATION

Local information: Charlotte's Got a Lot, 330 S. Tryon St., Charlotte 28202; (800) 231-4636; www.charlottesgotalot.com

Local events/attractions: Bechtler Museum of Modern Art, 420 S. Tryon St., Charlotte 28202; (704) 353-9200; www.bechtler.org. After checking out the handiwork of the beavers that live at RibbonWalk, check out the artwork at Bechtler.

Good eats: Derita Soda Shop & Grill, 2410 W. Sugar Creek Rd., Charlotte 28262; (704) 597-1659. Derita's offers great food, great service, and a great place to go after a hike.

Organizations: Girls on the Run International, 500 E. Morehead St., Suite 104, Charlotte 28202; (704) 376-9817; www.girlsontherun.com. Take your daughter on the trail with you, and if she is faster than you, consider this fabulous club.

Latta Plantation Nature Preserve: Mountain Island Lake

This route explores some of the most scenic trails in the northern half of Latta Plantation Nature Preserve. The hike starts on the Hill Trail but soon makes its way to the shore of Mountain Island Lake by following the Split Rock Trail. In this section you will have to alternate looking at the gorgeous lake views and staring at your feet, trying to navigate the rocky terrain. The hike returns briefly inland on better terrain, before once again skirting on the shoreline on the Cove Trail. After spotting freshwater clamshells and nesting birds on the Cove Trail, you will veer south and pass an old well and restoration site on the journey back to the trailhead.

Start: Latta Plantation Nature Center
Distance: 5.4-mile double balloon
Hiking time: About 2.5 hours
Difficulty: Moderate
Trail surface: Forested trail and dirt roads
Best season(s): Fall
Other trail users: Equestrians
Canine compatibility: Leashed dogs permitted
Land status: Mecklenburg County nature preserve

Fees and permits: None
Schedule: Open daily; 7 a.m. to sunset
Maps: USGS Mountain Island Lake; basic trail maps are available for free inside the nature center and at trailhead kiosks
Trail contacts: Latta Plantation Nature Preserve, 5226 Sample Rd., Huntersville 28078; (704) 875-1391; www.parkandrec.com

Finding the trailhead: From Charlotte take I-77 north. Latta Plantation Nature Preserve is marked off the interstate. Take exit 16B for Sunset Road West. Merge onto Sunset Road. When you arrive at the intersection with Beatties Ford Road, turn right (north). Travel 4.9 miles on Beatties Ford Road and then turn left (west) onto Sample Road. Stay on Sample Road and enter Latta Plantation Nature Preserve. The Mountain Island Lake trailhead is the first parking lot on the left, next to the nature center. GPS: N35 21.357' / W80 54.571'

THE HIKE

This hike begins at the parking lot of the Latta Plantation Nature Center. Be sure to stop inside the nature center before or after the hike to view the exhibits and talk with the ranger on duty. You might also consider doing a quick loop around the outside of the nature center to view the native plants that are labeled in the flower bed.

When you are ready to start walking, look for the black-blazed connector trail in the northeast corner of the parking lot, and follow it into the woods to its intersection with the Hill Trail. The connector trail intersects the Hill Trail just to the east of the Latta Equestrian Stables. At this junction you may want to take a quick side trip to the barn and view the horses or inquire about the trail riding program at Latta Equestrian Center.

Journeying past the stables on the Hill Trail, the route continues north on a gravel road. The road passes beside several open fields and under a set of power lines before arriving at the Split Rock Trail. Turn left on the Split Rock Trail and hike

An abandoned well sits near the trail.

west toward Mountain Island Lake. The Split Rock Trail begins as a gravel road, and like the Hill Trail, this path can become very hot in the summer due to the lack of shade. Thankfully, when you arrive at the shoreline of Mountain Island Lake, the path transitions into a single-track trail and stays well shaded under the canopy of the forest.

The tread of the Split Rock Trail near Mountain Island Lake becomes very rocky, and although you will want to spend most of your time looking up at the serene water and still landscape to your left, you will also need to focus on your footing and try not to trip. The trail at times comes close enough to the sandy edge of Mountain Island Lake that you can view freshwater clams gathered beneath the water.

When the Split Rock Trail veers away from the water, it also intersects the Hill Trail once again. By rejoining the Hill Trail, you will now travel to the northernmost portion of the preserve and once again return to the edge of Mountain Island Lake, this time on the Cove Trail. The footing on the Cove Trail is slightly better than on the Split Rock Trail and the quiet coves that define the path are often home to nesting waterfowl such as geese, ducks, and blue herons. Winter is the best time to spot a wide array of migrating duck species including mallards, northern pintails, and American black ducks.

Do not be misled on the Cove Trail by the many connecting trails that lead inward. The black-blaze connector trails serve as interconnecting spokes, but as long as you veer right and stay near the water, you will remain on the right path. On the north side of the Cove Trail, you will start to see houses and perhaps hear noises coming from the Latta Springs neighborhood to the north. The still cove that separates you from this development is a popular spot to see a handful of bass fisherman testing their luck.

When you complete the loop portion of the Cove Trail, return south on the Hill Trail and then reconnect with the Cove Trail on the perimeter of the Latta Restoration site. This protected area is home to the endangered Schweinitz's sunflower. By hiking on the outskirts of this open field, you will not only have the opportunity to view the rare wildflower, but you will also pass the stone remnants of an old well.

When the Cove Trail terminates at the Split Rock Trail, veer left and follow the southern boundary of the restoration area back to the Hill Trail, where you will then retrace your steps, past the equestrian center, to the nature center parking lot.

> 🌰 **Green Tip:**
> *Go out of your way to avoid birds and other animals that are mating or taking care of their young.*

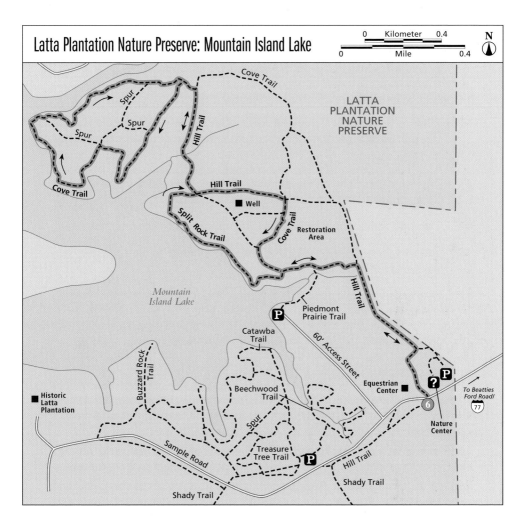

0   Kilometer   0.4

0   Mile   0.4

N

LATTA
PLANTATION
NATURE
PRESERVE

Cove Trail

Spur

Spur

Spur

Hill Trail

Cove Trail

Hill Trail

Well

Split Rock Trail

Cove Trail

Restoration
Area

Mountain
Island Lake

Piedmont
Prairie Trail

Hill Trail

Catawba
Trail

60' Access Street

Buzzard Rock Trail

Beechwood
Trail

Equestrian
Center

?

To Beatties
Ford Road/

Historic
Latta
Plantation

77

6

Nature
Center

Spur

Sample Road

Treasure
Tree Trail

Hill Trail

Shady Trail

Shady Trail

MILES AND DIRECTIONS

0.0   Locate the black-blazed connector trail in the northeast corner of the nature center parking lot and follow it into the woods.

0.1   Veer left on the connector trail to join the Hill Trail and continue to hike north.

0.5   Turn left (west) on the red-blazed Split Rock Trail.

0.6   Bypass the Piedmont Prairie Trail, then veer left where the Split Rock Trail splits in two.

1.4   After tracing the shoreline of Mountain Island Lake, the Split Rock Trail rejoins the Hill Trail. Turn left (east) on the Hill Trail.

1.8 When you arrive at a busy trail junction, cut back to your left (west), and head west to hike in a clockwise direction on the green-blazed Cove Trail.

2.2 A short out-and-back leads to a lookout point.

3.5 When you complete the loop portion of the Cove Trail, continue straight through the first trail junction, then turn right (south) to rejoin the Hill Trail and hike south.

3.9 Intersect the Split Rock Trail and turn left (east). Stay on the combined Split Rock and Hill Trail until you reconnect with the Cove Trail.

4.1 Turn right (south) on the Cove Trail and hike through the restoration area.

4.2 Turn left (east) on the Split Rock Trail and continue to veer left until you reach the Hill Trail.

4.7 Retrace your steps on the Hill Trail to the black connector trail that leads to the nature center.

5.4 Conclude your hike at the nature center parking lot.

HIKE INFORMATION

Local information: Town of Huntersville Town Hall, 101 Huntersville Concord Rd., Huntersville 28078; (704) 875-6541; www.huntersville.org. The website can help you find local attractions and information about Huntersville.

Local events/attractions: Historic Latta Plantation, 5225 Sample Rd., Huntersville 28078; (704) 875-2312; www.lattaplantation.org. The gorgeous Latta Plantation house, known as Latta Place, was built in 1800. It is open to the public and offers tours daily.

Good eats: Bennington Bagel and Coffee Co.; 8142 Mount Holly Huntersville Rd., Charlotte 28216; (704) 393-3733; www.benningtonbagels.com. Three words: Chocolate cream cheese . . . plus other good stuff.

Organizations: Charlotte-Mecklenburg Historic Landmarks Commission, 2100 Randolph Rd., Charlotte 28207; (704) 376-9115; www.cmhpf.org. This organization provides local historic information and suggested historic driving routes.

Latta Plantation Nature Preserve: Raptor Trail

This pleasant balloon hike is a great excursion for families. The path starts at the Latta Plantation Nature Preserve, where educational exhibits and native animal displays will get you excited about searching for specific plants and reptiles on the trail. From the nature center, the Hill Trail follows a rolling dirt road to connect with the Shady Trail. The Shady Trail makes a large 1.6-mile loop, and passes the main park road that provides close access to a picnic site and the Carolina Raptor Center. The raptor center provides a great place to rest and learn about birds of prey before completing the hike.

Start: Latta Plantation Nature Center
Distance: 2.6-mile balloon
Hiking time: About 1.5 hours
Difficulty: Easy
Trail surface: Forested trail and dirt road
Best season(s): Year-round
Other trail users: Equestrians
Canine compatibility: Dogs are not allowed at the raptor center.
Land status: Mecklenburg County nature preserve

Fees and permits: None
Schedule: Open daily; 7 a.m. to sunset
Maps: USGS Mountain Island Lake; basic trail maps are available for free inside the nature center and at trailhead kiosks
Trail contacts: Latta Plantation Nature Preserve, 5226 Sample Rd., Huntersville 28078; (704) 875-1391; www.parkandrec.com

Finding the trailhead: From Charlotte take I-77 north. Latta Plantation Nature Preserve is marked off the interstate. Take exit 16B for Sunset Road West. Merge onto Sunset Road. When you arrive at the intersection with Beatties Ford Road, turn right (north). Travel 4.9 miles on Beatties Ford Road and then turn left (west) onto Sample Road. Stay on Sample Road and enter Latta Plantation Nature Preserve. The Mountain Island Lake trailhead is the first parking lot on the left, next to the nature center. GPS: N35 21.357'/W80 54.571'

THE HIKE

This route, along with the Mountain Island Lake hike, both start at the Latta Plantation Nature Center parking lot, and it can only enhance your visit to stop by the nature center before or after the hike to view the exhibits and speak with the knowledgeable staff. It should also be noted before you start this trek that if you decide to take the optional side trip to visit the Carolina Raptor Center, you should allot more than the recommended 1.5 hours for this hike.

To begin your adventure, walk past the entrance of the Latta Nature Center, and then cross the main park road at the designated crosswalk. On the opposite side of the street, there is a dirt road that soon terminates at a locked gate. When you reach the gate, turn right and hike southwest on the orange-blazed Hill Trail. This wide dirt path is a popular trail for pedestrians and equestrians. You will need to watch your step to avoid the evidence of horses and also be warned that sections of this trail can become slick and muddy after a heavy rain.

The Hill Trail will parallel the main park road and a set of power lines for nearly half a mile before it intersects the Shady Trail. At the Shady Trail, turn left and follow the orange blazes clockwise. The Shady Trail is named for the ample hardwood trees that line the trail and provide a pleasant shadow with their deciduous leaves in the spring, summer, and fall. You will also notice a handful of pine trees mixed

A birdhouse sits aside the path.

within the forest. These longleaf pine, pitch pine, and Virginia pine trees give the forest a nice shade of green, even in the winter months.

Because of the ample amount of large trees, both growing toward the sky and littered on the ground from past storms and hurricanes, the Shady Trail is one of the best birding areas in the park. In anticipation of visiting the Carolina Raptor Center, keep your eyes peeled for owls, hawks, and vultures roosting in the high trees.

As you make your way around the Shady Trail loop, you might catch glimpses of Mountain Island Lake on your left. The lake fosters a rare habitat in much of the Latta Plantation Nature Preserve, known as a bottomland hardwood forest. A bottomland hardwood forest is much more damp and moisture-rich than a typical hardwood or mixed forest. Due to the added water, the bottomland hardwood forest is a popular habitat for amphibians, birds, and lizards. On the Shady Trail you will actually hike through a bottomland hardwood forest and upland hardwood forest, but most of the trail is spent in a transition zone between the two ecosystems.

After hiking 1.7 total miles, you will come to an intersection with the main park road. To the right you will notice a picnic ground with a covered gazebo. This is a great place to rest and have a snack, but it is also the side trail that leads to the Carolina Raptor Center. To access the facility, walk past the picnic area and look for the paved road to the left that provides access and parking for the raptor center. The raptor center is located outdoors on unpaved trails. Exploring the entire facility will add 0.8 mile to the total hike, but it is well worth the added time, distance, and entrance fee.

The Carolina Raptor Center is an educational facility that rehabilitates birds of prey. Upon visiting the facility you will learn that a raptor is distinguished from other birds of prey by the fact that it can hunt animals with the claws or talons on its feet. Native raptors of North Carolina include owls, hawks, vultures, and eagles. Although the birds within the facility constantly rotate, the educational exhibits and bird observatories always provide interesting facts and lasting memories.

After visiting, or just noting, the location of the raptor center, the hike continues across the main park road on the Shady Trail. Within the next 0.25 mile, the Shady Trail will intersect a Buzzard Trail connector and the Treasure Tree Trail. Be sure to stay straight at all intersections and continue to follow the orange triangles that mark the Shady Trail.

When you cross the main park road for the second time on the Shady Trail, the loop will conclude at a junction with the Hill Trail. At this intersection turn left and follow the Hill Trail back to your car at the nature center parking lot.

If you ever find an injured bird on the trail or in your neighborhood, you can call the Carolina Raptor Center at (704) 875-6521. If they are open, they will be able to provide guidance and assistance.

Latta Plantation Nature Preserve: Raptor Trail

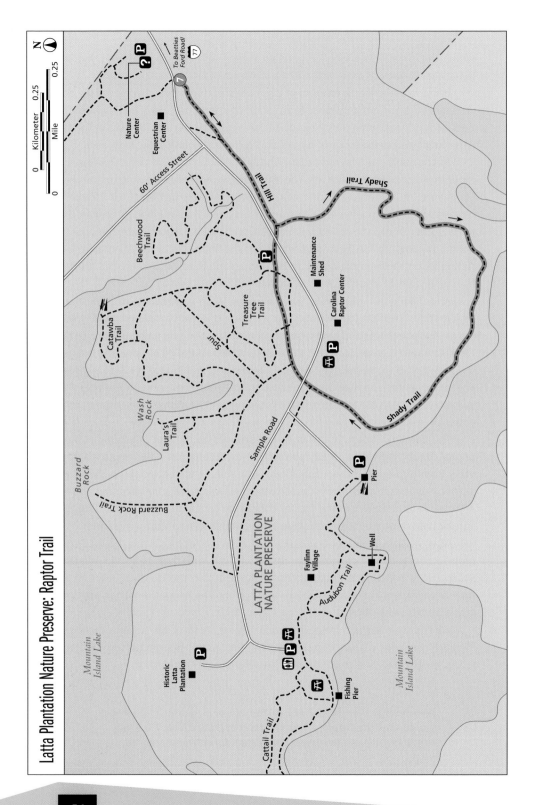

LATTA PLANTATION NATURE PRESERVE

Mountain Island Lake

Historic Latta Plantation

Cattail Trail

Fishing Pier

Faylinn Village

Audubon Trail

Well

Pier

Sample Road

Buzzard Rock

Buzzard Rock Trail

Laura's Trail

Wash Rock

Catawba Trail

Spur

Treasure Tree Trail

Maintenance Shed

Carolina Raptor Center

Shady Trail

Hill Trail

Beechwood Trail

60' Access Street

Nature Center

Equestrian Center

To Beatties Ford Road!

77

7

N

0   Kilometer   0.25

0   Mile   0.25

MILES AND DIRECTIONS

0.0   Hike west from the parking area and pass the front entrance of the nature center before turning left to cross the main park road and continuing on a dirt road.

0.2   The dirt road reaches a locked gate. Turn right (west) and follow the orange-blazed Hill Trail.

0.3   A spur trail that leads to the park road intersects the Hill Trail to the right. Continue straight.

0.5   The Hill Trail terminates at the Shady Trail. Turn left (south) and hike the Shady Trail loop in a clockwise direction.

1.7   The Shady Trail intersects the main park road. Cross the road to continue the hike, or follow the road to the right to access the picnic area and Carolina Raptor Center.

1.8   The Shady Trail crosses several intersecting trails including a Buzzard Rock connector and the Treasure Tree Trail. At each intersection continue straight on the wide dirt path that is marked with orange blazes.

2.0   The Shady Trail crosses the main park road near the horse trailer parking lot. Just past the road turn left (east) onto the Hill Trail.

2.2   Veer right to avoid a spur trail that leads to the road.

2.6   Arrive back at the nature center and trailhead parking lot.

HIKE INFORMATION

Local information: Town of Huntersville Town Hall, 101 Huntersville Concord Rd., Huntersville 28078; (704) 875-6541; www.huntersville.org. This website can help you find local attractions and information about Huntersville.

Local events/attractions: The Carolina Raptor Center, 6000 Sample Rd., Huntersville 28078; (704) 875-6521; www.carolinaraptorcenter.org. Learn about hawks, eagles, owls, and other raptors at this outdoor exhibit.

Good eats: Find a wide variety of restaurants at nearby Northlake Mall, 6801 Northlake Mall Dr., Huntersville 28078; (704) 599-6665; www.shopnorthlake.com.

Organizations: Arts & Science Council, 227 W. Trade St., Suite 250, Charlotte 28202; (704) 333-2272; www.artsandscience.org. Promoting "arts, science, history, and heritage" in Charlotte.

Latta Plantation Nature Preserve: Latta Loops

By combining four separate, short loop trails, this hike offers a wide variety of terrain and scenery. The first two loops leave from the horse trailer parking lot and take you on an information station hike on the Treasure Tree Trail, followed by a scenic and hilly traverse of the neighboring Beechwood Trail. Next, you will need to shuttle your car to the western boundary of the preserve, where the Audubon Trail and Cattail Trail explore the shoreline of Mountain Island Lake. The Faylinn Village portion of the Audubon Trail is a favorite with children, since they are encouraged to build an all-natural fairy hut on their hike through the forest.

Start: The horse trailer parking lot
Distance: 3.9-mile double figure eight
Hiking time: About 2 hours
Difficulty: Moderate
Trail surface: Forested trail
Best season(s): Year-round
Other trail users: Equestrians
Canine compatibility: Leashed dogs permitted
Land status: Mecklenburg County nature preserve

Fees and permits: None
Schedule: Open daily; 7 a.m. to sunset
Maps: USGS Mountain Island Lake; basic trail maps are available for free inside the nature center and at trailhead kiosks
Trail contacts: Latta Plantation Nature Preserve, 5226 Sample Rd., Huntersville 28078; (704) 875-1391; www.parkandrec.com

Finding the trailhead: From Charlotte take I-77 north. Latta Plantation Nature Preserve is marked off the interstate. Take exit 16B for Sunset Road West. Merge onto Sunset Road. When you arrive at the intersection with Beatties Ford Road, turn right (north). Travel 4.9 miles on Beatties Ford Road and then turn left (west) onto Sample Road. Stay on Sample Road and enter Latta Plantation Nature Preserve. The first trailhead is located at the horse trailer parking lot, past the nature center. GPS: N35 21.156'/W80 54.956'

The second trailhead is located at the west end of the preserve, past Latta Plantation. GPS: N35 21.103'/W80 55.808'

THE HIKE

I f variety is the spice of life, then this hike certainly is well seasoned. Although it is grouped together as one cumulative hike, this route actually combines four separate loop trails at Latta Plantation Nature Preserve. Those four trails are then split into two figure-eight hiking circuits that are connected by a short car shuttle. Each short loop presents a different feel and feature of the preserve, and due to the variety and short segments of this hike, it is considered a great outing for the entire family.

The first figure-eight loop starts at the horse trailer parking lot. Before venturing into the woods, approach the wooden information kiosk at the north end of the parking lot and look for a *Treasure Tree Trail Guide*. This free brochure will help lead you through the stations of the Treasure Tree Trail.

To begin the loop, hike west from the kiosk and locate the red blazes that lead into the woods. As you hike the trail, you will encounter a numbered station every few minutes. Take the time to stop and read the corresponding paragraph from the *Treasure Tree Trail Guide*. In doing so you will learn about tree identification, forestry practices, and leave-no-trace ethics. The brochure will also point out the

Watch out for wood nymphs in Faylinn Village.

large sourwood tree toward the end of the loop that is designated as a "Treasure Tree" by Mecklenburg County because of it's large size and maturity.

The only confusing portion of the loop comes when the trail briefly adjoins a dirt road blazed with black markers. Once you arrive at the road, immediately start looking for the Treasure Tree Trail and dart back into the forest on your right. Follow it to the completion of the loop, and then take a left to reenter the horse trailer parking lot.

When you have completed the Treasure Tree Trail, venture to the east end of the parking lot to locate the trailhead for the Beechwood Trail. Like the Treasure Tree Trail, this path soon splits and you will once again take a left and travel clockwise around the loop. The rolling terrain of the Beechwood Trail will lead you over several small streams that connect to nearby Mountain Island Lake. During the winter you can catch several glimpses of the lake through the golden brown leaves that are still hanging on to the beech trees. Unlike most deciduous trees, beech tree leaves do not contain the chemical that causes their leaves to detach in the fall. Therefore beech trees will hold on to their leaves throughout the winter, until a strong storm, wind, or spring bud causes them to fall off. There are copious young beech saplings that line this trail and also a handful of impressive mature beech trees.

A peaceful stream winds its way through fallen leaves.

At the conclusion of the Beechwood Trail, drive your car to the picnic area at the west end of the preserve. Visit the wooden information kiosk in the center of the picnic area, and then hike east to begin the Audubon Trail. The green-blazed trail will promptly split, and by veering left you will enter Faylinn Village. This imaginary fairy village is a favorite among children, and the park encourages visitors to use fallen sticks, leaves, and pinecones to build miniature homes for the Latta fairies to visit. Just remember not to break any branches or use anything living to build the forest dwellings. On the other end of Faylinn Village, continue east and hike to the terminus of the Audubon Trail at the public boat launch parking lot. From here, turn around and hike back to the picnic area on the Audubon Trail, but veer left at the first trail junction to return along the shoreline of Mountain Island Lake.

Once you are back at the picnic area, continue on the paved trail past the wooden kiosk, where you started, and follow it to the start of the Cattail Trail. Take a right on the Cattail Trail and follow it through the forest until it arrives at a marshland. This water habitat is a popular nesting site for herons and ducks. Continue along the shoreline past a rock outcropping, and follow the dirt path to its terminus at the wooden fishing pier. The paved trail at the fishing pier leads back to your car at the picnic area parking lot.

MILES AND DIRECTIONS

0.0 At the horse trailer parking lot, hike west to begin the red-blazed Treasure Tree Trail.

0.1 Turn left (south) where the trail splits.

0.2 Within the next 300 yards, you will intersect the Shady Trail twice. Be sure to continue straight at both intersections to remain on the Treasure Tree Trail.

0.8 Complete the loop and turn left (east) to return to the horse trailer parking lot.

0.9 Begin the Beechwood Trail at the east end of the parking lot.

1.0 The trail splits. Turn left (north).

The National Audubon Society has designated Latta Plantation Nature Preserve as part of the Mountain Island Lake Important Bird Area. The preserve's bottomland forest and sheltered coves attract a large number of songbirds and migratory waterfowl. Visit the Mecklenburg County Audubon Society website (http://meckbirds.org) to learn how to identify the birds that you see at Latta Plantation Nature Preserve.

Latta Plantation Nature Preserve: Latta Loops

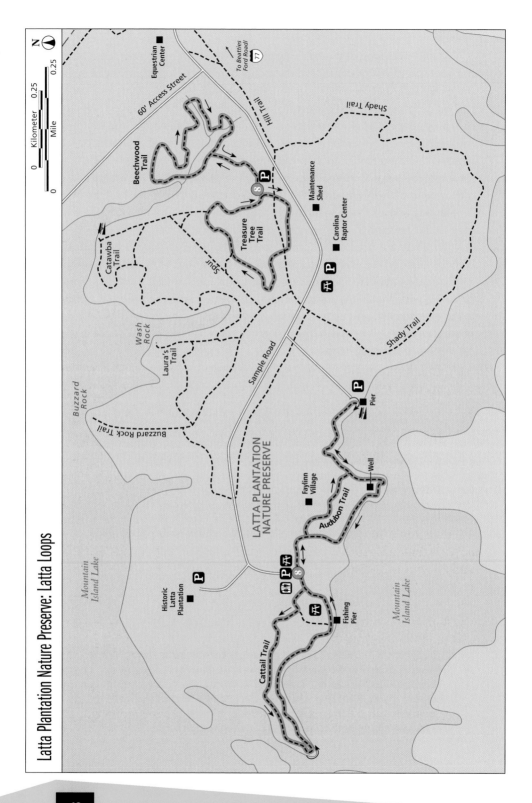

1.8 Complete the Beechwood Loop and turn left (west) to return to the parking area.

1.9 Reenter the horse trailer parking lot. To start the second figure eight, travel to the public picnic area and fishing pier at west end of the preserve. Locate the wooden information kiosk in the middle of the picnic area, then hike west on a paved trail.

2.0 The Audubon Trail starts at the edge of the forest, and shortly thereafter it splits. Veer left (east) to enter Faylinn Village. Consider building a fairy home while you are there!

2.3 Leave behind the magical Faylinn Village and continue straight on the Audubon Trail.

2.4 Reach the public boat launch parking area and turn around. At the subsequent Faylinn Village intersection, turn left (south) and hike toward Mountain Island Lake.

2.9 Conclude the Audubon Loop and turn left (west) toward the picnic area.

3.0 Pass the wooden information kiosk and follow the paved trail to the start of the Cattail Trail. Turn right (northwest) on the Cattail Trail.

3.8 Arrive at a marshy cove of Mountain Island Lake. Contour the shoreline.

3.9 The dirt path terminates at the fishing pier. Follow the paved trail back to the wooden information kiosk and trailhead parking.

HIKE INFORMATION

Local information: Town of Huntersville Town Hall, 101 Huntersville Concord Rd., Huntersville 28078; (704) 875-6541; www.huntersville.org. This website can help you find local attractions and information about Huntersville.

Local events/attractions: The Carolina Raptor Center, 6000 Sample Rd., Huntersville 28078; (704) 875-6521; www.carolinaraptorcenter.org. Learn more about hawks, eagles, owls, and other raptors at this outdoor exhibit.

Good eats: Find a wide variety of restaurants at nearby Northlake Mall, 6801 Northlake Mall Dr., Huntersville 28078; (704) 599-6665; www.shopnorthlake.com.

Organizations: Charlotte Folk Society, Regional History Consortium, PO Box 36864, Charlotte 28236; (704) 372-3655; www.folksociety.org. This organization helps to carry on modern and traditional folk culture in the North Carolina piedmont.

Latta Plantation Nature Preserve: Buzzard Rock

If sitting on a large solitary boulder warmed by the sun and overlooking a beautiful lake sounds like a nice way to spend the afternoon, then this hike is for you. The path starts at the Buzzard Rock trailhead and immediately travels out to the Buzzard Rock outcropping and viewing area on Mountain Island Lake. And if you like this spot, you will love the hike's next waterfront destination at the secluded Wash Rock Overlook. Beyond Wash Rock, the trail travels through the forest to reach one final lake destination at the Catawba Trail boating dock, before looping back around to the trailhead.

Start: Buzzard Rock trailhead

Distance: 3.1-mile balloon

Hiking time: About 1.5 hours

Difficulty: Moderate

Trail surface: Forested trail and dirt roads

Best season(s): Year-round

Other trail users: Equestrians

Canine compatibility: Leashed dogs permitted

Land status: Mecklenburg County nature preserve

Fees and permits: None

Schedule: Open daily; 7 a.m. to sunset

Maps: USGS Mountain Island Lake; basic trail maps are available for free inside the nature center and at trailhead kiosks

Trail contacts: Latta Plantation Nature Preserve, 5226 Sample Rd., Huntersville 28078; (704) 875-1391; www.parkandrec.com

Finding the trailhead: From Charlotte take I-77 north. Latta Plantation Nature Preserve is marked off the interstate. Take exit 16B for Sunset Road West. Merge onto Sunset Road. When you arrive at the intersection with Beatties Ford Road, turn right (north). Travel 4.9 miles on Beatties Ford Road and then turn left (west) onto Sample Road. Stay on Sample Road and enter Latta Plantation Nature Preserve. The Buzzard Rock trailhead is located on the right, past the Carolina Raptor Center. GPS: N35 21.231'/W80 55.556'

THE HIKE

This hike traces the shoreline of Mountain Island Lake and touches the water at three separate view points that overlook the serene lake. The route is one of the most scenic at Latta Plantation Nature Preserve, and past Buzzard Rock it is one of the least traveled as well.

The hike begins at the Buzzard Rock parking area. Before beginning your hike make sure that you pick up a free trail map at the nature center or one of the trailhead kiosks. This will help you better navigate the intersecting trails.

When you are ready to start hiking, locate the trail leading into the woods at the northeast end of the parking area and follow it into the forest. Within a few minutes you will arrive at your first trail junction. Veer left and continue toward Buzzard Rock. This short out-and-back leads to a beautiful wooden viewing platform that overlooks Mountain Island Lake.

Mountain Island Lake is the drinking-water source for more than 800,000 residents in Gaston and Mecklenburg Counties. No matter how inviting the still waters below may look, especially on a hot summer day, remember that swimming is not allowed at Latta Plantation Nature Preserve. Splashing or wading near the shoreline may disturb nesting waterfowl.

A boulder sits on the shore of Mountain Island Lake.

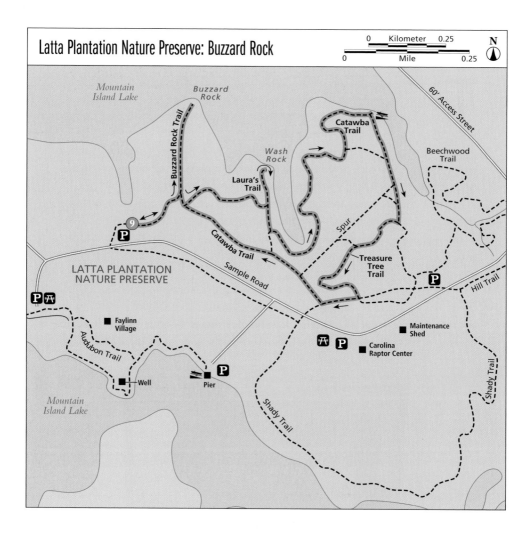

Latta Plantation Nature Preserve: Buzzard Rock

When you are ready to leave Buzzard Rock, backtrack to the nearby trail junction and then turn left and head east on the Catawba Trail. You will only stay on the Catawba Trail momentarily before you veer off to the left to join Laura's Trail. The blue-blazed Laura's Trail will quickly lead to Wash Rock, your second overlook of Mountain Island Lake. Unlike Buzzard Rock, there is not a wooden viewing area at Wash Rock, but there are several diorite boulders where you can sit and enjoy the scenery. A diorite rock contains very low levels of quartz, compared to a high composition of quartz in granite. The smooth rounded diorite boulders at the end of Laura's Trail are named Wash Rock because it is believed that early settlers used to wash and dry their clothes on these sunbathed rocks.

Once you leave Wash Rock, veer left at the next intersection to rejoin the Catawba Trail. At this point follow the orange-blazed path inland through a forest of towering tulip poplar trees. You can usually identify the tulip poplars by searching for the tallest, straightest trees in the forest, or you can look for their unique four-lobbed leaf. These trees require a large amount of sunlight to survive, and that is why they shoot toward the sky as young trees, hoping to outgrow the competition.

At mile 1.2 the trail briefly exits the forest and enters a power-line clear-cut. Rather than crossing the field, hug the western edge of the forest and then dive back into the woods on the continuing Catawba Trail. Past the power lines, the Catawba Trail splits. Veer left and follow the trail to the third and final Mountain Island Lake viewpoint, which coincides with the Latta Plantation Nature Preserve boat dock. During the summer months the Latta staff offers guided paddling trips on the lake. Check at the nature center for schedule information.

The access road leads under a set of power lines. Just past this opening, turn right and join a connector trail that will take you back into the forest and soon connect with the Treasure Tree Trail. By following the Treasure Tree Trail west, you will once again rejoin the Catawba Trail and follow it to the completion of the hike at the Buzzard Rock trailhead.

MILES AND DIRECTIONS

0.0 The Buzzard Rock Trail is blazed in red and leaves from the northeast corner on the parking lot.

0.1 Veer left (north) at the trail junction to continue on the Buzzard Rock Trail.

0.3 You will arrive at Buzzard Rock overlook. When you are ready to leave, retrace your steps to the last trail junction.

0.5 Turn left (east) on the Catawba Trail.

0.6 Veer left (north) to join the blue-blazed Laura's Trail.

0.7 Veer left (north) to remain on Laura's Trail.

0.8 Arrive at Wash Rock. When you are ready to leave Wash Rock, retrace your steps to the last trail junction.

0.9 Turn left (east) and rejoin the Catawba Trail.

1.1 Enter an open field with power lines, continue on the west side of the field for 100 yards, and then delve back into the forest, remaining on the Catawba Trail.

1.5 The Catawba Trail splits. Go left (west).

1.8 Arrive at the boat dock. Hike south on the gravel access road past the boathouse.

2.0 Cross under the power lines and turn off the road and join a black connector trail to your right (west). An alternate connector trail hugs the edge of the power-line field, but you should take the shaded path.

2.1 Turn right (west) on the Treasure Tree Trail.

2.4 At a four-way intersection, turn right (west) to briefly join the orange-blazed Shady Trail.

2.5 Before arriving at the main park road, turn right (west) on a black-blazed connector trail and follow it north, under a set of power lines.

2.6 Turn left (west) on the Catawba Trail.

3.0 Turn left (south) again, at the Buzzard Rock Trail intersection.

3.1 Complete the hike at the Buzzard Rock trailhead.

A peaceful bench at Buzzard Rock is a great place to sit and enjoy the scenic view of Mountain Island Lake.

Local information: Town of Huntersville Town Hall, 101 Huntersville Concord Rd., Huntersville 28078; (704) 875-6541; www.huntersville.org. The website can help you find local attractions and information about Huntersville.

Local events/attractions: Historic Latta Plantation, 5225 Sample Rd., Huntersville 28078; (704) 875-2312; www.lattaplantation.org. The gorgeous Latta Plantation house, known as Latta Place, was built in 1800. It is open to the public and offers tours daily.

Good eats: Lancaster's Bar-B-Que, 9230 Beatties Ford Rd.; Huntersville 28078; (704) 394-1464; www.lancastersbbq.com. If you are hungry after the hike, try one of their pulled-pork sandwiches.

Organizations: Charlotte Regional History Consortium; PO Box 33113, Charlotte 28233; www.charlotteregionalhistory.org. This group is dedicated to "preserving, promoting, and interpreting the history of the Charlotte region."

Discover More

Latta Place at Latta Plantation is separate from Latta Plantation Nature Preserve. Latta Place is the beautiful early-nineteenth-century house on the plantation. Latta Nature Preserve is comprised of the scenic hills, fields, forest, and shoreline that surround the house. Both are worth visiting. The white plantation house, Latta Place, was built in 1800 by James Latta. The surrounding 742 acres were used primarily to grow cotton. The operation had all the traditional aspects of Southern farm life, including more than thirty-four enslaved people. After James Latta passed away, the land changed hands twice before being bought by a subsidiary of Duke Power in the 1900s. Duke Power bought the land due to its proximity to the Catawba River and did very little to preserve the plantation home. In the 1970s a group of concerned citizens who saw the potential of Latta Plantation came together and formed Latta Place Inc. This group secured funds to buy the plantation house, restore the property, and ultimately open it to the public in the 1970s. Today it is a living farm and museum that is open to the public and hosts more than 10,000 schoolchildren every year.

Although McDowell Nature Preserve has great trails along Lake Wylie, it also features beautiful wooded paths that are terrific places to go bird watching or to simply stretch your legs. This trail starts at the McDowell Nature Center and then immediately dives into the woods on the Sierra Trail. The path travels a narrow corridor through a mixed forest of oak, maple, cedar, and pine. Eventually the route connects with the Creekside Trail and follows the fern-filled banks of Porter Branch, before veering up to meet Cedar Ridge. The trail then loops back to the nature center through a verdant forest with verdant undergrowth and stunning seasonal wildflowers.

Start: McDowell Preserve Nature Center

Distance: 2.8-mile balloon

Hiking time: About 1.5 to 2 hours

Difficulty: Moderate

Trail surface: Forested trail

Best season(s): Fall

Other trail users: None

Canine compatibility: Leashed dogs permitted

Land status: Mecklenburg County nature preserve

Fees and permits: None

Schedule: Open daily; 7 a.m. to sunset

Maps: USGS Lake Wylie; basic trail maps are available for free at the trailhead kiosk and inside the nature center

Trail contacts: McDowell Nature Preserve, 15222 York Rd., Charlotte 28278; (704) 588-5224; www.parkandrec.com

Finding the trailhead: From Charlotte take I-77 southbound to exit 90. Turn west on Carowinds Boulevard and drive 2.0 miles to South Tryon Street/NC 49. Take a left (south) on South Tryon Street and drive 4.0 miles to the entrance of McDowell Nature Preserve. Turn right (west) into the preserve and then follow the signs to the nature center. GPS: N35 06.047'/W81 01.205'

THE HIKE

The Woodland Forest Trail starts at the McDowell Nature Center. Be sure to stop by the facility before or after the hike to view the terrariums and aquariums. While you are there you can also view the informational displays and ask the ranger on duty about the native flora and fauna that you will see on your hike. The first, very short segment of trail, takes place on the Sierra Trail, and there is an informational pamphlet to accompany the path that is available in the nature center.

When you are ready to start walking, locate the trailhead kiosk to the northwest of the nature center. Follow the spur trail behind the information board into the woods to a small amphitheater of benches. Turn right here to start the green-blazed Sierra Trail. If you picked up a brochure at the nature center, you can use it to help identify the trees along the path. The sweet gum, oak, and black-cherry trees that line the tread way are all deciduous hardwood trees. Deciduous trees have leaves that change color and detach each fall.

> **🌿 Green Tip:**
> *If you see someone else littering, muster up the courage to ask them not to.*

Moss and a Christmas fern poke through the fall folliage.

McDowell Nature Preserve: Woodland Forest Trail

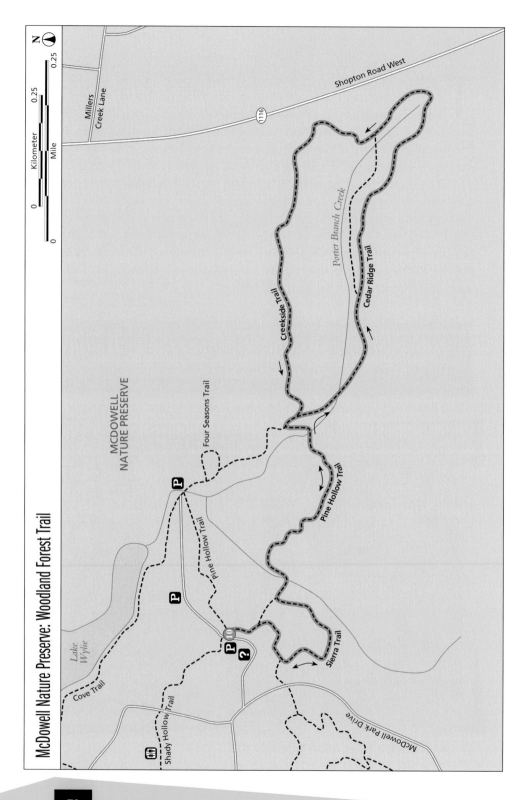

As you turn onto the Pine Hollow Trail and travel deeper into the woods, the trees along the path transition from hardwood to evergreen trees. Even in winter the different varieties of pine trees, holly trees, and towering cedars that line the path will form a green tunnel through the woods. Although the trail is in great shape, this path also passes ruts in the forest where heavy storm runoff has formed erosion ditches alongside the trail.

The path travels up and down several short climbs and crosses a small seasonal stream before arriving at the gurgling Porter Branch Creek. The rocks jutting out of the creek are covered in moss and the shoreline is decorated with green Christmas ferns. Cross the creek on a wooden footbridge and then turn right to follow the water upstream on the Creekside Trail. This quiet trail in a remote portion of the reserve is a great place to look for wildlife, including native birds such as the owl, hawk, or woodpecker.

The path will briefly leave the stream and cross through an open field filled with power lines before reentering the forest. At this point, if you prefer staying on a level path and enjoy the creek side walking then feel free to continue straight on the blue-blazed trail, however if you want to add a challenging ascent to your hike, then veer right on the Cedar Ridge Trail. This climb will take you above the bottomland forest to a lovely ridge lined with young beech trees. Through the beech leaves, you will catch glimpses of the creek bed to the north, and straight ahead you may spot a car whizzing by on Shopton Road West, a brief reminder that you have not entirely escaped civilization.

The Cedar Ridge Trail ends with a short, steep descent back to the Creekside Trail. This downhill portion of the hike can be very slick and muddy after a storm, so be careful, or you may be sliding on your bum. The faint hum of nearby traffic will continue on the northern half of the Creekside Trail, but this will not detract from the beautiful green underbrush and wildflowers lining the path. You may also want to keep your eyes peeled for the remains of an old wooden outhouse to the left of the trail.

At the completion of Creekside Trail, you will find yourself back at the wooden bridge that crosses Porter Branch Creek. Cross the bridge and retrace your steps on the Pine Hollow Trail. This path may feel more difficult than you may remember, as the return trip is slightly uphill. Press on and soon you will reach the Sierra Trail. A left or right turn on this short loop will lead you back to the trailhead at the McDowell Nature Center in a matter of minutes.

MILES AND DIRECTIONS

0.0 The trail starts at the wooden information kiosk to the northwest of the nature center. Within the first 50 feet, the path will split. Turn right to enjoy a brief detour on the Sierra Trail.

0.1 Pass a connector trail on your right. Continue straight (east) on the Sierra Trail.

0.2 At the trail intersection, turn right (east) and follow the Pine Hollow Trail.

0.8 Arrive at Porter Branch Creek. Cross the water on a wooden bridge and turn right on the Creekside Trail. In 30 yards the trail will split. Veer right (southeast) across a second bridge to travel the ensuing loop in a counter-clockwise direction.

0.9 Pass through a power-line field.

1.0 Veer right (southeast) on the red-blazed Cedar Ridge Trail.

1.4 Rejoin the Creekside Trail and turn right (north).

2.0 At the conclusion of the Creekside Trail loop, retrace your steps on the Pine Hollow Trail.

2.5 Veer left (southwest) on the Sierra Trail.

2.8 Conclude your hike at the McDowell Nature Preserve.

MILES AND DIRECTIONS

Local information: Lake Wylie Chamber of Commerce, 264 Latitude Lane, Suite 101, Lake Wylie, SC 29710; (803) 831-2827; www.lakewyliesc.com. Lake Wylie is both a lake and a town. Check it out.

Local events/attractions: Daniel Stowe Botanical Garden, 6500 S. New Hope Rd., Belmont 28012; (704) 829-1240; www.dsbg.org. Didn't get your fill of wild-flowers at McDowell Nature Preserve? Check out the manicured flower beds at Daniel Stowe Botanical Garden. There is a charge for admission.

Good eats: Luigi's Pizza, 13551 Steelecroft Pkwy., #100, Charlotte 28278; (704) 587-6010; www.luigis-pizza.com. Enjoy New York–style pizza in a great family-friendly atmosphere.

Organizations: Catawba Riverkeeper Foundation, 421 Minuet Lane, Suite 205, Charlotte 28217; (704) 679-9494; www.catawbariverkeeper.org. Help to preserve and protect the Catawba River.

> *Hike this trail in various seasons and different weather conditions to observe Lake Wylie's color change to varying tones of blue. It can be very murky after a rainstorm and almost appear orange. When the sky is cloudy or dark, the lake sometimes looks dark blue or brown. Typically the lake appears a beautiful sapphire color when the sky is blue.*

McDowell Nature Preserve: Cove Loop

This route explores a scenic and undeveloped cove at Lake Wylie. It starts by first taking a warm-up loop on the handicapped-accessible Four Seasons Trail, and then follows the nearby creek to its marshy tributary. At this point the Cove Trail will lead you past the wetlands area and to the shoreline of Lake Wylie. This quiet waterside trek will often reveal nesting waterfowl or even a freshwater otter. After tracing the shoreline the trail veers inland and follows the undulating Shady Hollow Trail back to the visitor center, where a brief downhill hike will lead you back to your car at the Four Seasons trailhead.

Start: The Four Seasons trailhead
Distance: 2.2-mile figure eight
Hiking time: About 1 hour
Difficulty: Moderate
Trail surface: Forested trail
Best season(s): Fall, winter, early spring
Other trail users: None
Canine compatibility: Leashed dogs permitted
Land status: Mecklenburg County nature preserve

Fees and permits: None
Schedule: Open daily; 7 a.m. to sunset
Maps: USGS Lake Wylie; basic trail maps are available for free at the trailhead kiosk and inside the nature center
Trail contacts: McDowell Nature Preserve, 15222 York Rd., Charlotte 28278; (704) 588-5224; www.park andrec.com

Finding the trailhead: From Charlotte take I-77 southbound to exit 90. Turn west on Carowinds Boulevard and drive 2.0 miles to South Tryon Street/NC 49. Take a left (south) on South Tryon Street and drive 4.0 miles to the entrance of McDowell Nature Preserve. Turn right (west) into the preserve and then follow the signs to the nature center. Continue past the nature center and picnic pavilion parking until the road dead-ends at the Four Seasons trailhead. GPS: N35 06.099'/W81 01.019'

The majority of the Cove Loop hike is one large circle that encompasses the Lake Wylie shoreline and the inland forest at McDowell Nature Preserve. However, before venturing out on the main trail, the hike completes a very short loop on the Four Seasons Trail. This paved path travels briefly through the forest before returning to the trailhead along the banks of Porter Branch Creek. It is a very scenic hike and the fact that it is paved makes it handicapped-accessible. It even has a wheelchair ramp that leads down to the creek for better views of the water. Some hikers may turn their noses up at a paved hiking trail, but it is important to remember that the woods should be accessible to everyone, even those with limited mobility.

After a short but pleasant hike on the Four Seasons Trail, locate the Cove Trail at the west end of the parking lot. Make sure that you do in fact start down the single-track dirt path and not the gravel road that veers off to the north of the parking lot. The Cove Trail follows the transitioning Porter Branch Creek into a wetland area that is often home to muskrats and beavers. And even if you don't spot a beaver, you will probably be able to view their handiwork in a gnawed tree trunk or a log dam. If you see a horizontal pile of trees and twigs in the water, then you have spotted a beaver's home, called a lodge. But beware! The still murky water can also be home to mosquitoes in the late spring and early summer, so come prepared!

See this rocky creek bed near the Four Seasons Trail.

Eventually the water levels deepen and the marshy area evolves into a well-defined lakeshore. Unlike the southern banks of McDowell Nature Preserve, this section of trail reveals mostly undeveloped shoreline. There are a handful of understated lake houses on the opposite side of the cove, but nothing that compares to the large lakefront mansions that dominate other portions of the waterfront. The trail now hugs very closely to the shoreline, and the quiet ins and outs of the cove will often reveal ducks, a heron, or perhaps even a playful otter. The clear water will also provide glimpses of freshwater clams and darting minnows.

After hiking just over a mile, the path leaves the serene cove and veers inland. You will then climb a short but steep hill to arrive at the main park road. Located diagonally to your right is a parking area. You will need to walk to the far west end of that parking lot to resume the hike on the Shady Hollow Trail.

The Shady Hollow Trail features an undulating forested hike that weaves its way through towering pine trees. The path will leave the woods one more time to cross the main park road before arriving at its terminus at the nature center. Feel free to make a pit stop to visit the nature center to make use of the facilities and view the educational exhibits on display.

When you are ready to conclude your hike, travel to the north of the nature center and turn left on the Pine Hollow Trail. Follow this path past sourwood and maple trees on a gentle downhill grade. Within a few minutes you will arrive at the scenic Porter Branch Creek. Veer left to access to the Four Seasons trailhead and the nearby parking lot.

Discover More

Did you know that in 2008 the Catawba River was named one of the most endangered rivers in America? In 2010 it also made the list of top ten endangered places in the Southeast, as determined by the Southern Environmental Law Center. Some of the biggest threats to the river are pollution, dumping, and development. The Catawba River includes many inland lakes such as Lake Norman, Mountain Island Lake, and Wylie Lake. The high metal content and PCBs in these lakes and near the Charlotte-Mecklenburg area also affect the water quality downstream when the Catawba becomes the Wateree River. The Catawba Riverkeepers are dedicated to preserving and protecting this natural resource. Formed in 1997, this nonprofit organization trains cove keepers and volunteers to protect the river by picking up litter from the water and the banks. Volunteers also complete water-quality tests and try to garner positive publicity for the lake and the Riverkeepers' environment campaign. Consider financially supporting the group or joining them on one of their upcoming workdays! Contact Catawba Riverkeepers, 421 Minuet Lane, Suite 205, Charlotte 28217; (704) 679-9494; www.catawbariverkeeper.org.

McDowell Nature Preserve: Cove Loop

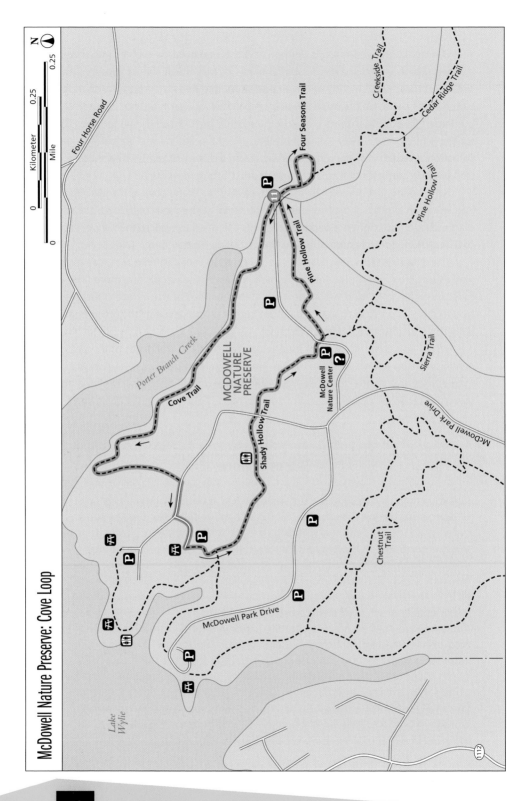

0.0 Locate the red-blazed Four Seasons Trail to the east of the parking lot. Follow the paved trail south into the woods along Porter Branch Creek.

0.1 The trail splits. Veer left (east) to complete this loop in a clockwise direction.

0.4 Complete the Four Seasons Trail and return to the parking lot. Continue hiking west on the blue-blazed Cove Trail.

1.3 The Cove Trail terminates at the paved Park Road. Hike diagonally to your right (northwest) to access a nearby parking lot.

1.4 Locate the Shady Hollow trailhead at the north end of the parking lot. Follow it into the woods.

1.5 Remain on the Shady Hollow Trail by turning left (southeast) at the intersection with a connector trail.

2.0 Arrive at the McDowell Nature Center. To continue the hike, walk to the south of the building and turn left (northeast) on the Pine Hollow Trail.

2.2 Connect to the Four Seasons trailhead. The trailhead and parking lot are a few dozen feet to your left.

HIKE INFORMATION

Local information: Lake Wylie Chamber of Commerce, 264 Latitude Lane, Suite 101, Lake Wylie, SC 29710; (803) 831-2827; www.lakewyliesc.com. Lake Wylie is both a lake and a town. Check it out.

Local events/attractions: Enjoy some bluegrass music at Allison Creek. It meets the first and third Thursday of every month at Allison Creek Presbyterian Church, 5780 Allison Creek Rd., York, SC 29745; www.allisoncreekbluegrass.com.

Good eats: Rey Azteca, 4052 Charlotte Hwy., Clover, SC 29710; (803) 831-9277; www.aztecamex.com. Head across the border (of South Carolina) for some great Mexican food.

Organizations: Catawba Riverkeeper Foundation, 421 Minuet Lane, Suite 205, Charlotte 28217; (704) 679-9494; www.catawbariverkeeper.org. Help to preserve and protect the Catawba River.

> 🍃 **Green Tip:**
> *Use the sun to recharge backcountry electronics.*

McDowell Nature Preserve: Lake Wylie Trail

This hike combines the best of McDowell Nature Preserve: beautiful hardwood forests and dramatic lakefront views. By starting at the nature center, the route will first travel through a woodland forest to the nearby Chestnut Trail. The path in this section is lined with beech trees and thin seasonal creeks. Eventually you will come out of the forest at the banks of Lake Wylie. Here you will trace the shoreline past the McDowell waterfront all the way to the picnic shelter and pier at the northern portion of the preserve. There are plenty of lakeside benches on which to sit and rest before retracing the shoreline back to the Chestnut Trail. A connector trail will then lead you back through the woods and toward the McDowell Nature Center to conclude your hike.

Start: McDowell Preserve Nature Center

Distance: 3.1-mile balloon

Hiking time: About 1.5 to 2 hours

Difficulty: Moderate

Trail surface: Forested trail and dirt roads

Best season(s): Spring, fall

Other trail users: None

Canine compatibility: Leashed dogs permitted

Land status: Mecklenburg County nature preserve

Fees and permits: None

Schedule: Open daily; 7 a.m. to sunset

Maps: USGS Lake Wylie; basic trail maps are available for free at the trailhead kiosk and inside the nature center

Trail contacts: McDowell Nature Preserve, 15222 York Rd., Charlotte 28278; (704) 588-5224; www.parkandrec.com

Finding the trailhead: From Charlotte take I-77 southbound to exit 90. Turn west on Carowinds Boulevard and drive 2.0 miles to South Tryon Street/NC 49. Take a left (south) on South Tryon Street and drive 4.0 miles to the entrance of McDowell Nature Preserve. Turn right (west) into the preserve and then follow the signs to the nature center. GPS: N35 06.047' / W81 01.205'

THE HIKE

This route is a terrific sampler of McDowell Nature Preserve. By passing through hardwood forests, beside the lake, and through picnic and recreation areas, the hike appeals to people of many different ages and interests. The trail starts at the McDowell Nature Center. To locate the trail, walk to the north of the nature center and locate the wooden information kiosk. Behind the kiosk is a dirt path. Follow it into the woods and then turn right on the Sierra Trail. You will notice numbered signposts lining the Sierra Trail. Rangers use these signposts to identify the different types of trees. See how many trees you can identify without a ranger there.

One tree in particular on the Sierra Trail will grab your attention. The tree at signpost #3 is a common northern red oak, but what makes it unique is the gargantuan bump growing on its trunk. This bump, called a burl, is the tree's version of a Band-Aid. The cause of burls, including this one, are still a mystery and may be due to bacteria, fungi, injury to the tree, or genetic mutation. Just think of it as a scar—a particularly big scar!

When the Sierra Trail intersects a black-blazed connector trail, turn left and follow the short connector across the main park entrance to join the Chestnut Trail.

The fishing pier extends into Lake Wylie.

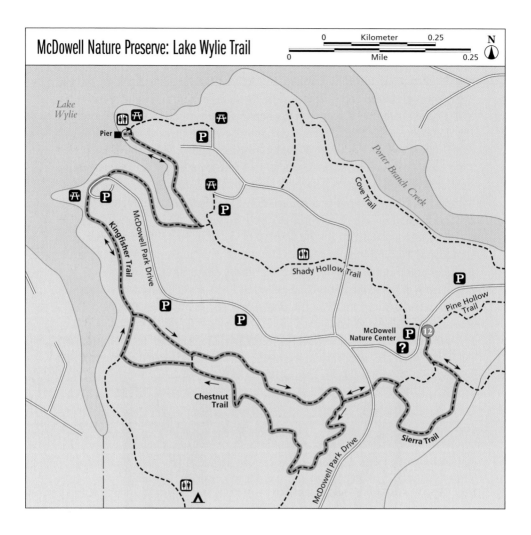

The Chestnut Trail forms a loop. Veer left to travel the southern portion of the trail through a hardwood forest and above a narrow valley. The trail will come very close to a seeping stream located in the valley before intersecting with another black connector trail. Once again veer left on the connector trail and follow it to the Kingfisher Trail on the banks of Lake Wylie.

At the shoreline you will immediately notice the large lakefront houses located to the north, and if the weather is nice, you may see motorboats cruising around the lake as well. By hiking north on the Kingfisher Trail, you will soon encounter the Lake Wylie waterfront. At this time swimming is not permitted at Lake Wylie, but this scenic stop does make a great place to enjoy a snack. Past the waterfront the route briefly skirts a park road to rejoin the Kingfisher Trail and then continues to the shore of a quiet lake cove. Treasure the silence along the shoreline of the small cove, because just past this wooded area, you will start to encounter picnic benches along the path, and within minutes you will pop out of the woods at the parks picnic pavilion. If you brought food on the hike, this is a great place to enjoy it. Or you might want to hike east to enjoy a bite to eat on a lakeside bench or perhaps even on the nearby pier.

When you are ready to head back toward the nature center, retrace your steps along the Kingfisher Trail. Past the waterfront area there will be a black connector trail to your left. Take this to join the Chestnut Trail and hike the northern portion of this path. It will display several large trees that were felled by hurricanes that occurred over the past two decades. After completing the second half of the Chestnut Trail, travel across the park road to rejoin the Sierra Trail and return to the McDowell Nature Center.

MILES AND DIRECTIONS

0.0   Locate the trailhead kiosk to the north of the nature center. Follow the dirt path, behind the wooden information board into the woods. In 20 yards the trail splits. Turn right and then take an immediate left (south) on the Sierra Trail.

0.2   Remain on the green-blazed Sierra Trail and follow it uphill to a black connector trail. Turn left (west) on the connector trail.

0.3   Cross a paved park road.

0.4   At the intersection with the Chestnut Trail, veer left.

0.8   Arrive at a junction with another connector trail. The Chestnut Trail turns north to cross a small creek bed, but you will continue east on the unnamed black-blazed trail.

0.9   On the banks of Lake Wylie, turn left (north) on the wide and well-groomed Kingfisher Trail.

1.2   Pass the preserves waterfront and then hike diagonally to the east. In 50 yards look for the Kingfisher Trail to resume on the north shoulder of the paved path.

1.6   Arrive at the McDowell picnic shelter and follow the recreation trail west to the pier. When you head back, retrace your route on the Kingfisher Trail.

2.3   Past the waterfront turn left (east) on a black connector trail.

2.4   When the connector trail intersects the Chestnut Trail, hike east on the red-blazed path.

2.8   Connect to the start of the Chestnut Trail and then turn left (east) to retrace your steps across the park road to the Sierra Trail.

2.9   Turn right on the Sierra Trail. (***Side trip:*** You can turn left if you want to complete the entire Sierra Trail loop.)

3.1   Emerge from the woods at the nature center.

HIKE INFORMATION

Local information: City of Tega Cay, PO Box 3399, Tega Cay, SC 29708; (803) 548-3512; www.tegacaysc.org. Tega Cay is located off the banks of Lake Wylie in South Carolina.

Local events/attractions: McCelvey Center, 212 E. Jefferson St., York, SC 29745; (803) 684-3948; www.chmuseums.org. A great place to enjoy the performing arts in York County. Check the website for upcoming shows.

Good eats: Jim 'n Nick's Bar-B-Q, 13840 Steele Creek Rd., Charlotte 28278; (704) 930-2290; www.jimnnicks.com. The cheese biscuits at Jim and Nick's are a terrific post-hike treat.

Organizations: Catawba Riverkeeper Foundation, 421 Minuet Lane, Suite 205, Charlotte 28217; (704) 679-9494; www.catawbariverkeeper.org. Help to preserve and protect the Catawba River.

> 🌿 **Green Tip:**
> *If you're driving to or from the trailhead, don't allow passengers to throw garbage out the window. Keep a small bag in the car that you can empty properly at home.*

If you can't get enough of McDowell Nature Preserve, consider spending the night in their public campground. Visit the park office for information and to make a reservation.

Reedy Creek Park and Nature Preserve: Robinson Rockhouse Ruins

This hike travels past modern sports fields and picnic pavilions in Reedy Creek Park, before accessing the remote southeast corner of Reedy Creek Nature Preserve. The majority of the hike follows the peaceful Sierra Trail through pine and holly trees to reach the Robinson Rockhouse Trail. From there it is a short trek out to the 200-year-old ruins of a Mecklenburg County farmhouse. Take your time exploring the house's remnants of the foundation and fireplace before retracing your steps back to the trailhead.

Start: At the dog park near the Rocky River Road entrance

Distance: 4.2-mile out and back

Hiking time: About 2 hours

Difficulty: Moderate

Trail surface: Dirt road and forested trail

Best season(s): Year-round

Other trail users: None

Canine compatibility: Leashed dogs permitted

Land status: Mecklenburg County park and nature preserve

Fees and permits: None

Schedule: Open daily; 7 a.m. to sunset

Maps: USGS Harrisburg; basic trail maps are available for free at the Reedy Creek Nature Center

Trail contacts: Reedy Creek Park and Nature Preserve, 2000 Rocky River Rd., Charlotte, 28215; (704) 598-8857; www.parkandrec.com

Finding the trailhead: From Charlotte take I-85 to exit 45-A (East W. T. Harris Boulevard). Continue on East W. T. Harris Boulevard to the fourth traffic light, at Rocky River Road. Take a left (east) and follow Rocky River Road for 0.5 mile. After veering left at a traffic light, turn right (south) into Reedy Creek Park and Nature Preserve. Trailhead parking is found immediately inside the park entrance, to the east of the dog park. GPS: N35 16.539'/W80 43.019'

THE HIKE

This hike starts near the entrance of Reedy Creek Park and Nature Preserve, at a large wooden kiosk near the dog park. If you decided to bring your four-legged friend on this hike, it might be a good idea to let your pooch run free for a few minutes inside the dog park, since Fido will need to stay on a leash during the hike.

When you are ready to begin your trek, follow the wide dirt path along the eastern outskirts of the dog park. In a few minutes the dirt path will lead you to the main park road near the baseball field. Cross over the paved road and follow the dirt trail clockwise around the baseball diamond. After making a semicircle around right field, the trail veers south and skirts the boundary of a soccer field. On a Saturday morning or warm spring evening, these athletic fields will be bustling with activity, but on a cold winter morning, this portion of the hike can be as silent as a trail leading through the woods.

Past the soccer field, the dirt road will enter the forest and travel through the Frisbee golf course before arriving at the nearby picnic pavilions. This is a good spot to stop and enjoy a snack or use the nearby restrooms before the trail transi-

Robinson Rockhouse has been in ruins since the 1890s.

tions into a remote single-track path. When you are ready to leave the amenities of the park behind you and enter Reedy Creek Nature Preserve, locate the black-blazed Sassafras Trail to the east of the picnic pavilions and follow it to the nearby Sierra Trail. At the Sierra Trail junction, turn left and follow the yellow-blazed path past a thick patch of boulders to the left.

The Sierra Trail was constructed by volunteers from the Central Piedmont's Sierra Club chapter. It presents an undulating path that weaves its way through hardwood trees and pine trees, and it provides one of the best places in the park to look for regional birds such as a Carolina wren or white-breasted nuthatch.

After traveling 1.1 miles on the Sierra Trail, you will approach a wooden bridge and trail intersection. Just before the bridge turn left onto the Robinson Rockhouse Trail and follow the path southeast, along the north shore of Reedy Creek, for 0.4 mile. At the end of the trail, you will arrive at the foundation of Robinson Rockhouse. The Robinson Rockhouse is one of two such rock houses in Mecklenburg County that dates back to the eighteenth century. The structure is located on the former property of John Robinson and is thought to have been built in 1790.

The Robinson Rockhouse was occupied until the end of the nineteenth century, at which point it was abandoned. Since that time Mother Nature has taken a toll on the farmhouse—several major storms and hurricanes have contributed to its decay. However, the greatest cause of damage to the house came when a large elm tree fell across the remaining stone walls. The large trunk of the elm tree can still be seen near the ruins, and it's just as impressive as the historic building.

A small circular path leads around the ruins and passes the remnants of a former outer building and the banks of Reedy Creek. Because of its level terrain and close proximity to a water source, this location would have been considered an ideal spot for a farmhouse in the 1700s. Furthermore, the dense forest that now surrounds the rockwork has protected the house from vandals. Some artifacts discovered at this site are on display in the Reedy Creek Nature Center, and further archaeological digs are planned for the future.

Remember while visiting the ruins that children, young and old, should not play on the historic remains. If you need something more modern to climb on, there is a fabulous playground adjacent to the nature center. When you are ready to leave the ruins, retrace your steps to the Sierra Trail and follow it back through the woods to reach Reedy Creek Park and the dirt road that leads through the sports fields and back to your car.

Each fall the annual summer Hummingbird Festival at Reedy Creek gives visitors a chance to learn about the ruby-throated hummingbird and view the bird as it makes its yearly winter migration to Mexico.

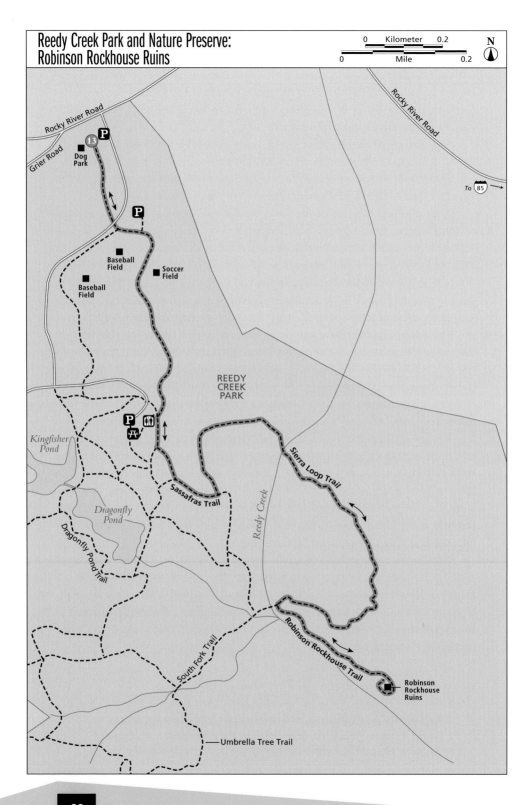

Reedy Creek Park and Nature Preserve:
Robinson Rockhouse Ruins

0   Kilometer   0.2

0   Mile   0.2

N

Rocky River Road

Rocky River Road

Grier Road

To 85

P

13

Dog Park

P

Baseball Field

Soccer Field

Baseball Field

REEDY CREEK PARK

P

Kingfisher Pond

Sassafras Trail

Sierra Loop Trail

Dragonfly Pond

Reedy Creek

Dragonfly Pond Trail

Robinson Rockhouse Trail

South Fork Trail

Robinson Rockhouse Ruins

Umbrella Tree Trail

0.0 From the wooden information kiosk at the northeast end of the dog park, follow the dirt path that parallels the dog park fence to the south.

0.2 Cross over the main park road and veer left (southeast) to travel clockwise around the baseball field.

0.4 After completing a semicircle around the baseball field, continue south along the western edge of the soccer field.

0.6 Upon arriving at the picnic pavilions and restroom facilities, veer left (east) and stay near the forest to locate the black-blazed Sassafras Trail.

0.8 The Sassafras Trail comes to a trail junction with the Sierra Trail. Turn left (east) and follow the Sierra Trail.

1.7 The Sierra Trail arrives at a wooden bridge and trail junction. Turn left (southeast) on the Robinson Rockhouse Trail, just before the bridge.

2.1 Explore Robinson Rockhouse, then retrace your steps along the banks of Reedy Creek to the Sierra Trail.

2.5 Turn right (east) on the Sierra Trail.

3.6 At the conclusion of the Sierra Trail, turn right (west) on the Sassafras Trail.

3.8 Arrive at the picnic pavilions at Reedy Creek Park and veer right (north) to retrace your steps through the athletic complex.

4.2 Conclude your hike at the dog park parking lot and trailhead.

HIKE INFORMATION

Local information: Charlotte Visitor Info Center, 330 S. Tryon St., Charlotte 28202; (704) 331-2700; www.visitcharlotte.com

Local events/attractions: Barkingham Park at Reedy Creek, 2900 Rocky River Rd., Charlotte, 28215; (704) 336-3854. Your dog needs exercise too! Bring him to the off-leash park at Reedy Creek so that he can run around and meet new friends.

Good eats: Hungry Howie's Pizza, 8806 University East Dr., Charlotte 28213; (704) 598-4744; www.hungryhowies.com. It's popular with local UNCC college students and hungry hikers!

Organizations: Charlotte Disk Golf Club, 615 Elmhurst Rd., Apt A, Charlotte 28209; www.charlottedgc.com. Play disk golf at Reedy Creek Park and Nature Preserve or at several other locations around Charlotte with this local club.

Reedy Creek Park and Nature Preserve: Preserve Loop

This hike explores the southwest corner of Reedy Creek Nature Preserve. The route starts at the Reedy Creek Nature Center parking area and veers left toward Dragonfly Pond. After exploring the water habitat on the south shore of the pond, the hike then travels south to pass underneath deciduous magnolia trees on the Umbrella Tree Trail. The Umbrella Tree Trail then connects with the Big Oak Trail. The Big Oak Trail is aptly named for the beautiful century-old oaks that line the path and grow amid a garden of tall boulders. The hike nearly touches Plaza Road before looping back to conclude at the Reedy Creek Nature Center. There is always an awesome and informative exhibit inside the nature center that will interest both children and adults.

Start: Reedy Creek Nature Center parking area

Distance: 2.8-mile loop

Hiking time: About 1.5 hours

Difficulty: Easy

Trail surface: Forested trail

Best season(s): Year-round

Other trail users: None

Canine compatibility: Leashed dogs permitted

Land status: Mecklenburg County park and nature preserve

Fees and permits: None

Schedule: Open daily; 7 a.m. to sunset

Maps: USGS Harrisburg; basic trail maps are available for free at the Reedy Creek Nature Center

Trail contacts: Reedy Creek Park and Nature Preserve, 2000 Rocky River Rd., Charlotte 28215; (704) 598-8857; www.parkandrec.com

Finding the trailhead: From Charlotte take I-85 to exit 45-A (East W. T. Harris Boulevard). Continue on East W. T. Harris Boulevard to the fourth traffic light, at Rocky River Road. Take a left (east) and follow Rocky River Road for 0.5 mile. After veering left at a traffic light, turn right (south) into Reedy Creek Park and Nature Preserve. Trailhead parking is located at the Reedy Creek Nature Center parking area. GPS: N35 15.769'/W80 43.206'

THE HIKE

This hike starts at the nature center parking lot at Reedy Creek Preserve. The fact that Reedy Creek is both a park and a nature preserve can sometimes be confusing to visitors. The majority of the facility, 727 acres, is designated as a nature preserve and takes the shape of the letter U. The filling in the middle of that U, 116 acres, makes up the park. Both the park and the preserve are open to pedestrians, but in the park you will hike past sports fields and picnic pavilions, whereas the trails within the preserve stay within the confines of the forest. The Reedy Creek Loop stays almost entirely within the nature preserve.

To begin the hike, locate the Dragonfly trailhead in the northeast corner of the parking lot. Follow the green-blazed trail into the woods. Within a few minutes you will pass a fence and shed to your right. Shortly past this landmark the trail will split in two. By opting to go straight you can visit the east bank of the Kingfisher Pond, but the Reedy Creek Loop continues to the right. Soon the trail will open up to the north to reveal views of Dragonfly Pond.

The path meanders along the south side of Dragonfly Pond. There are a handful of wooden benches placed near the shoreline where you can take a break from

A serene bench overlooks a still Dragonfly Pond.

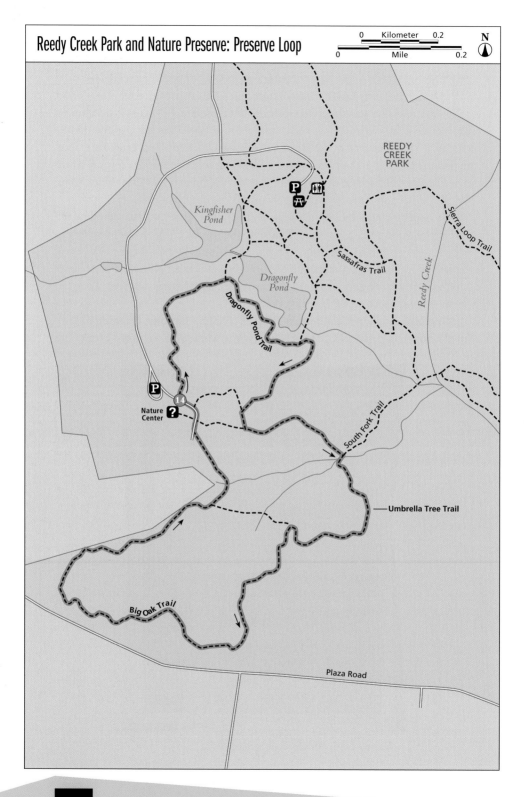

Reedy Creek Park and Nature Preserve: Preserve Loop

REEDY CREEK PARK

Kingfisher Pond

Dragonfly Pond

Dragonfly Pond Trail

Sassafras Trail

Reedy Creek

Sierra Loop Trail

P

14

Nature Center

South Fork Trail

Umbrella Tree Trail

Big Oak Trail

Plaza Road

0   Kilometer   0.2

0   Mile   0.2

N

hiking and stop to enjoy the tranquil view. You may be able to spot a fisherman casting his bait from the pier on the opposite side of the lake. Fishing is permitted in Dragonfly Pond, but if you are over the age of 16, you are required to provide a valid North Carolina fishing license. If you are interested in fishing but did not bring a pole with you, you can rent fishing gear from the Reedy Creek Nature Center.

At the east end of Dragonfly Pond, the trail comes to a T intersection. Turn right to continue on the Dragonfly Pond Trail. In another 0.1 mile you will come to another trail junction—but this one is very easy to miss. After traveling around a gradual bend that redirects the trail to the northwest, you will notice a faint spur trail to the left. This unmarked path is the connector to the Umbrella Tree Trail. Take this shortcut through the woods and then turn left on the yellow-blazed path. Don't fret if you miss this turnoff. The Dragonfly Pond Trail will soon conclude at the nature center, and from here you can easily hike east on the Umbrella Tree Trail to rejoin the Reedy Creek Loop.

The Umbrella Tree Trail is home to the umbrella magnolia, or the magnolia tripetala. Aptly named, this shrublike tree is comprised of bare branches that host a collective bunch of leaves at the end. The circular leaf arrangements give the impression of an open umbrella. And in the late spring, the center of the umbrella formation is crowned with a white flower that is similar to the bloom of a Frasier magnolia or southern magnolia. Since the umbrella magnolia is deciduous, it is harder to identify in the winter when the leaves fall out, but can still be pinpointed by its smooth bark, which is often lined with small wart-size bumps.

When the Umbrella Tree Trail intersects the South Fork Trail, stay straight and continue up a set of steps to remain on the yellow-blazed path. However, at the next intersection, with the Big Oak Trail, you will turn left and temporarily leave the Umbrella Tree Trail.

The Big Oak Trail is, once again, all about the trees. Large, mature oak trees dominate the forest canopy and shade the adolescent pine, holly, and beech trees underneath its branches. Large rocks also line the path, and it is intriguing to view some of the towering oak trees seemingly growing between boulders or on a field of rocks. At the southernmost portion of the Big Oak Trail, you will be able to hear the traffic from nearby Plaza Road. However, when the trail bends north, the car noise disappears and soon you are once again connected with the Umbrella Tree Trail.

The Umbrella Tree Trail will lead to the conclusion of your hike at the Reedy Creek Nature Center, but just because the walk is over doesn't mean that the fun has to end. Before you leave the preserve, take time to visit some of the displays and resident animals inside the visitor center. And if you are hiking with kids, they will almost certainly want to explore the adjacent playground, which includes a birdhouse jungle-gym and eco-friendly tree maze. These two attractions combine to create the final icing on top of an already enjoyable outing.

0.0   Find the start of the green-blazed Dragonfly Trail at the northeast corner of the Reedy Creek Nature Center parking lot and follow it north into the woods.

0.3   Veer right (east) to stay on the Dragonfly Trail. (**Side trip:** If you veer to the left, the path will take you to the east shore of Kingfisher Pond.)

0.7   Reach the east bank of Dragonfly Pond and turn right (east).

0.8   Take a left (south) on an unmarked spur trail to join the Umbrella Tree Trail. Turn left (east) on the Umbrella Tree Trail.

1.1   Bypass the South Fork Trail and continue south up the wooden steps to stay on the Umbrella Tree Trail.

1.5   Turn left (south) on the Big Oak Trail.

2.5   Veer left (north) and travel clockwise on the Umbrella Tree Trail.

2.8   Conclude your hike at the Reedy Creek Nature Center and playground.

HIKE INFORMATION

Local information: Charlotte Visitor Info Center, 330 S. Tryon St., Charlotte 28202; (704) 331-2700; www.visitcharlotte.com

Local events/attractions: The Hummingbird Festival at Reedy Creek, 2990 Rocky River Rd., Charlotte 28215; (704) 336-3854; www.charmeck.org (search for Hummingbird Festival). Have fun and learn more about the ruby-throated hummingbird at this annual fall festival.

Good eats: Hungry Howie's Pizza, 8806 University East Dr., Charlotte 28213; (704) 598-4744; www.hungryhowies.com. It's popular with local UNCC college students and hungry hikers!

Organizations: The Storytellers Guild of Charlotte, 9904 Avensong Crossing Dr., Charlotte 28215; (704) 568-6940. A great place to share a story about your hike!

Learn more about the plants and animals found along the trail by visiting the Reedy Creek Nature Center. A ranger is available to answer your questions.

US National Whitewater Center: Lake Trail

The Lake Trail travels south from the US National Whitewater Center headquarters and weaves through a shaded pine forest to reach the banks of several lakes in the southeast corner of the property. Though the first and last part of this hike travel through exposed terrain, most of the route falls under the shade of the forest. The water found on this trek is still and peaceful, unlike the fast-moving Catawba River to the east of the Whitewater Center. The route also provides terrific opportunities to look for nesting waterfowl as well as frogs, water snakes, beavers, and muskrats. The trees along the second half of the hike are heavily covered in vines, which add intrigue and dimension to the towering tree trunks. And at 3.5 miles this hike can easily accent or highlight a full day of activities at the Whitewater Center.

Start: US Whitewater Center trailhead in the southeast corner of the parking area
Distance: 3.5-mile loop
Hiking time: About 1.5 to 2 hours
Difficulty: Moderate
Trail surface: Mostly single-track dirt trail, with some road beds
Best season(s): Year-round
Other trail users: Mountain bikes
Canine compatibility: Leashed dogs permitted
Land status: US National Whitewater Center
Fees and permits: Parking fee; annual passes available
Schedule: Open daily; 7 a.m. to 10 p.m.
Maps: USGS Mount Holly; US National Whitewater Center Trail maps are available at the center's outfitter store for a small fee.

Trail contacts: US National Whitewater Center, 5000 Whitewater Center Pkwy., Charlotte 28214; (704) 391-3900; www.usnwc.org
Trail status: Trails may be inaccessible at times due to inclement weather, trail maintenance, or scheduled events. Check the trail status prior to your visit on Twitter (@usnwctrails), at the USNWC website (www.usnwc.org), or over the phone at (704) 391-3900, ext. 1.

Finding the trailhead: From Charlotte travel south on I-85. Next, take I-485 North to exit 12 (Moore's Chapel Road). Take a left (west) onto Moore's Chapel Road and then turn right (north) onto Rhyne Road. Travel Rhyne Road to Belmeade Road. Turn left (northwest) onto Belmeade Road. After driving 1.0 mile on Belmeade Road, turn left (south) onto Whitewater Center Parkway. The Whitewater Center Parkway leads to the entrance gate, Whitewater Center, and the parking lot. (Look for signs leading to the Whitewater Center. The route is well marked off the interstate.) The trailhead is located at the southeast corner of the parking lot. It is marked with a green flag. GPS: N35 16.205'/W81 00.258'

THE HIKE

The US National Whitewater Center offers an extensive trail network with nearly 15 miles of connecting dirt paths. Mountain bikers and hikers share all of the routes at the Whitewater Center. It is recommended that hikers, who normally do not want to constantly be passed by spandex-wearing two-wheel riders, try to plan their hikes for weekdays, when the trails are less traveled. There is a small fee to enter the facility, but it gives access to the trails and provides holders with privileges to many of the other park facilities as well. And the yearly fee still costs far less than a gym membership.

To begin the hike, locate the green flag at the southeast corner of the parking lot. This is the common starting point for all of the trails at the Whitewater Center. Follow the wide dirt path downhill to arrive at a trail junction. This is where the north and south trails at the center divide. Turn left to join the south trails network and follow the path uphill through an open power-line field. In this section you will probably hear the buzz of the electrical lines intermingled with the natural sound of crickets and sometimes katydids.

At the top of the hill, veer left and follow green signs marking the lake trail to the boundary of the forest. If it is warm day, this first 0.4 mile of hiking will feel hot under the bright sun. It comes as a welcome relief to enter the forest and travel underneath a canopy of pine, sycamore, sweet gum, and holly trees. Once inside the sanctuary of the forest, the single-track trail will intersect several old roadbeds. At each crossing continue straight and follow the faint narrow path across each brief opening.

After hiking 0.7 mile, you will arrive at the first and largest lake of the hike. The trail now contours the lakeshore. If you keep your eyes peeled and walk softly, there is a good chance that you will spot a sunning turtle, frog, or duck resting on a fallen log near the shallow banks of the lake. Pine trees surround the water and the path now has a soft bed of pine needles cushioning the hard-packed earth. The route travels along the south shore of the lake and then crosses a land bridge to explore a smaller pond to the east.

Once the trail tours the north shore of the pond, it crosses over a second land bridge and returns to the confinement of the forest. At mile 1.3 the trail reaches a fence and makes a hard left turn. Notices on the fence and trail remind hikers that a portion of this hike travels on private property and it is of utmost importance that hikers and bikers travel only on the path. Remember, veering off-trail on private property could close the trail for everyone—for good.

After another 0.25 mile the trail returns to the water and travels the northeast shore of the easternmost lake. The path almost completes a full loop around the lake before veering north and returning to the forest. There are multiple vines decorating the trees in this portion of the hike. Native plants crawl up the tree trunks in search of sunlight as do invasive exotic plants such as Japanese kudzu. Mature trees can often bear the extra weight of the vines. However, the twisting, fast-growing plants often harm younger trees with their weight and sun-blocking properties.

At mile 2.0 the trail visits the fourth and final lake on the hike. It then returns to the north shore of the first lake, before making a sharp right-hand turn away from the

A beautiful sky is reflected in the water along the Lake Trail.

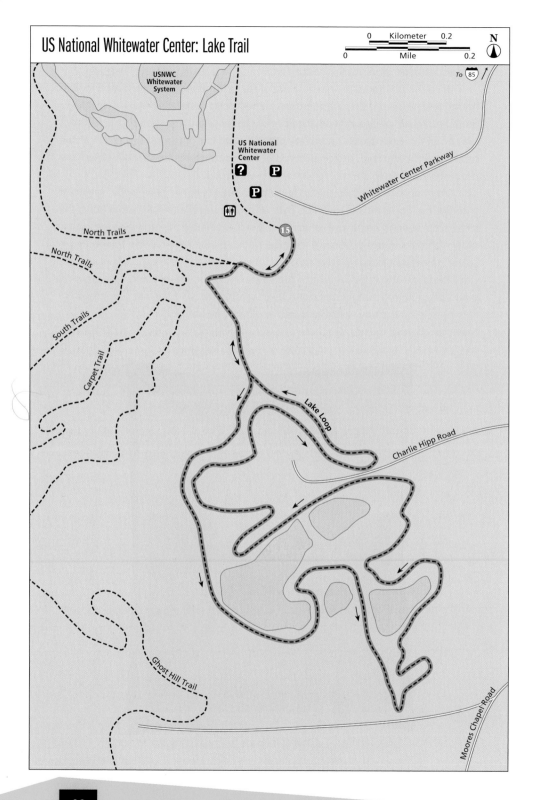

US National Whitewater Center: Lake Trail

0 Kilometer 0.2

0 Mile 0.2

N

To 85

USNWC
Whitewater
System

US National
Whitewater
Center

P

P

Whitewater Center Parkway

15

North Trails

North Trails

South Trails

Carpet Trail

Lake Loop

Charlie Hipp Road

Ghost Hill Trail

Moores Chapel Road

water. The trail now takes you on a circuitous route that first parallels the first portion of the Lake Trail, before jutting 0.25 mile southeast and looping back to add distance to the outing. After walking a total of 3.1 miles, the path completes the loop portion of the hike and leaves the forest. From here you will need to retrace your steps through the field of power lines back to the trailhead to conclude your hike.

After your trek be sure to check out the many amenities and facilities of the Whitewater Center—including showers and a restaurant!

MILES AND DIRECTIONS

0.0   Begin your hike at the southeast corner of the parking lot below the green flag. Follow the wide dirt path downhill and away from the Whitewater Center.

0.1   Arrive at a trail intersection that divides the north trails network from the south trails. Turn left (south) and follow the signs pointing toward the south trails.

0.3   At the top of a hill, turn left (east) and pass close to a power-line tower to reach the forest boundary on the east side of the clearing.

0.7   Arrive at the first lake on the trail. Continue to travel south and then veer left (east) to contour the south shore of the water.

0.9   Hike north across a land bridge and then quickly turn right (east). Almost immediately you will turn right again and hike south across a second, larger land bridge.

1.3   Reach a chain link fence and make a hard left turn to veer away from the fence and back into the forest.

1.5   Return to the water for 0.25 mile before delving back into the woods, where multiple vines hang off the trees that border the trail.

2.0   Visit the fourth and final lake on the hike.

2.2   Return to the north shore of the first lake and then take a sharp right turn (northeast) away from the water.

3.1   Complete the loop portion of the hike and retrace your steps to the north trails junction.

3.4   At the intersection with the north trails network, turn right (east) and hike uphill toward the parking lot.

3.5   Conclude your hike at the southeast corner of the parking lot.

15

HIKE INFORMATION

Local information: There is a lot of information about Lake Norman and the Catawba River at www.bestoflakenorman.com. Be sure to check out the History link, which tells about the first inhabitants to live along this lush river valley.

Local events/attractions: Interested in running the rapids at the Whitewater Center, zip-lining, or experiencing the Canopy Tour, which opened in 2011. Extend your visit at this facility and experience all that the US National Whitewater Center has to offer!

Good eats: Why not eat lunch or dinner at the Whitewater Center? They have a great restaurant with yummy sweet potato fries. River's Edge Bar and Grill is located underneath the ticket office. You can check out their menu online at www.usnwc.org/rivers-edge-bar-and-grill/.

Organizations: Catawba Riverkeeper Foundation, 421 Minuet Lane, Suite 205, Charlotte 28217; (704) 679-9494; www.catawbariverkeeper.org. Help to preserve and protect the Catawba River.

Discover More

The trails at the US National Whitewater Center are not just a popular place to go hiking or biking—they are also the perfect spot to try out trail running. If you are already a hiker, trail running might be right up your alley. In fact, most trail races involve a fair bit of hiking—especially uphill. The dirt of the trail is better for your joints than running down a concrete sidewalk. Furthermore, the roots and rocks of the trail keep your mind occupied and can help pass the time far better than cracks in the asphalt. If you want to try trail running, start slow, have fun, and incorporate as much hiking as you want. When you are ready for some company or competition, consider signing up for the Charlotte Running Club Trail Race at the Whitewater Center (http://usnwc.org/2010/12/charlotte-running-company-trail-race/). There are 4-mile, 9-mile, and 13-mile options.

🍃 Green Tip:
Consider citronella as an effective natural mosquito repellent.

The North Trails at the US National Whitewater Center provide a very scenic and interesting route along the north end of the property. The trail travels through the woods under the Canopy Tour (opened in 2011) and then along the east end of the Whitewater Center's man-made river. Past the rushing rapids, the trail reenters the woods and follows the figure-eight loop. This winding circuit contains several bridges, boardwalks, and short, steep descents, which make it a technical trail for mountain bikers. However, hikers should have no trouble navigating the obstacles and rejoining the primary North Trail. From here, the path travels through a wetland area that is often filled with the sound of chirping frogs. The hike then contours up to a nearby ridge that provides views of the Catawba River to the west. The trail dives down to visit the river near the center's boat launch area and then weaves its way back under canopy zip-line platforms to conclude at the parking lot.

Start: US Whitewater Center trailhead in the southeast corner of the parking area

Distance: 4.0-mile loop

Hiking time: About 2 to 2.5 hours

Difficulty: Moderate

Trail surface: Mostly single-track dirt trail, with some road beds

Best season(s): Year-round

Other trail users: Mountain bikes

Canine compatibility: Leashed dogs permitted

Land status: US National Whitewater Center

Fees and permits: Parking fee; annual passes available

Schedule: Open daily; 7 a.m. to 10 p.m.

Maps: USGS Mount Holly; US National Whitewater Center Trail maps are available at the center's outfitter store for a small fee.

Trail contacts: US National Whitewater Center, 5000 Whitewater Center Pkwy., Charlotte 28214; (704) 391-3900; www.usnwc.org

Trail status: Trails may be inaccessible at times due to inclement weather, trail maintenance, or scheduled events. Check the trail status prior to your visit on Twitter (@usnwctrails), at the USNWC website (www.usnwc.org), or over the phone at (704) 391-3900, ext. 1.

Finding the trailhead: From Charlotte travel south on I-85. Next, take I-485 North to exit 12 (Moore's Chapel Road). Take a left (west) onto Moore's Chapel Road and then turn right (north) onto Rhyne Road. Travel Rhyne Road to Belmeade Road. Turn left (northwest) onto Belmeade Road. After driving 1.0 mile on Belmeade Road, turn left (south) onto Whitewater Center Parkway. The Whitewater Center Parkway leads to the entrance gate, Whitewater Center, and parking lot. (Look for signs leading to the Whitewater Center. The route is well marked off the interstate.) The trailhead is located at the southeast corner of the parking lot. It is marked with a green flag. GPS: N35 16.206'/W81 00.262'

THE HIKE

The US National Whitewater Center opened its doors to the residents of Charlotte and beyond in 2006. Since that time, outdoors enthusiasts have flocked to the center to enjoy rafting, kayaking, paddling on the river, geocaching, rock climbing, zip-lining, biking, and, of course, hiking! The facility is the equivalent of an outdoor amusement park for folks that love off-road sports. And it brings some of the best aspects of the wilderness to the city-dwellers of Charlotte.

Hiking at the Whitewater Center can be combined with so many other activities that everyone in the family will enjoy visiting the complex. Exploring the center's north trails system is a great early morning activity to enjoy. The cool morning temperatures are perfect for hiking, and after 4 miles of undulating terrain, you will be more than ready to enjoy one of the many water activities that afternoon.

This route begins at the southeast corner of the parking area. If you are having trouble finding the trailhead, look for the green flags and trash receptacle that mark the trail entrance. The wide dirt path immediately travels downhill, and within the first 0.1 mile, you will arrive at a trail junction. This is where the north trails network splits from the south trails. Veer right and follow the signs pointing toward the north trails.

The next part of the hike travels west under the Canopy Tour. You will definitely be able to spot the wooden platforms built in the trees, and perhaps even a person flying through the air on a zip-line!

Past the canopy platforms the path travels through a predominantly hardwood forest of beech, sourwood, and oak trees. Enjoy the shade and stillness of the forest, because soon you will climb a gradual rise and exit the forest at southwest corner of the man-made whitewater canal. If you are hiking in the warmer months, there is a good chance rafts full of smiling paddlers will be traveling over the fast currents of the narrow channel. Contour the outside of the water park in a clockwise direction. You will pass beside a bridge that leads pedestrians back to the main complex. If anyone in the group needs to bail, this is the best place to do so. Otherwise, continue on the dirt path and arrive at a large wooden gateway, with a rusted sign that indicates the continuation of the north trails system.

Back inside the confines of the forest, you will soon arrive at a junction with the figure-eight trail. Turn right to travel this path in a counterclockwise direction. Although this route is rated highly technical for bike riders, hikers will have little trouble traversing the wooden boardwalks and traveling down the short, steep descents that cause the mountain bikers to catch air.

At the conclusion of the figure-eight trail, you will rejoin the primary north trail. The path now takes you on the outskirts of a wetland area where the croaking of frogs fills the air. If you hike this trail in late spring or early summer, mosquitoes might also fill the air, so come prepared and wear bug repellant. At mile 2.1 you have the opportunity to travel a short spur trail down to a nearby pier that spans across the nearby marsh. Take this opportunity to walk quietly to the wooden dock and search the nearby environment for frogs, turtles, and waterfowl.

Past the pier the trail reaches a switchback and veers south to reach a nearby ridge. There are views of the Catawba River as you climb to the crest of the hill, and glimpses of the water continue as you hike along the narrow ridgeline. This is also the portion of the Whitewater Center where some hikers participate in geocaching activities.

A wooden bridge crosses a creek on the figure-eight portion of the North Trails.

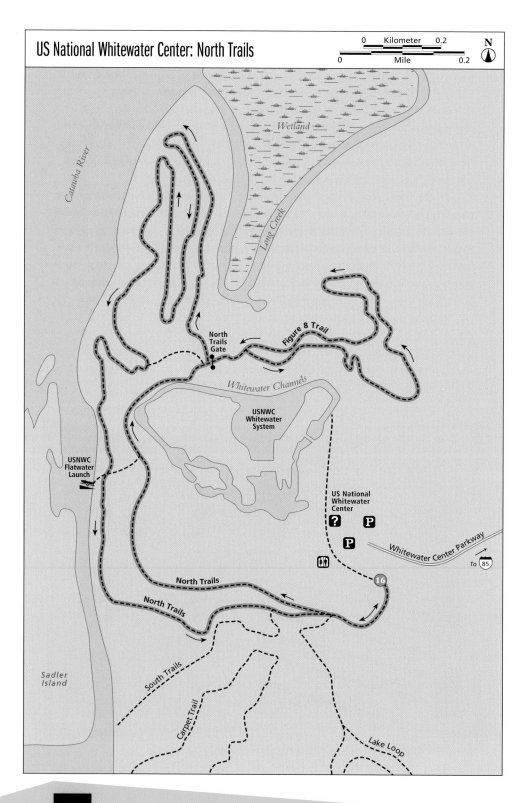

US National Whitewater Center: North Trails

0   Kilometer   0.2
0   Mile   0.2

N

Catawba River

Wetland

Long Creek

Figure 8 Trail

North
Trails
Gate

Whitewater Channels

USNWC
Whitewater
System

USNWC
Flatwater
Launch

US National
Whitewater
Center

P

P

Whitewater Center Parkway

To 85

16

North Trails

North Trails

Sadler
Island

South Trails

Carpet Trail

Lake Loop

When the trail descends off the ridge, it travels down to the banks of the river and passes the Whitewater Center's river launch. You will most likely be able to see the resting yellow, red, and blue kayaks lying on the shore. This is the best place to access the Catawba River on the hike, so feel free to travel to the water to take pictures and look for local paddlers.

Past the Catawba access, the trail travels gently uphill and eventually reaches an old roadbed. The route now continues on the roadbed and passes back underneath the facility's Canopy Tour. When the trail reaches the intersection with the south trails network, the loop portion of this hike will conclude. At this point retrace your steps to the trailhead and conclude your hike.

MILES AND DIRECTIONS

0.0 Start at the trailhead at the southeast corner of the parking area that is marked with green flags. Follow the solitary dirt path leaving the trailhead downhill.

0.2 The path splits in two and separates into the north and south trails network. Veer right (northwest) and travel into the forest and under the Whitewater Center's Canopy Tour.

0.5 The trail climbs a small rise where views of the Catawba River can be seen in the winter months.

0.6 The path exits the woods and travels around the outer whitewater channel in a clockwise direction.

0.9 The route reenters the forest under the North Trails sign and travels slightly downhill.

1.1 Shortly after the trail returns to the woods, it reaches a junction with the figure-eight trail. Veer right (east) to travel the figure-eight path in a counterclockwise direction.

2.0 The figure-eight loop concludes. Veer right (west) to continue on the north trail and follow the path on the outskirts of a nearby wetland area.

2.1 Travel a short spur trail to a nearby boardwalk that provides great views of the surrounding marsh.

2.2 The trail turns south at a long switchback and climbs up to a nearby ridge to reveal views of the Catawba River.

3.2 The path travels very close to the western shore of the Catawba River and passes the Whitewater Center's flat-water kayak launch.

3.8 Complete the north trails route and return to the trail junction with the south trails. Veer left (east) and retrace your steps to the primary trailhead.

4.0 Conclude your hike at the southeast corner of the Whitewater Center parking lot.

HIKE INFORMATION

Local information: There is a lot of information about Lake Norman and the Catawba River at www.bestoflakenorman.com Be sure to check out the History link, which tells about the first inhabitants to live along this lush river valley.

Local events/attractions: Interested in running the rapids at the Whitewater Center, zip-lining, or experiencing the Canopy Tour, which opened in 2011. Extend your visit at this facility and experience all that the US National Whitewater Center has to offer!

Good eats: Why not eat lunch or dinner at the Whitewater Center? They have a great restaurant with yummy sweet potato fries. River's Edge Bar and Grill is located underneath the ticket office. You can view their menu online at www .usnwc.org/rivers-edge-bar-and-grill/.

Organizations: Catawba Riverkeeper Foundation, 421 Minuet Lane, Suite 205, Charlotte 28217; (704) 679-9494; www.catawbariverkeeper.org. Help to preserve and protect the Catawba River.

> 🌿 **Green Tip:**
> *When you just have to go, dig a hole 6 to 8 inches deep and at least 200 feet from water, camps, and trails. Carry a ziplock bag to carry out toilet paper, or use a natural substitute such as leaves instead (but not poison ivy!!!). Fill in the hole with soil and other natural materials when you're done.*

> *The U.S. Whitewater Center has an outdoor concert series. Check out what bands are playing online (http://usnwc.org/riverjam/), and then bring your friends and enjoy a day of outdoor activities and an evening of music.*

West Region

Reeds rise out of the shallow water near the shoreline (hike 18).

Some of the best hiking near Charlotte is found an hour west of the city. Crowders Mountain State Park is typically one of the most popular hiking destinations in the piedmont region of North Carolina. The park offers a wide variety of trails to suit all age and skill levels. The views from Kings Pinnacle and Crowders Mountain are some of the best in the region, and Kings Pinnacle is the tallest peak included in this book. The rocky summits at Crowders Mountain State Park offer hikers the opportunity to scramble and practice fancy footwork, especially on the Rocktop portion of the Crowders Mountain Ridge Trail. Another highlight of traveling to Crowders Mountain State Park to hike is stopping afterward to explore the nearby town of Kings Mountain, or traveling a little farther west to enjoy some of the state's best barbecue in Shelby.

Just across the North Carolina–South Carolina border from Crowders Mountain State Park, you can explore Kings Mountain State Park and Kings Mountain National Military Park. These two neighboring facilities offer another great network of hiking trails, including the 16-mile Kings Mountain National Recreation Trail. You can explore portions of this path on the Clarks Creek Trail and Browns Mountain Trail. Another trail, the Ridgeline Trail, connects these two South Carolina parks with Crowders Mountain State Park to the north. The Buzzards Roost Trail not only crosses the border on the Ridgeline Trail, but also crosses through all three neighboring parks.

The historic highlight of this region is the Kings Mountain National Military Park Battlefield Trail. This paved route explores the perimeter of the Revolutionary War battlefield where the loyalist militia defeated a well-trained Patriot army. The many information plaques and monuments along the route will delight both the historian and the hiker. Another colonial jewel that can be explored nearby is the Living History Farm. This short hike explores a re-created nineteenth-century farm, complete with restored and reconstructed buildings, gardens, tools, and everyone's favorite—farm animals!

Another advantage of the west region is that most of the hikes are located very close to each other, so if one adventure is not enough for you, consider starting early and fitting two outings into your day. You won't regret it!

A blue bird feather on the path.

Crowders Mountain State Park: Kings Pinnacle

Kings Pinnacle is one of the most recognizable peaks surrounding Charlotte. This hike takes you on a challenging uphill climb from the visitor center at Crowders Mountain State Park to the jagged summit of Kings Pinnacle. The last section of trail, leading to the pinnacle, provides a technical but enjoyable rock scramble. On top of Kings Pinnacle, hikers are greeted with beautiful views to the north and east. The mountain also provides a glimpse of cars driving 65 mph on I-85. However, from the top of the mountain, the vehicles look like small toys moving much slower than they really are. Everything seems to move slower on Kings Mountain. After embracing the peace and stillness of the mountain, retrace your steps to the Turnback Trail. Once on the Turnback Trail, you will descend the south slope of the mountain through a mixed forest and beside a quiet creek on your return to the visitor center.

Start: Crowders Mountain State Park Visitor Center

Distance: 4.0-mile balloon

Hiking time: About 2.5 hours

Difficulty: Strenuous

Trail surface: Forested trail

Best season(s): Year-round

Other trail users: None

Canine compatibility: Leashed dogs permitted

Land status: State park

Fees and permits: None

Schedule: 8 a.m. to 6 p.m. Nov through Feb; 8 a.m. to 8 p.m. Mar, Apr, Sept, and Oct; 8 a.m. to 9 p.m. May through Aug

Maps: USGS Kings Mountain; basic trail maps are available for free inside the Crowders Mountain State Park Visitor Center

Trail contacts: Crowders Mountain State Park, 522 Park Office Lane, Kings Mountain 28086; (704) 853-5375; www.ncparks.gov

Finding the trailhead: From Charlotte take I-85 southbound toward Gastonia. Take exit 13 and turn left (south) onto Edgewood Road. Follow Edgewood Road to the US 74 intersection. Turn right (west) onto US 74 and travel 3.0 miles before turning left (south) onto Sparrow Springs Road. From Sparrow Springs Road follow the park signs leading toward the park office and visitor center. GPS: N35 12.820' / W81 17.604'

The aptly named "Crowders" Mountain State Park is a popular destination for hikers. On weekends and holidays the trails are bustling with activity. If you long for a more solitary experience, try to visit the park on a weekend or at 8 a.m. when the gates first open.

Located between Shelby and Charlotte, Crowders Mountain State Park is the ideal retreat for a day hike. With more than 15 miles of trails, the park offers more hiking and adventures than can be experienced in one day. But if you do only have one day, then don't miss the Kings Pinnacle Trail.

The Kings Pinnacle Trail takes you from the Crowders Mountain State Park Visitor Center to the highest point in the park. To start the hike, locate the wooden information kiosk to the north of the visitor center. Follow the wide dirt trail that starts at the kiosk into the forest. After 200 yards the trail splits. Turn left and follow the orange-blazed Pinnacle Trail to the west.

The trail immediately begins gaining elevation, but the grade is so gradual that you will hardly notice the gently uphill ascent. At 0.7 mile you will notice a spur trail on your right that descends off the ridge and away from the Pinnacle Trail. This path leads to the park's designated campsites and may be worth exploring if you're considering turning your next park visit into an overnight adventure.

Past the campground spur, the trail becomes more technical. For a short distance the tread way is littered with rocks and jagged stone outcroppings on the south side of the trail. These geological formations provide a small sample of the rugged cliffs that are found on top of the pinnacle.

After hiking 1.0 mile the path once again smoothes out and passes an adjoining trail on the left. Although you will remain on the Pinnacle Trail, take special notice as you pass the white-blazed Turnback Trail. This will serve as your return route to the visitor center.

Forging ahead, the trail becomes more difficult as it nears the summit. At mile 1.6 you will pass the Ridgeline Trail on your left. Bypass this footpath to South Carolina and continue just a little farther on the Pinnacle Trail to reach the base of a 10-foot rock wall. A sign indicates that this is the end of the trail, and on a stormy or wet day, it is wise to end your adventure here. However, if the conditions are nice, you can scramble up the rocks to the top of Kings Mountain Pinnacle.

On top of Kings Mountain Pinnacle, views to the north reveal level farmland and buildings on the outskirts of Kings Mountain. You will also notice the busy interstate that travels across the valley floor. However, on top of the mountain, the hustle and bustle of everyday life seems as far away as those tiny cars that seem to inch their way down I-85. There is a good chance the drivers of those cars are also looking up at you. Although they won't be able to make out a person on top of the mountain, they will be able to see the peak's resemblance to a king's crown. This particular shape is what gave the mountain its name.

If you follow the spine of the Pinnacle to the west, you will also be able to catch glimpses of the Charlotte skyline to the east, another reminder that a tall mountain offers a much different view and feeling than a visit to the top floor of a skyscraper.

At the top of the Pinnacle, you will notice the cement base of an old antenna that once served as a beacon to planes flying overhead. This also marks the highest point in the park, at 1,705 feet above sea level. Kings Pinnacle is also one of the highest mountains east of Shelby in North Carolina.

When you are ready to return down the mountain, retrace your steps on the Pinnacle Trail, past the Ridgeline Trail, to the junction with the Turnback Trail. Turn right on the Turnback Trail and follow the path down the mountain through a mixed forest of pine and hardwood trees.

At mile 3.3 you will notice a trickling creek to the right of the trail. The path continues to parallel the creek until its junction with the Fern Trail at mile 3.5. At the intersection, turn left and continue on the Turnback Trail for another 0.5 mile to reach the visitor center parking lot and the conclusion of your hike.

Note: Due to the rock ledges and steep drop-offs at Kings Mountain Pinnacle, families with small children should be extra-cautious on the mountain summit.

The jagged rocks of Kings Mountain Pinnacle and a view spanning the city limits of Kings Mountain below.

Crowders Mountain State Park: Kings Pinnacle

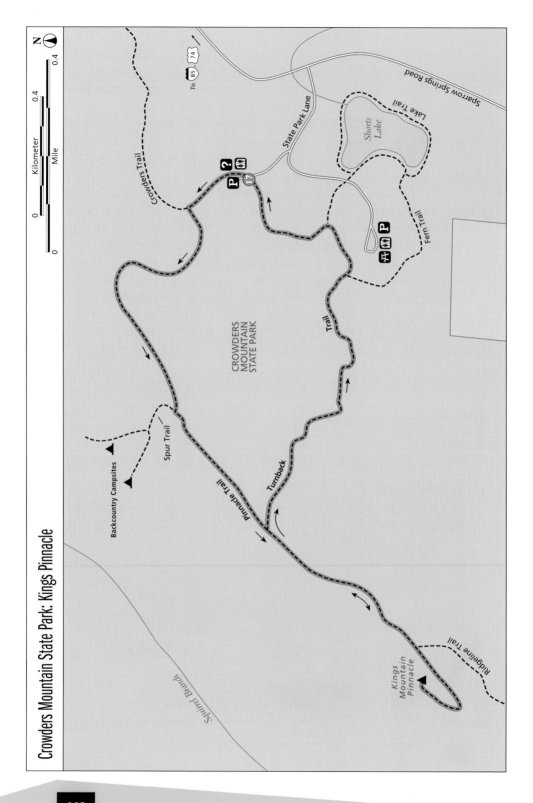

0.0 The trail begins to the north of the visitor center at the wooden kiosk.

0.1 The single dirt path splits in two. Turn left (west) on the Pinnacle Trail and begin a gradual uphill climb.

0.7 A spur trail on the right leads to campsites. The path becomes increasingly rocky as it continues up the ridgeline.

1.0 The Turnback Trail intersects the Pinnacle Trail on the left. Remain on the Pinnacle Trail and continue hiking along the ridge.

1.6 Veer right to remain on the Pinnacle Trail and bypass the Ridgeline Trail on your left. (Unless you want to hike to South Carolina!)

1.9 Arrive at the tip top of Kings Mountain Pinnacle and at the cement base of a former antenna. When you are ready to leave, retrace your steps to arrive at the Turnback Trail.

2.8 Turn right (south) on the Turnback Trail and descend off the ridge.

3.5 Veer left to stay on the Turnback Trail, which briefly joins the Fern Trail.

3.7 Leave the Fern Trail and continue north on the Turnback Trail.

4.0 Arrive back at the visitor center to conclude your hike.

HIKE INFORMATION

Local information: The City of Kings Mountain, P.O. Box 429, Kings Mountain 28086; (704) 734-0333; www.cityofkm.com

Local events/attractions: Kings Mountain Historical Museum, 100 E. Mountain St., PO Box 552, Kings Mountain 28086; (704) 739-1019; www.kingsmountain museum.org. Exhibits including period clothing, war memorabilia, and textile machines tell the history of Kings Mountain and the surrounding region.

Good eats: Cup and Saucer Tea Room, 107 W. King St., Kings Mountain 28086; (704) 730-0384. This place serves a light but delicious menu of soups, salads, quiche, and sandwiches.

Organizations: The Southern Arts Society, PO Box 334, Kings Mountain 28086; (704) 739-5585; www.southernartssociety.org. Dedicated to promoting the arts in Kings Mountain.

Crowders Mountain State Park: Fern and Lake Trails

This hike combines two of the most kid-friendly trails in Crowders Mountain State park into a fun-filled figure-eight hike that is perfect for families. The trail starts at the Crowders Mountain Visitor Center and then follows the Turnback Trail to join the Fern Trail. The Fern Trail shows off its lush underbrush before detouring onto the lake trail. A pleasant stroll around the lake can reveal fish, frogs, and waterfowl before rejoining with the Fern Trail to return to the trailhead.

Start: Crowders Mountain State Park Visitor Center
Distance: 1.8-mile figure eight
Hiking time: About 1 hour
Difficulty: Easy
Trail surface: Forested trail
Best season(s): Year-round
Other trail users: None
Canine compatibility: Leashed dogs permitted
Land status: State park
Fees and permits: None

Schedule: 8 a.m. to 6 p.m. Nov through Feb; 8 a.m. to 8 p.m. Mar, Apr, Sept, and Oct; 8 a.m. to 9 p.m. May through Aug
Maps: USGS Kings Mountain; basic trail maps are available for free inside the Crowders Mountain State Park Visitor Center
Trail contacts: Crowders Mountain State Park, 522 Park Office Lane, Kings Mountain 28086; (704) 853-5375; www.ncparks.gov

Finding the trailhead: From Charlotte take I-85 southbound toward Gastonia. Take exit 13 and turn left (south) onto Edgewood Road. Follow Edgewood Road to the US 74 intersection. Turn right (west) onto US 74 and travel 3.0 miles before turning left (south) onto Sparrow Springs Road. From Sparrow Springs Road follow the park signs leading toward the park office and visitor center. GPS: N35 12.775' / W81 17.635'

Green Tip:
As a reminder to children, young and old, the lizards, fish, frogs, and birds that live near water should not be picked up, petted, or fed.

THE HIKE

This hike starts at the Crowders Mountain State Park Visitor Center. It is a good idea to spend some time at the visitor center before venturing on the trail, so that you can view the fun and informative displays that teach you about some of the native plants and animals that you will encounter on your hike.

When you are ready to set off on your adventure, travel to the southeast corner of the visitor parking lot. Here the white-blazed Turnback Trail traces the edge of a forest through a small clearing that in the spring is filled with wildflowers such as golden rod.

Stay on the Turnback Trail for 0.2 mile until it intersects the Fern Trail. At this point turn left on the red-blazed Fern Trail and follow the shaded path near the banks of a tricking creek. You will immediately notice the beautiful green shoots that line the path and give the trail its name. Though several varieties of ferns can be found along the path, Christmas ferns are the most common. You can identify a Christmas fern by its leaves, which resemble Christmas stockings.

At 0.3 mile you will cross over a paved road. Take extra care with young children as this is one of the main roads inside Crowders Mountain State Park and cars often come zipping around the bend. Back inside the safety of the woods, you will notice a picnic shelter to your right. If anyone needs a quick snack, this is a great place to sit and rest in the shade.

The fishing pier stretches into a calm lake.

Crowders Mountain State Park: Fern and Lake Trails

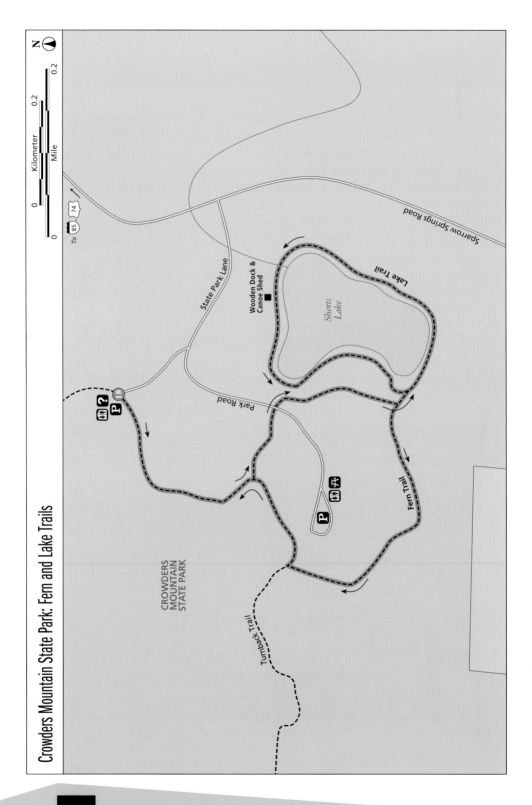

Past the pavilion the trail arrives at a four-way intersection. This is where you will depart the Fern Trail and travel southwest over a wooden bridge to join the Lake Trail. Immediately after hiking across the bridge, veer left to trace the perimeter of the lakeshore. At first you will only catch glimpses of the water through the trees. But by the time you arrive on the east shore, you will be able to enjoy uninterrupted views of the lake and can even stick your toes in it if you want to. But be careful if you venture off-trail, as the marshland surrounding the lake can often be deceptively muddy.

After hiking 0.9 mile you will arrive at a wooden pier across from the boathouse. Often there are Canada geese or mallards swimming beside the pier. This floating platform is also a great place to look for fish or tadpoles that live near the shore. You may even spot a nearby fisherman reeling in a small bass or carp. If you have a North Carolina fishing license, you may want to bring your fishing pole back to the lake to test your luck on a future visit to the park.

When the Lake Trail completes its 0.8-mile loop, you will rejoin the Fern Trail and follow it west through the forest. (At the intersection with the Fern Trail and Lake Trail, be sure to take a right and then an immediate left, or you will end up in a nearby parking lot.) This final stretch of trail is a great place to try to locate one last forest animal, such as a chipmunk, squirrel, or owl. But don't get too distracted looking for forest critters, as you will need to pay attention when the Fern Trail once again meets the Turnback Trail and then veers northeast toward the parking lot and visitor center to conclude the hike.

MILES AND DIRECTIONS

0.0   Locate the Turnback Trail at the southeast corner of the visitor center parking lot. Follow the narrow dirt path next to a stand of trees on your left and an open field on your right.

0.2   The Turnback Trail intersects the Fern trail. Turn left (southeast) to join the Fern Trail. The path now travels parallel to a small trickling creek.

0.3   Cross a paved park road. If you are having trouble locating where the trail reenters the forest, simply follow the slanted white crosswalk painted on the road.

0.5   Cross the wooden bridge and then immediately veer left (southeast) to travel around the park lake in a counterclockwise direction.

0.9   Arrive at the wooden dock and canoe shed. This is a good spot to stop and rest or to watch a fisherman reel in a carp.

1.2 Conclude the Lake Loop. At the four-way intersection with the Fern Trail, turn right (north) and then take an immediate left (west). You should now be on the Fern Trail, hiking away from the lake.

1.6 Conclude the Fern Trail Loop. Turn left (north) and retrace your steps to the visitor center on the Turnback Trail.

1.8 Arrive at the visitor center parking lot to conclude your hike.

HIKE INFORMATION

Local information: The City of Kings Mountain, PO Box 429, Kings Mountain 28086; (704) 734-0333; www.cityofkm.com

Crowders Mountain State Park is also very close to both Shelby and Gastonia.

City of Shelby, City Hall, 300 S. Washington St., Shelby 28150; (704) 484-6800; www.cityofshelby.com

City of Gastonia, Gaston County Tourism, 620 N. Main St., Belmont 28012; (704) 824-4044; www.visitgaston.org

Local events/attractions: Did you enjoy the small lake at Crowders Mountain State Park? Consider visiting the much larger Moss Lake, also known as Kings Mountain Reservoir. The lake is located forty-five minutes west of Crowders Mountain State Park. John H. Moss Lake, 2621 Oak Grove Rd., Shelby 28150; (704) 482-7926; www.mosslake-nc.com

Good eats: Oak Grove Grill, 1053 Oak Grove Rd., Kings Mountain 28086 (704) 739-6441. Located between Crowders Mountain State Park and Moss Lake, this American-style eatery offers great burgers to satisfy your appetite after a long hike.

Nearby campgrounds: There is also a campground at Moss Lake. The small fee includes water and electric hookup. The address and phone number for the campground is the same as the Moss Lake information listed under Local events/attractions above.

> *Crowders Mountain State Park often offers free educational programs and workshops to the general public. Before you visit the park, call or check their online calendar to coordinate your hike with a ranger presentation. www.ncparks .gov/Visit/parks/crmo/events*

Crowders Mountain State Park: Crowders Mountain Ridge Trail

This is one of the most technical and exciting hikes in the Charlotte area. It starts at the Crowders Mountain Visitor Center and follows the Crowders Trail through a dense forest of oak, cedar, and pine trees. After crossing Sparrow Springs Road, the route skirts the west side of Crowders Mountain. When the path comes to an intersection with the Backside Trail, you will turn south and face a challenging and stair-filled ascent to reach the top of the mountain. Your effort is rewarded with gorgeous views in three directions. From the summit the route follows the rocky Ridgeline Trail. This path will require some fancy footwork to navigate and you will be thankful to once again reconnect with the well-groomed Crowders Trail at the base of the mountain.

Start: Crowders Mountain Visitor Center

Distance: 5.2-mile balloon

Hiking time: About 2.5 to 3 hours

Difficulty: Strenuous

Trail surface: Forested trail and dirt road

Best season(s): Fall, winter, spring

Other trail users: None

Canine compatibility: Leashed dogs permitted

Land status: State park

Fees and permits: None

Schedule: 8 a.m. to 6 p.m. Nov through Feb; 8 a.m. to 8 p.m. Mar, Apr, Sept, and Oct; 8 a.m. to 9 p.m. May through Aug

Maps: USGS Kings Mountain; basic trail maps are available for free inside the Crowders Mountain State Park Visitor Center

Trail contacts: Crowders Mountain State Park, 522 Park Office Lane, Kings Mountain 28086; (704) 853-5375; www.ncparks.gov

Finding the trailhead: From Charlotte take I-85 southbound toward Gastonia. Take exit 13 and turn left (south) onto Edgewood Road. Follow Edgewood Road to the US 74 intersection. Turn right (west) onto US 74 and travel 3.0 miles before turning left (south) onto Sparrow Springs Road. From Sparrow Springs Road follow the park signs leading toward the park office and visitor center. GPS: N35 12.782' / W81 17.613'

S imilar to other great mountains—Everest, McKinley, Ranier—there is more than one route leading to the summit of Crowders Mountain. Thankfully, no matter which trail you take to the summit, you will be able to leave your technical gear at home. But that doesn't mean that this path isn't challenging. In fact, it requires more fancy footwork than any other trail in the Charlotte area.

The beginning of the hike is relatively gentle and offers a steady warm-up for more challenging obstacles to come. Leaving from the visitor center, the path travels north into the woods and then turns right on the Crowders Trail. This first part of the path travels up and down several small hills and across two seasonal streams to reach Sparrow Springs Road. Take a moment before crossing the road to look both right and left, but not just for cars. Note that to your right is a small dirt path descending to the opposite shoulder. This is the Rocktop Trail, your return route. To the left you should be able to spot another single-track trail veering northeast. This is the continuation of the Crowders Trail.

When you are sure that there is no oncoming traffic, hike across the road and follow the Crowders Trail into the forest. The next 1.8 miles travel through a for-

The rocky summit of Crowders Mountain.

est comprising hardwood and pine trees. Pine is the state tree of North Carolina. Although several different varieties of this towering conifer line the trail, it is easy to identify two of the most common species. The eastern white pine contains five 3-to-5-inch-long needles in every bundle, while the Virginia pine only contains two 1-to-3-inch needles per bundle.

Toward the end of the Crowders Trail, the hike will become more strenuous as you gain elevation to meet the ridge of Crowders Mountain. When you arrive at the spine of the mountain, you will leave the Crowders Trail and turn right to follow the Backside Trail toward the summit. The Backside Trail presents a steady climb that is heightened near the summit, where a seemingly endless staircase leads to the top of the mountain.

By putting one foot in front of the other and taking several pauses, you will eventually arrive at the jagged summit. The vista from Crowders Mountain is breathtaking, and on a clear day you can easily see the Charlotte skyline to the east.

Take time to rest and enjoy the view, before continuing south on the Rocktop Trail. At this point you will be happy to know that almost all of your climbing is behind you. But that said, the next 1.4 miles of trail certainly isn't easy.

The Rocktop Trail features an engaging pathway that is comprised of rocks and boulders. The best thing to do on this trail is to go at your own pace! If you are hiking with a group, don't feel like you need to keep up with your friends. Concentrate on your footing and enjoy the journey at whatever speed you are comfortable with. And If you are afraid of heights or of suffering a sprained ankle, you may want to consider backtracking on the Crowders Trail. Also, the Rocktop Trail travels the high ridge of the mountain and should never be attempted in bad, slightly bad, bad-looking bad, or recently bad weather.

So on a nice day take your time and enjoy the challenging footwork. The narrow gauntlet will have you laughing and smiling as you leap, balance, and skip across the rock surface. But remember to take the time to look up every now and then, as this trail provides the most consistent views in the park.

When you finally return to Springs Sparrow Road, you will feel more like a mountain goat than a hiker. Cross the street and retrace your steps on the Crowders Trail, back to the visitor center and trailhead.

> ### 🌿 Green Tip:
> *When hiking with your dog, stay in the center of the path and keep Fido close by. Dogs that run loose can harm fragile soils and spread invasive exotic plants by transferring the seeds, as well as lead to unintentional confrontations and citations by park rangers.*

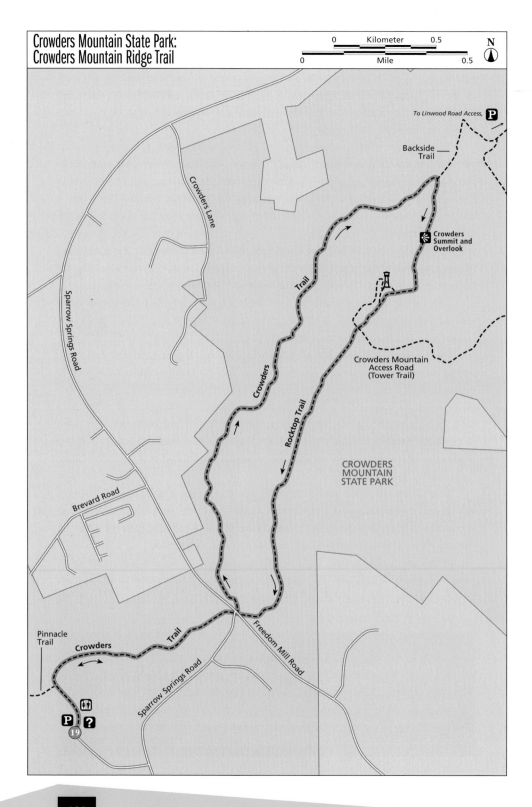

Crowders Mountain State Park:
Crowders Mountain Ridge Trail

0 Kilometer 0.5

0 Mile 0.5

N

To Linwood Road Access, **P**

Backside Trail

Crowders Summit and Overlook

Crowders Lane

Crowders _____ Trail

Crowders Mountain Access Road (Tower Trail)

Sparrow Springs Road

Crowders

Rocktop Trail

CROWDERS MOUNTAIN STATE PARK

Brevard Road

Pinnacle Trail

Crowders _____ Trail

Freedom Mill Road

Sparrow Springs Road

P **?** 19

0.0   Begin your hike at the trailhead kiosk to the north of the visitor center. Follow the wide dirt path into the woods.

0.1   The path splits. Turn right (east) to follow the Crowders Trail.

0.8   Arrive at Sparrow Springs Road. Cross the road and veer left to stay on the Crowders Trail. (Do not veer right—you will end up on the Rocktop Trail.)

2.6   The Crowders Trail terminates at the Backside Trail. Turn right (south) on the Backside Trail and begin a gradual climb toward the summit.

3.0   The climb is no longer gradual—stairs! Lots of stairs! Count them, crawl up them, do whatever you need to do to make it to the top, where fantastic views await from the top of Crowders Mountain.

3.1   You did it! Rest and enjoy the view. When you are ready to continue, hike south on the red-blazed Rocktop Trail.

3.2   Pass a large radio tower and continue on the Rocktop Trail.

3.4   Cross a dirt road and continue straight into the forest. Continue to follow the red blazes.

4.4   After continuing down the south slope of Crowders Mountain, arrive back at Sparrow Springs Road. Cross the road and retrace your steps on the Crowders Trail toward the visitor center.

5.1   At the final junction be sure to turn left and hike south toward the visitor center. Do not continue straight on the orange-blazed Pinnacle Trail.

5.2   Conclude your hike at the Crowders Mountain Visitor Center.

HIKE INFORMATION

Local information: The City of Kings Mountain, PO Box 429, Kings Mountain 28086; (704) 734-0333; www.cityofkm.com

Local events/attractions: The Gateway Festival celebrates Kings Mountain! For information contact Kings Mountain Special Events Director, PO Box 429, Kings Mountain 28086; (704) 730-2103; www.cityofkm.com.

Good eats: Love's Fish Box, 1104 Shelby Rd., Kings Mountain 28086; (704) 739-4036. Mmmmm, fish and chips!

Organizations: The Southern Arts Society, PO Box 334, Kings Mountain 28086; (704) 739-5585; www.southernartssociety.org. Dedicated to promoting the arts in Kings Mountain.

Discover More

Based in Gastonia, the nonprofit Friends of Crowders Mountain loves Crowders Mountain. They do all that they can to promote, preserve, and protect the nearby state park. In fact, if it were not for this small group of caring citizens, Crowders Mountain—arguably the most popular hiking destination near Charlotte—might not be open to the public. Known as the Gaston Conservation Society, the group lobbied hard during the 1970s to protect the land from proposed mining operations. Thankfully, they were successful, and the Gaston Conservation Society became the Friends of Crowders Mountain. Today the group frequently volunteers their time and talents at the nearby state park. The members in the organization aid with trail maintenance and help lead educational outreach programs. They lend an invaluable hand to the very busy staff at the state park. Even if you don't join the Friends of Crowders Mountain State Park, be sure to thank them when you see them busy at work inside the park.

Friends of Crowders Mountain, PO Box 1881, Gastonia 28053; www .friendsofcrowdersmountain.org

Seated atop Crowders Mountain, you may feel like you're on top of the world.

Crowders Mountain State Park: Summit Trail

This route starts at the Linwood Road parking lot, at the north end of Crowders Mountain State Park. The hike then follows the Tower Trail up the east face of Crowders Mountain. This trail will often provide great views of mountain climbers trying to ascend the Crowders rock face. When you reach the ridgeline, you will briefly connect with the Rocktop Trail. It will then lead to the summit where expansive views of the North Carolina piedmont and the Charlotte skyline await. When you are ready to leave the jagged mountaintop, you will follow the backside trail down a long staircase and past the Crowders Trail to return to your car at the trailhead parking lot.

Start: Tower Trail trailhead at the Linwood Road parking area
Distance: 2.9-mile loop
Hiking time: About 1.5 to 2 hours
Difficulty: Strenuous
Trail surface: Forested trail and dirt road
Best season(s): Fall, winter, spring
Other trail users: None
Canine compatibility: Leashed dogs permitted
Land status: State park
Fees and permits: None

Schedule: 8 a.m. to 6 p.m. Nov through Feb; 8 a.m to 8 p.m. Mar, Apr, Sept, and Oct; 8 a.m. to 9 p.m. May through Aug
Maps: USGS Kings Mountain; basic trail maps are available for free inside the Crowders Mountain State Park Visitor Center
Trail contacts: Crowders Mountain State Park, 522 Park Office Lane, Kings Mountain 28086; (704) 853-5375; www.ncparks.gov

Finding the trailhead: From Charlotte take I-85 southbound toward Gastonia. Take exit 13 and turn left (south) onto Edgewood Road. Follow Edgewood Road for 0.7 mile. Edgewood Wood becomes Archie Whiteside Road. Continue on Archie Whiteside Road for 1.7 miles, until it dead-ends at Linwood Road. Turn left (east) on Linwood Road, and then take an immediate right into the Crowders Mountain Linwood Road access area. GPS: N35 14.449'/W81 16.171'

I f you want to hike to the top of Crowders Mountain but don't have the time or energy to take the 5.2-mile Ridge Trail, this hike will get you there in half the time and almost half the distance. But just because the hike is shorter doesn't mean it's any less spectacular.

By beginning the hike at the Linwood Road parking lot, you will avoid most of the park visitors, who travel to the heart of Crowders Mountain State Park. And whereas this parking lot is a well-kept secret among hikers, it is a common meeting place for climbers. That is one of the best aspects of this hike: Not only are you walking to the top of Crowders Mountain, but you also have the opportunity to engage and observe the many rock climbers that use this route to access the sheer east face of Crowders Mountain. Perhaps the experience will pique your interest in rock climbing, or if you are like me, you will be even more appreciative of the well-groomed trails at Crowders Mountain State Park that don't require any ropes, harnesses, or upper body strength.

Steps lead up to Crowders Mountain.

To begin the hike, follow the Tower Trail from the parking lot into the woods. This path is a wide gravel road that is easy to follow. As soon as you depart the parking area, you will slowly begin to gain elevation, but the start of the climb is extremely gradual and goes almost unnoticed for the first mile.

As you draw closer to the summit, you will notice more and more rock formations appearing under the canopy of the forest. The exposed rock and primitive feeling of Crowders Mountain is part of what makes the park so appealing. As outlining mountains to the Appalachian mountain chain, Crowders Mountain and neighboring Kings Mountain are included among some of the oldest peaks in the world. And the outcropping of worn rocks that litter the path speak to the mountains' age and wisdom.

The second mile of the hike is the most difficult. The grade increases and will offer little respite until you reach the summit. Take your time climbing up to the ridge and remember to stop and try to peak through the branches for the climbers, who are faced with an even more difficult ascent.

The Tower Trail terminates at set of radio towers that crown Crowders Mountain. The structures are built on a small plot of privately held land on top of the mountain, and the first tower was erected in 1940s. The current structure relays radio, phone, and emergency signals. There is always controversy when a man-made structure sits on top of a mountain, and environmental groups have worked very hard to reject or delay plans to increase the size of the main tower on top of Crowders Mountain.

At the end of the Tower Trail, continue along the ridge of the mountain on the Rocktop Trail to reach Crowders Mountain's summit. This dominating peak once marked the boundary between Cherokee and Catawba hunting grounds. Today it is a favorite spot among Charlotte-area hikers and recreationalists. Even if there are multiple people on the summit, there are enough isolated rocks to find a peaceful picnic spot. Just don't untie the ropes that you find attached to those rocks—remember, there are probably climbers attached to them!

Also, be sure to keep a close eye on children and pets. Do not let them wander too close to the edge of Crowders Mountain. There are several steep drop-offs around the summit.

When you are ready to return to the parking lot, follow the long set of stairs down the north slope of Crowders Mountain and follow the Backside Trail to complete the hike at the Linwood Road parking area.

> *If you hike with children, try to make the uphill sections easier by playing games. A quick round of I Spy or Follow-the-Leader can turn mountains into molehills.*

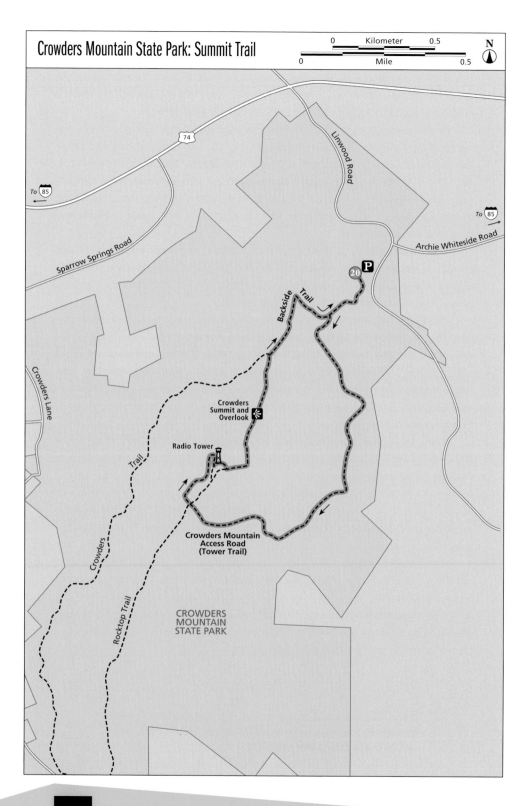

Crowders Mountain State Park: Summit Trail

0 Kilometer 0.5

0 Mile 0.5

N

74

To 85

Linwood Road

Sparrow Springs Road

Archie Whiteside Road

To 85

20 P

Backside Trail

Crowders Lane

Crowders Summit and Overlook

Radio Tower

Trail

Crowders

Crowders Mountain Access Road (Tower Trail)

Rocktop Trail

CROWDERS MOUNTAIN STATE PARK

MILES AND DIRECTIONS

0.0   Locate the Tower Trail trailhead at the southwest corner of the parking lot. Follow the dirt path behind the trail sign to a wide dirt road.

0.1   The Backside Trail veers off to the right, but you will continue straight (south) on the blue-blazed Tower Trail.

1.0   The trail becomes more strenuous as it begins its final push to the summit.

1.4   Where the Rocktop Trail intersects the Tower Trail, continue straight on the gravel Tower Trail.

1.8   Arrive at the radio towers on top of Crowders Mountain. The gravel road terminates. Continue north along the ridge on the Rocktop Trail.

1.9   Crowders Mountain Summit provides expansive views. From the top of the mountain, hike north and descend a long series of wooden steps on the Backside Trail.

2.3   Intersect the Crowders Trail on your left. Continue straight on the wide Backside Trail.

2.7   Reconnect to the main spur trail leading to the parking lot. Turn left (north).

2.9   Conclude your hike and locate your car.

HIKE INFORMATION

Local information: The City of Kings Mountain, PO Box 429, Kings Mountain 28086; (704) 734-0333; www.cityofkm.com

Crowders Mountain State Park is also very close to both Shelby and Gastonia.

City of Shelby, City Hall, 300 S. Washington St., Shelby 28150; (704) 484-6800; www.cityofshelby.com

City of Gastonia, Gaston County Tourism, 620 N. Main St., Belmont 28012; (704) 824-4044; www.visitgaston.org

Local events/attractions: Nearby Shelby is a hotbed for local barbecue. Consider attending the annual Hog Happnin' weekend in the fall. The event is held at the Cleveland County Fairground, 1751 E. Marion St., Shelby 28152. For more information visit www.hoghappnin.com.

Good eats: You're in the mood for barbecue, but it's not Hog Happnin' weekend? No problem! Check out Bridges Barbecue, 2000 E. Dixion Blvd., Shelby 28150; (704) 482-8567; www.bridgesbbq.com.

Organizations: The Trust for Public Land, Charlotte Office, 1200 E. Morehead St., Suite 290, Charlotte 28104; (704) 376-1839; www.tpl.org (search for Charlotte)

Kings Mountain National Military Park: Browns Mountain

If you want to escape the crowds and monuments at the Kings Mountain National Military Park Visitor Center, consider taking this scenic out-and-back hike to the solitary summit of Brown Mountain. As part of the 16-mile Kings Mountain National Scenic Trail, this path travels over several hills and beside a small seasonal creek to reach the slopes of Browns Mountain. Browns Mountain, like Crowders Mountain and Kings Mountain Pinnacle, is an outlying monadnock. It has not been worn down to the level of the surrounding farmland because of its dense quartzite composition. And while its elevation creates a challenging ascent to the summit, it also provides uninterrupted views of the valley that surrounds Kings Mountain National Military Park.

Start: Kings Mountain National Military Park

Distance: 5.6-mile out and back

Hiking time: About 2.5 to 3 hours

Difficulty: Moderate

Trail surface: Forested trail

Best season(s): Year-round

Other trail users: None

Canine compatibility: Leashed dogs permitted

Land status: National park

Fees and permits: None

Schedule: Open 9 a.m. to 5 p.m.

Maps: USGS Grover; basic trail maps are available for free online at http://www.nps.gov/kimo/planyourvisit/upload/KIMOmap1.pdf

Trail contacts: King Mountain National Military Park, 2625 Park Rd., Blacksburg, SC 29702; (864) 936-7921; www.nps.gov/kimo

Finding the trailhead: From Charlotte take I-85 southbound toward Gastonia. Take exit 2, turn left (south), and join NC 216.
Follow NC 216 south across the North Carolina–South Carolina border (where it becomes SC 216). After 3.5 miles 216 becomes Battleground Road. Follow park signs to the visitor center inside the National Military Park.
GPS: N35 8.498'/W81 22.651'

THE HIKE

I n order to be designated as a National Scenic Trail, a path must contribute to health, conservation, and recreation. The Kings Mountain National Recreation Trail that leads to Browns Mountain does just that. And not only does it conserve the forest and our natural resources, but it also preserves an important part of American history. By fully encompassing Kings Mountain National Military Park and battlefield, the larger recreation trail serves as a garrison that protects the story and the legacy of the land.

The hike begins at Kings Mountain National Military Park Visitor Center. Feel free to explore the visitor center or tour the 1.5-mile Battlefield Trail before beginning your journey to Browns Mountain. When you are ready to start your trek, locate the spur trail behind the visitor center restrooms and follow it into the woods. You will bypass the Battlefield Trail on your left and then you will intersect the Kings Mountain Recreation Trail. A right will take you to nearby Kings Mountain State Park, but you will turn left and hike west toward Browns Mountain.

As an interesting aside, Kings Mountain National Military Park is not only home to a national recreation trail, it is also the southern terminus of the Overmountain Victory National Historic Trail. The historic trail travels through Virginia, Tennessee, North Carolina, and South Carolina. It combines dirt paths and paved

View from Browns Mountain's Summit.

Kings Mountain National Military Park: Browns Mountain

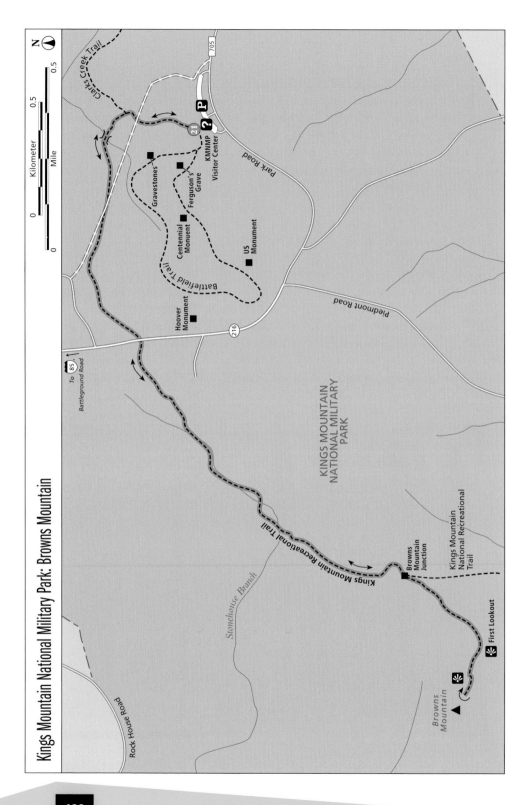

roads to roughly retrace the route of the Patriot militia that traveled, mostly by foot, to fight at Kings Mountain. It is a long and difficult process to incorporate a trail or route into the national trail system, and it is really unique that this hike touches two of them.

Your journey now descends downhill. You will cross a small creek on a wooden footbridge and then hike on a relatively level path that cuts through a forest filled with oak, Virginia pine, beech, and holly trees. After crossing a bridle path, you will start to gain elevation and eventually cross SC 216. Past the paved road, the trail will climb a little higher before quickly descending back down to the valley floor. The path contours a creek bed through the valley floor that is often bone dry. You will notice the forest start to transition in this section as you hike across a fire boundary. The National Park Service uses controlled burns to help regenerate the forest, and a portion of the woods in this area has been burned to reduce underbrush, revitalize the soil, and control insects and disease that affect the forest. Depending on the park's burn schedule, you may see this effect on other portions of this hike as well.

When the trail leaves the creek bed, you will begin a challenging uphill climb. The path briefly levels out on a broad ridge before arriving at an intersection with the Browns Mountain spur. Turn right and follow this side trail uphill to an open summit with several benches, where you can sit and rest. But don't get too comfortable, because the true high point of Browns Mountain lies another 0.25 mile to the west! Follow the trail as it descends down to a small saddle and then quickly regains its elevation to reach the top of Browns Mountain. You will know that you are at the highest peak when you see the four separate cement blocks that once served as the foundation to a fire tower.

Browns Mountain, like Crowders Mountain and Kings Mountain Pinnacle, is composed of kyanite-quartzite. The dense makeup of Browns Mountain, and its northern neighbors, has allowed the mountain to stand tall and proud over the surrounding farmland despite several hundred million years of potential erosion.

After taking in the views from the summit, retrace your steps to the visitor center to conclude your hike.

MILES AND DIRECTIONS

0.0 Start at the Kings Mountain National Military Park Visitor Center and follow the spur trail leading north behind the facility's restrooms.

0.2 At an intersection with the Kings Mountain National Recreation Trail, turn left (west) and follow signs pointing toward Browns Mountain.

1.1 Cross SC 216 and continue to follow the blue blazes up a short, steep hill.

2.0 Leave behind the meandering creek bed in the valley floor and start your climb up the slopes of Browns Mountain.

2.3 Turn right (summit) to leave the recreation trail and follow the spur trail to Browns Mountain.

2.6 You will reach a false summit. Veer west and descend into a nearby saddle to stay on the trail.

2.8 Arrive at the true summit of Browns, where the cement base of a former fire tower is located. When you are ready to return to the trailhead, start to backtrack along the Browns Mountain spur trail.

3.0 When you arrive back at the recreation trail, turn left and hike northeast back toward the visitor center.

5.4 You will need to take one more right turn (south) on the spur trail that leads to the visitor center. Otherwise you will be on your way to Kings Mountain State Park!

5.8 Arrive at the visitor center to conclude your hike.

HIKE INFORMATION

Local information: SC Welcome Center in Blacksburg, located at mile marker 103 on I-85 southbound; (864) 839-6742

Blacksburg Town Hall, 105 S. Shelby St., Blacksburg, SC 29702; (864) 839-2333

Local events/attractions: Cowpens National Battlefield, 4001 Chesnee Hwy., Chesnee, SC 29323; (864) 461-2828; http://cowpens.areaparks.com. Visit this nearby Revolutionary War battlefield.

Can't get enough Revolutionary War history? Check out Historic Brattons-ville, 1444 Brattonsville Rd., McConnells, SC 29726; (803) 684-2327; www.chmu seums.org.

Good eats: Bailey's Fish Camp, 606 N. Shelby St., Blacksburg, SC 29702; (864) 839-6023. Don't flounder with this decision. Go to Bailey's Fish Camp!

Organizations: Overmountain Victory Trail Association, 2517 Shipe Rd., Knox-ville, TN 37924; (770) 387-1945; www.ovta.org

> *If you want to read more about National Historic Trails, scenic trails, and recreation trails, check out www.nps.gov/nts/.*

Kings Mountain National Military Park: Battlefield Trail

The historic Battlefield Trail starts at Kings Mountain National Military Park Visitor Center and retraces the significant plot of land where the Patriots defeated the Loyalists in a critical victory that turned the tide of the American Revolution in the South. The paved trail is technically handicapped-accessible, but all hikers should be prepared for the brief steep climb to the summit of Kings Mountain. There are two monuments along the short ridgeline of the mountain. The first, located at the summit of the mountain, is the Centennial Monument—erected by the descendants of the valiant Patriots who fought at Kings Mountain. The second is a tall white obelisk, commissioned by Congress and dedicated in 1909. Beyond the two, the entire journey is filled with information plaques, Major Patrick Ferguson's gravestone, and other significant points of interest.

Start: Kings Mountain National Military Park
Distance: 1.5-mile loop
Hiking time: About 1 to 1.5 hours
Difficulty: Moderate
Trail surface: Paved trail
Best season(s): Year-round
Other trail users: None
Canine compatibility: Leashed dogs permitted
Land status: National park

Fees and permits: None
Schedule: Open 9 a.m. to 5 p.m.
Maps: USGS Grover; basic trail maps are available for free online at http://www.nps.gov/kimo/planyourvisit/upload/KIMOmap1.pdf
Trail contacts: King Mountain National Military Park, 2625 Park Rd., Blacksburg, SC 29702; (864) 936-7921; www.nps.gov/kimo

Finding the trailhead: From Charlotte take I-85 southbound toward Gastonia. Take exit 2, turn left (south) and join NC 216. Follow NC 216 south across the NC/SC border (where it becomes SC 216). After 3.5 miles 216 becomes Battleground Road. Follow park signs to the visitor center inside the National Military Park. GPS: N35 8.488'/W81 22.641'

THE HIKE

This hike explores one of the most prominent mountains in South Carolina. Kings Mountain is a small geological bump in South Carolina that rises 150 feet above the surrounding terrain near the border of York County and Cherokee County. It does not share the impressive height or regional significance of Crowders Mountain and Kings Pinnacle to the north. However, on October 7, 1780, something very big happened at Little Kings Mountain that changed the course of US history.

The American Revolution began in 1775, and after five years of fighting, the British decided to refocus their efforts to the southern colonies, where they believed there was a strong following of loyalists. The British quickly secured the port of Charleston, South Carolina, and then focused their campaign to the north. General Charles Cornwallis instructed his best marksman, Major Patrick Ferguson, to recruit residents from southern Appalachia for the Loyalist Army. It was understood that if the men resisted, there would be consequences. In fact, Major Ferguson sent a letter to the residents of this remote region threatening to "hang your leaders, and lay waste your country by fire and sword."

Two gravestones line the Battlefield path.

As you might imagine, this was not received well by the individuals of Scotch-Irish descent that farmed the rural Appalachian Mountains. They quickly organized into a militia and started the 300-mile trek over the mountains to fight Major Ferguson. Several hundred men journeyed across challenging terrain and difficult conditions that included early season snow. None of the men were paid soldiers—all of them were volunteers.

On October 7, 1780, the militia forces, armed with their hunting rifles, surrounded Ferguson's army, which was camped on top of Little Kings Mountain. A little over one hour after the first shot was fired, Major Ferguson was dead and the trained Loyalist Army had completely surrendered to the resilient Patriot militia.

Historians now agree that this battle not only changed the tide of the Revolutionary War in the Southeast, but also heavily contributed to the end of the war and the British surrender at York, Virginia—twelve months and twelve days after the Battle at Kings Mountain.

The public walking trail that explores this battlefield may not be significant in length or views, but it will leave a lasting impact on everyone that takes the time to walk the paved trail and visit the information plaques, gravesite, and memorials along the route. (As a side note, although the path is made of asphalt to allow accessibility to this historic site, be warned that the trail is anything but flat and it would be very difficult to push a wheelchair up the 150-foot incline leading to the top of Kings Mountain.)

By traveling the trail in a counterclockwise direction, you will parallel a stream as you travel past the spot where militia leaders William S. Cleveland, James Williams, and Campbell Shelby commanded their troops. The summit of Kings Mountain rises above you to the north, and when you leave the stream, you will start your steep but short ascent to the summit.

A worthy side trip, that both breaks up the challenging uphill climb and adds to the hike, is the Hoover Monument spur trail. This very brief detour, which adds less than 0.1-mile to the total hike, leads to a rock monument that marks the place where President Herbert Hoover gave a speech to over 75,000 people on the 150th anniversary of the Battle of Kings Mountain. It was directly after that speech that Congress designated the battlefield as a National Military Park and it was opened to the public the following spring.

When you reach the top of the ridge on the Battlefield Trail, you will be able to view the 28-foot Centennial Monument that was dedicated in 1880, a hundred years after the Battle of Kings Mountain. A little farther down the ridgeline, the spectacular Kings Mountain US Monument will appear on the horizon. This 83-foot white obelisk was constructed in 1909 and dedicated to the American patriots who fought at Kings Mountain. The structure looks strikingly similar to the much larger Washington Monument, which was built in 1884 and stands 555 feet tall on the Mall in Washington, D.C.

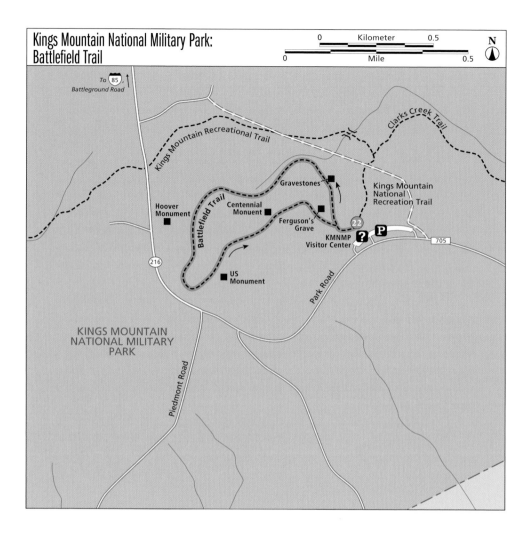

Kings Mountain National Military Park:
Battlefield Trail

0   Kilometer   0.5

0   Mile   0.5

N

To 85,
Battleground Road

Kings Mountain Recreational Trail

Clarks Creek Trail

Gravestones

Kings Mountain
National
Recreation Trail

Hoover
Monument

Battlefield Trail

Centennial
Monuent

Ferguson's
Grave

22

P

KMNMP
Visitor Center

705

216

US
Monument

Park Road

KINGS MOUNTAIN
NATIONAL MILITARY
PARK

Piedmont Road

Past the obelisk, you will journey beside Major Patrick Ferguson's grave on the descent to the visitor center, where an informational movie and small museum reveal more insight into the Battle of Kings Mountain.

Green Tip:
When choosing trail snacks, go with homemade goodies without the industrial packaging.

MILES AND DIRECTIONS

0.0 Start at the visitor center. Turn right and travel north to hike the Battlefield Trail in a counterclockwise direction.

0.3 Arrive at a small stream and pass the Chronicle Markers to your the right. The worn-down stone represents the second-oldest Revolutionary War monument in existence.

0.8 A spur trail to the right (west) leads to the Hoover Monument.

1.0 Arrive at the Centennial Monument, located on the Kings Mountain Summit.

1.2 The trail passes beside the imposing 83-foot Kings Mountain US monument.

1.3 There is a stone cairn (rock pile) beside the trail that marks Major Patrick Ferguson's grave. A memorial marker stands nearby.

1.5 Conclude the hike at the visitor center.

HIKE INFORMATION

Local information: SC Welcome Center in Blacksburg, located at mile marker 103 on I-85 southbound; (864) 839-6742

Blacksburg Town Hall, 105 S. Shelby St., Blacksburg, SC 29702; (864) 839-2333

Local events/attractions: There is a wreath-laying ceremony every year at Kings Mountain National Military Park. The event takes place at the Kings Mountain US Monument on the Battlefield Trail. The date always falls on the anniversary of the battle, October 7. For more information call the park office.

Good eats: Papa G's, 101 S. John St., Blacksburg, SC 29702; (864) 839-3938; Yes, they have pizza. But more important, they have ice cream!

Organizations: Overmountain Victory Trail Association, 2517 Shipe Rd., Knoxville, TN 37924; (770) 387-1945; www.ovta.org

> *Every fall, there is a two-week march/drive that traces the route taken by the Overmountain Men during the American Revolution. On October 7 each year, there is a wreath-laying ceremony at the Kings Mountain US Monument on Kings Mountain. The event is designed to commemorate the men who fought at Kings Mountain. It is free and open to the public.*

Kings Mountain State Park: Living History Farm

This is a fabulous hike for families. It starts at the Lake Crawford Lodge, which was built in the 1930s by the Civilian Conservation Corps. From there it travels to the south end of the lake, where a rock-hop beneath the lake dam will help you cross the water outlet while keeping your feet dry. The path then travels slightly uphill through a hardwood forest to reach the Living Farm at Kings Mountain State Park. This recon-structed 1800s farm is an outdoor museum, complete with 200-year-old farming equipment, a small garden, and everyone's favorite—farm animals! Take your time to walk around the outer buildings and visit the chickens, cows, and donkeys before retracing your steps back to Lake Crawford.

Start: Kings Mountain State Park Crawford Lake parking area
Distance: 1.8-mile out and back
Hiking time: About 1 to 1.5 hours
Difficulty: Easy
Trail surface: Forested trail
Best season(s): Spring, fall
Other trail users: None
Canine compatibility: Leashed dogs permitted
Land status: State park
Fees and permits: Day-use fee required. Pay at park entrance.

Schedule: Open 8 a.m. to sunset
Maps: USGS Kings Mountain; very basic trail maps are available for free at www.southcarolina parks.com/files/State%20Parks/Kings%20Mtn/KM_Current-Trail -Map.jpg
Trail contacts: Kings Mountain State Park, Park Road, Blacksburg, SC 29702; (803) 222-3209; www.southcarolinaparks.com/park-finder/state-park/945.aspx

Finding the trailhead: From Charlotte take I-85 southbound toward Gasto-nia. Take exit 8 and turn left (south) onto US 161. Follow US 161 across the North Carolina–South Carolina bor-der. The state park entrance will be on your right (west) just past the state line. GPS: N35 8.952' / W81 20.718'

THE HIKE

For such a short trail, this hike has a lot to offer. By starting at the Lake Crawford parking area in Kings Mountain State Park, hikers are immediately greeted by a large wooden lodge with a stone patio that was built in the 1930s by the Civilian Conservation Corps. The east side of the lodge provides great views of Lake Crawford, and there are picnic benches near the convenient lake if you want to stop and enjoy a snack before or after the hike.

To find the trail, walk to the southeast corner of the parking area that is located just uphill from the brown lodge. In the corner of the lot, there is a sign for the Farm Trail. Follow the path behind the sign into the woods and downhill to the Lake Crawford Dam. The dam is beautiful and hidden from the sight of most park visitors. The beautiful stonework is once again a feature designed by the CCC in the 1930s. The water flowing out of Lake Crawford, over the dam, and into the creek below gives the feel of a quaint waterfall or serene rock fountain.

Even though it will be tempting to step out on the rockwork to gain a closer view of the thin cascade of water, playing or walking on the dam is prohibited. Remember this structure is very old and very slick and best enjoyed when observed from the trail. Plus, your desire to play on rocks will be satiated below the dam, where you have to hop from stone to stone to successfully cross the creek with dry feet.

A donkey greets visitors at the Living Farm.

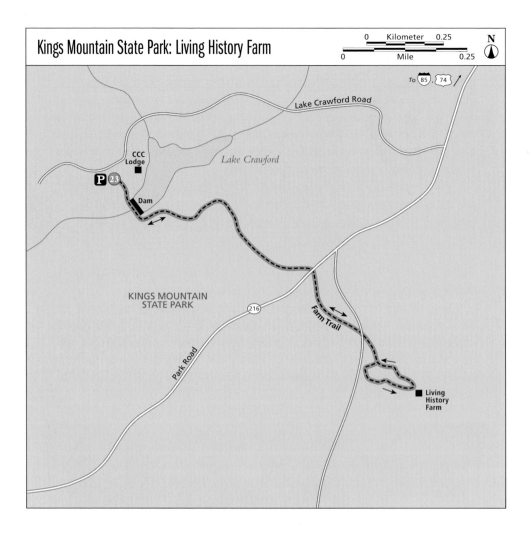

0   Kilometer   0.25

N

0   Mile   0.25

To 85, 74

Lake Crawford Road

CCC
Lodge

Lake Crawford

P 23

Dam

KINGS MOUNTAIN
STATE PARK

216

Farm Trail

Park Road

Living
History
Farm

On the east side of the dam, the path continues uphill and then veers north. You quickly leave behind views of the lake and soon cross over a seasonal stream on a wooden bridge. Past the bridge the route travels through a forest comprised of holly, oak, and pine trees. This portion of the hike is mostly uphill, but the grade is gentle and it comes early enough in the hike that little legs should still have the energy and enthusiasm to keep hiking.

After hiking for 0.5 mile, you will cross a paved park road. On the other side of the road, the trail levels out and travels a little farther under the shade of the trees, before exiting the forest at the Living Farm parking area.

If you and your family are the only ones at the site, it will feel as if you have experienced some type of time warp in the forest and traveled back to the 1800s. More likely, you will be reminded of the current age by SUVs in the parking lot and visitors toting digital cameras. But still, it is amazing to just walk out of the woods and onto a nineteenth-century farm.

Take time to explore the highly educational and entertaining farmstead. By starting in the main courtyard, you will be able to visit several of the outbuildings, including the carpenter shop, blacksmith shop, smokehouse, and the ever-popular outhouse. Some of these buildings were constructed by the park, but other structures predate the Civil War and were moved here to become part of this outdoor museum.

Underneath the barn you will be able to view 200-year-old farming equipment, in particular a cotton gin that's on display for the public to see. Invented by Eli Whitney in 1794, this machine was once integral to the success of farming and textile operations in the South. The farm typically even has a few rows of cotton growing to the east of the barn for the public to see.

Beyond the barn and cotton rows, you will also want to visit the small vegetable garden, and if you have kids with you, you will have no choice but to observe the wonderful farm animals that bring the site to life.

After spending ample time at the Living Farm, feel free to retrace your steps on the Farm Trail on a mostly downhill journey back to Lake Crawford.

Cotton grows outside of the historic barn.

MILES AND DIRECTIONS

0.0 Start at the wooden lodge on the east shore of Lake Crawford and locate the Farm Trail sign to the south.

0.1 Arrive at the Lake Crawford Dam and cross the stream located to the south of the dam.

0.3 Cross a small seasonal stream.

0.5 Cross a paved park road.

0.7 Exit the woods at the entrance for the Kings Mountain State Park Living Farm.

0.9 Explore the courtyard of the Living Farm and visit the resident farm animals before backtracking to the parking lot on the Farm Trail.

1.8 Return to your car at the trailhead parking lot.

HIKE INFORMATION

Local information: The Town of Clover, 114 Bethel St., Clover, SC 29710; (803) 222-9495; www.cloversc.info. Clover is known as "the town with 'love' in the middle."

Local events/attractions: If you need something to do in early June, or if you want an excuse to wear a kilt, check out Clover Scottish Games and Scotch-Irish Festival at Clover Memorial Stadium, 320 Clinton Ave., Clover, SC 29710. For more information visit www.cloverscottishgames.com.

Good eats: Eagles Nest, 507 N. Main St., Clover, SC 29710; (803) 222-7461. Enjoy traditional American fare in a laid-back atmosphere.

Organizations: Friends of Kings Mountain State Park, 1277 Park Rd., Blacksburg, SC 29702; (803) 222-3209. Find Friends of Kings Mountain State Park on Facebook.

Kings Mountain State Park participates in the Discover Carolina program, which offers age-appropriate lesson plans based on state academic programs. Learn more about the program and view some of the lesson plans at www.discover carolina.com/html/s01overview.html.

Kings Mountain State Park: Clarks Creek Trail

This trail leads from the scenic, recreation-filled Kings Mountain State Park to the historic and inspiring Kings Mountain National Military Park. The route starts by exploring a hardwood forest and then descends to the beautiful banks of Clarks Creek. The waterway is filled with intriguing rock formations. Lush mountain laurel trees, long strands of dog hobble, and Christmas ferns keep the shoreline looking green and lush throughout the year. When the path leaves the creek, it travels up a short hill and then exits the forest at the Kings Mountain National Military Park Visitor Center, where fascinating historic displays and information plaques tell the story of the pivotal Revolutionary battle of Kings Mountain.

Start: Kings Mountain State Park Crawford Lake parking area
Distance: 6.0-mile out and back
Hiking time: About 3 to 3.5 hours
Difficulty: Moderate
Trail surface: Forested trail
Best season(s): Year-round
Other trail users: None
Canine compatibility: Leashed dogs permitted
Land status: State park and national park
Fees and permits: Day-use fee required. Pay at park entrance.
Schedule: Open 8 a.m. to sunset
Maps: USGS Kings Mountain; very basic trail maps are available for free at www.southcarolina parks.com/files/State%20Parks/Kings%20Mtn/KM_Current-Trail -Map.jpg
Trail contacts: Kings Mountain State Park, 1277 Park Rd., Blacksburg, SC 29702; (803) 222-3209; http://www.southcarolinaparks .com/park-finder/state-park/ 945.aspx
King Mountain National Military Park, 2625 Park Rd., Blacksburg, SC 29702; (864) 936-7921; www.nps.gov/kimo

Finding the trailhead: From Charlotte take I-85 southbound toward Gastonia. Take exit 8 and turn left (south) onto US 161. Follow US 161 across the North Carolina–South Carolina border. The state park entrance will be on your right (west) just past the state line. GPS: N35 8.957' / W81 20.728'

While hiking is now mostly done for fun and exercise, 200 years ago people often walked long distances with limited supplies to escape persecution or fight for their freedom. By starting at the recreation facilities at Kings Mountain State Park, which include a boating lake, picnic pavilions, and playground, and then traveling to nearby Kings Mountain National Military Park, where war monuments, grave markers, and Revolutionary War relics await, you will realize that while our reasons for walking have evolved, hiking through the woods can also serve as a connection to our past.

Kings Mountain State Park is a great place to start and end this journey. The amenities at the park make this a great spot to enjoy a picnic and spend a lazy afternoon outdoors. However, before that laziness overtakes your body, enjoy a scenic and historic hike on the Clarks Creek Trail. The path takes form near the picnic pavilions and immediately descends down to a nearby creek. Once you cross over the wooden bridge that spans the water, you will intercept the Kings Mountain National Recreation Trail. This loop trail travels over 16 miles and connects the

A wooden bridge near the start of the hike keeps your feet high and dry.

state park with the National Military Park. A few ambitious hikers will try to complete the entire trail in one day. If this is on your to-do list, make sure you get an early start, as it is typically an eight-to-ten-hour trek.

Today, you will only need a few hours of daylight to travel a portion of this trail. Turn right and follow the path uphill and past a backcountry campsite to your left. Past the campsite, the trail will weave through a mature upland forest filled with beech, Virginia pine, oak, and maple trees. After walking for almost a mile, you will arrive at a trail junction with the Ridgeline Trail. This is a strenuous 8.7-mile trail that continues north across the state line to its terminus on the south slope of Kings Mountain Pinnacle in Crowders Mountain State Park. Once again, any attempt to hike the Ridgeline Trail should start early in the morning. Bypass this route and continue to follow the blue blazes to the banks of Clarks Creek. This scenic waterway is surrounded by a green tunnel of laurel, ferns, and underbrush. At normal water levels the creek will reveal jagged rock formations jutting up out of the water. But after a heavy rain the creek will conceal the rocks and sometimes overflow onto the trail!

The hike remains almost entirely level as it traces the shore of Clarks Creek, but you will still need to pay attention to the multiple roots and rocks that litter the trail. After covering a little over 2.0 miles of terrain, the trail will leave the creek and veer uphill. After a brief climb the path will turn toward the south and arrive at a trail junction. The recreation trail continues to the right toward Browns Mountain, but you will go straight and follow the signs leading to the nearby Kings Mountain National Military Park Visitor Center.

When you arrive at the facility, you will be at the halfway point of the hike. From here, you just need to turn around and retrace your steps along Clarks Creek back to the state park. However, you will not want to start back until you take ample time to explore the visitor center, which could also be considered a Revolutionary War museum. Inside the building there are artifacts from the Battle of Kings Mountain, as well as informational displays and a brief educational film that runs every thirty minutes. If at this point you want to expand your knowledge, extend your visit, and lengthen your hike, consider tacking on the 1.5-mile Battlefield Trail to your journey.

> *On a hot summer day, the cool waters of Lake Crawford will look very appealing. Although there is no swimming allowed at the lake, you can rent a canoe or paddleboat to take out on the water. Call the park or visit the website for more information.*

Kings Mountain State Park: Clarks Creek Trail

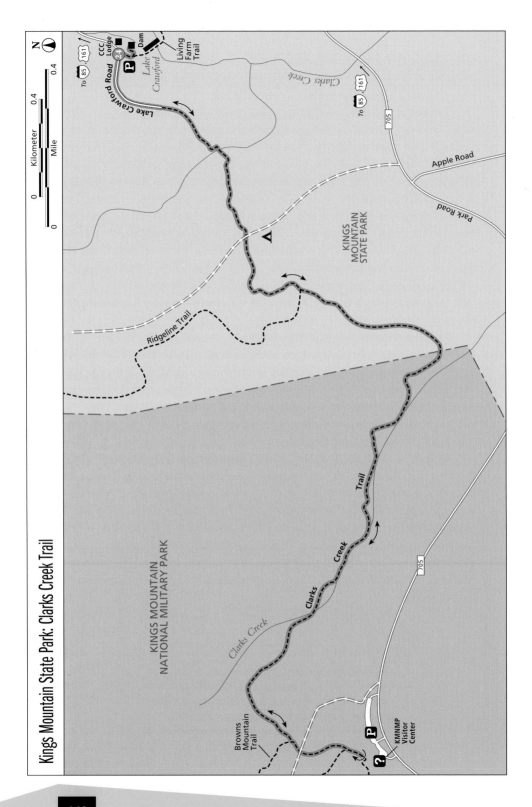

MILES AND DIRECTIONS

0.0 Start at the wood lodge on the west shore of Lake Crawford and hike west and slightly uphill through the parking lot.

0.1 Take the stairs that lead from the parking lot to the park road. Turn left (south) and follow the road south toward the picnic area.

0.2 The road terminates and the path begins. Follow it past the picnic pavilions and restrooms.

0.3 Cross over a wooden bridge and turn right (west) on the Kings Mountain National Recreation Trail. Continue uphill past a primitive campsite.

0.9 Bypass the Ridgeline Trail to your right and continue hiking straight on the recreation trail.

2.7 You will arrive at a three-way junction. Continue straight (south) and follow signs pointing toward the visitor center.

3.0 Take time to enjoy the Kings Mountain National Military Park Visitor Center and then retrace your steps toward Kings Mountain State Park.

3.3 Veer right (east) to rejoin the National Recreation Trail and follow it east toward Clarks Creek.

5.1 Pass the Ridgeline Trail on your left.

5.7 Cross a wooden footbridge and then follow the path uphill and to the left (north).

6.0 End your hike at the lodge overlooking Lake Crawford.

HIKE INFORMATION

Local information: The Town of Clover, 114 Bethel St., Clover, SC 29710; (803) 222-9495; www.cloversc.info. Clover is known as "the town with 'love' in the middle."

Local events/attractions: If you need something to do in early June, check out Clover Scottish Games and Scotch-Irish Festival at Clover Memorial Stadium, 320 Clinton Ave., Clover, SC 29710. For more information visit www.cloverscottish games.com.

Good eats: Jackson's Kitchen, 304 N. Main St., Clover, SC 29710; (803) 222-7461. It's a tucked-away restaurant that is worth discovering. Be sure to try the delicious lunch specials.

Organizations: Friends of Kings Mountain State Park, 1277 Park Rd., Blacksburg, SC 29702; (803) 222-3209. Find Friends of Kings Mountain State Park on Facebook.

Kings Mountain State Park: Buzzards Roost

This is a strenuous but enjoyable full-day hike. The trail starts near Lake Crawford at Kings Mountain State Park and immediately heads for the woods, where the route travels through a hardwood forest on single-track trail and old roadbeds. After traveling along a relatively level grade, the route comes to a clearing that marks the South Carolina/North Carolina state line. There is always something very rewarding about hiking from one state to another, but the journey doesn't end there! Instead, the path continues over increasingly rolling terrain. After crossing the paved Bethlehem Road, the trail travels one more challenging hill to reach Buzzards Roost. Take time to explore the dramatic boulder-laden ridgeline that overlooks the farmland to the northwest, before retracing your steps to Kings Mountain State Park.

Start: Kings Mountain State Park Lake Crawford parking area
Distance: 9.6-mile out and back
Hiking time: About 5 to 6 hours
Difficulty: More challenging, based on length
Trail surface: Forested trail
Other trail users: None
Best season(s): Year-round
Canine compatibility: Leashed dogs permitted
Land status: State park and national military park
Fees and permits: Day-use fee required. Pay at park entrance.
Schedule: The park is open from 8 a.m. to sunset. The hours at Kings Mountain National Military Park and Crowders Mountain State Park vary slightly, but if you arrive back at the state park 30 minutes before sunset, you should be fine.
Maps: USGS Kings Mountain; online trail maps available at www.southcarolinaparks .com/files/State%20Parks/ Kings%20Mtn/KM_Current-Trail -Map.jpg and www.ncparks .gov/Visit/parks/crmo/pics/park map.pdf
Trail contacts: Kings Mountain State Park, 1277 Park Rd., Blacksburg, SC 29702; (803) 222-3209; www.southcarolinaparks.com/ park-finder/state-park/945.aspx
   Crowders Mountain State Park, 522 Park Office Lane, Kings Mountain 28086; (704) 853-5375; www.ncparks.gov

Finding the trailhead: From Charlotte take I-85 southbound toward Gastonia. Take exit 8 and turn left (south) onto US 161. Follow US 161 across the North Carolina–South Carolina border. The state park entrance will be on your right (west) just past the state line. GPS: N35 8.957' / W81 20.728'

THE HIKE

How rewarding is it to return home after a long day hike and tell all your friends that you hiked from South Carolina to North Carolina?! This hike, which travels on the Ridgeline Trail, will not only guide you across the state line but also provide terrific views and a unique setting at Buzzards Roost.

The hike starts at Kings Mountain State Park, where you'll park at the day-use lot near Lake Crawford. You will need to start your hike by following the park road on foot to the picnic pavilions, at which point a dirt path will take shape. Follow the dirt path past the picnic pavilions and down a steep hill to reach a creek. Cross the creek on a wooden footbridge and then turn right on Clarks Creek Trail (Kings Mountain National Recreation Trail). Follow the blue blazes uphill and past a primitive campsite. This is a popular campsite with scouting groups, and if you pass the tents of a local troop early Saturday morning, there is a good chance you will smell bacon and coffee as you pass by. Luckily the aromas won't be too terribly tempting since you are at the very beginning of your hike.

Past the campsite the path continues on a single track, through a forest of pine, beech, cedar, and holly trees. Almost a mile into the hike, you will reach an intersection with the Ridgeline Trail. Turn right on this red-blazed path and follow it north. The Ridgeline Trail, constructed in 2009, joins Kings Mountain State Park and

Nature's rocky playground is on display at Buzzards Roost.

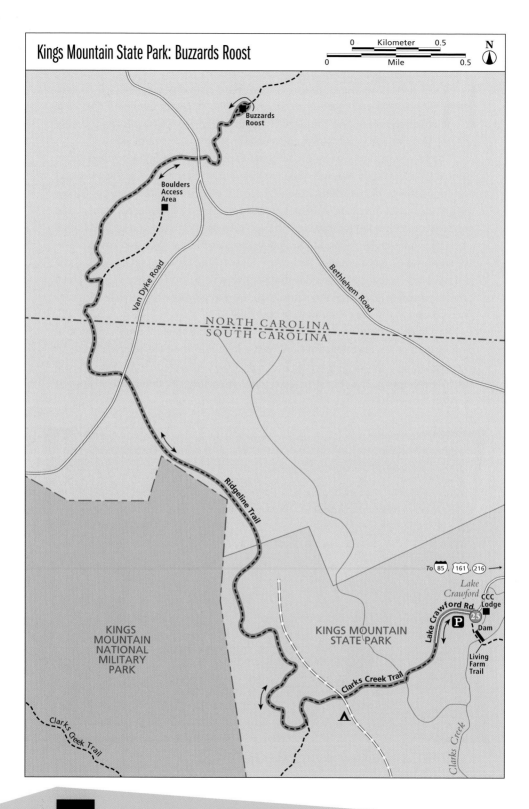

Kings Mountain State Park: Buzzards Roost

Kilometer

Mile

N

Buzzards Roost

Boulders Access Area

Van Dyke Road

Bethlehem Road

NORTH CAROLINA
SOUTH CAROLINA

Ridgeline Trail

KINGS MOUNTAIN NATIONAL MILITARY PARK

Clarks Creek Trail

Clarks Creek Trail

To 85 161 216

Lake Crawford

CCC Lodge

Lake Crawford Rd.

P

25

Dam

KINGS MOUNTAIN STATE PARK

Living Farm Trail

Clarks Creek

Kings Mountain National Military Park with Crowders Mountain. The trail spans 2.5 miles in South Carolina and another 6.2 miles in North Carolina, for a total length of 8.7 miles. However, the larger impact of the path is that it now connects three parks and an even larger network of hiking trails.

The Ridgeline Trail offers a combination of single-track paths and old road-beds. Be sure to pay close attention to the red blazes in order to stay on the right track. After hiking a little over 3.0 miles, the trail will enter a brief clearing. It will quickly return to the woods and when it exits at the next clear-cut boundary, you will be at the state line. An informative marker near the boundary states that for many years the actual location of the North Carolina/South Carolina state line was in dispute until modern instruments could clearly define the 35-degree latitude line, on which this portion of the border rests.

Once you are in North Carolina, you will quickly come to a trail junction. Veer left to continue on the Ridgeline Trail and avoid a detour to the nearby Boulders Access Area parking lot. In the future if you want to return to Buzzards Roost on a shorter hike, this access area will allow you to reach the spectacular rocks on a 2.0-mile out-and-back hike. A few minutes past the trail junction, the path exits the woods and crosses Bethlehem Road. Be sure to look both ways before proceeding as cars travel very quickly down this paved two-lane road. Past Bethlehem Road the trail travels a short uphill to reach another intersection. Turn left to access Buzzards Roost. The first set of large rocks will be to your left, but other even more impressive formations continue up the ridgeline to the north. There are faint rabbit trails that explore the rocks in both directions.

This compilation of ridgeline boulders is dramatic, and the view from the top of the rocks is stunning. That said, be cautious as you explore this natural play-ground. Do not climb technical or slick rocks. Views of the surrounding valley floor are available on the northern half of Buzzards Roost, without any rock climbing. Take your time at the overlook to enjoy the view and rest on one of the warm, sun-baked rocks. When you are ready to commence the second half of your hike, turn around and retrace your steps back to Kings Mountain State Park.

Did you know that Buzzards Roost is a popular place to practice bouldering? You should never attempt this activity on your own, but if you want to learn more about rock climbing and bouldering, consider joining a group or practicing at a local gym like Inner Peaks (http://innerpeaks.com).

MILES AND DIRECTIONS

0.0   Start at the wood lodge on the west shore of Lake Crawford and hike west and slightly uphill through the parking lot.

0.1   Take the stairs that lead from the parking lot to the park road. Turn left and follow the road south toward the picnic area.

0.2   The road terminates and the path begins. Follow it past the picnic pavilions and restrooms.

0.3   Cross over a wooden bridge and turn right on Clarks Creek Trail (Kings Mountain National Recreation Trail). Continue uphill past a primitive campsite.

0.9   Take a right (north) on the red-blazed Ridgeline Trail.

2.2   The trail intersects an old roadbed. Turn left (west).

3.0   The Ridgeline Trail leaves the roadbed and continues on a single-track trail.

3.4   Enter North Carolina!

4.0   The trail splits. Veer left (northwest) to continue on the Ridgeline Trail.

4.4   Cross Bethlehem Road.

4.7   Leave the Ridgeline Trail and veer left (west) on a spur trail to access Buzzards Roost.

4.8   Explore Buzzards Roost before retracing your steps on the Ridgeline Trail.

6.2   Reenter South Carolina.

8.7   Turn left (east) to rejoin the Kings Mountain National Recreation Trail.

9.3   Cross a stream on a wooden bridge, then turn left. Leave the recreation trail and hike north.

9.6   Return to your car at the parking lot nearest to Lake Crawford.

🌱 Green Tip:
For rest stops, go off-trail so others won't have to get around you. Head for resilient surfaces that don't contain vegetation.

HIKE INFORMATION

Local information: The Town of Clover, 114 Bethel St., Clover, SC 29710; (803) 222-9495; www.cloversc.info. Clover is known as "the town with 'love' in the middle."

Local events/attractions: If you need something to do in early June, check out Clover Scottish Games and Scotch-Irish Festival at Clover Memorial Stadium, 320 Clinton Ave., Clover, SC 29710. For more information visit www.cloverscottish games.com.

Good eats: Victoria's Diner, 102 N. Main St., Clover, SC 29710; (803) 222-3310. Fast and delicious Southern cuisine.

Organizations: Friends of Kings Mountain State Park, 1277 Park Rd., Blacksburg, SC 29702; (803) 222-3209. Find Friends of Kings Mountain State Park on Facebook.

Discover More

This hike crosses the North Carolina–South Carolina border, however, the two states were not always separate entities. For twenty years Charleston served as the capital of Carolina. It wasn't until 1711 that the two states separated, and since that time there have been countless disagreements concerning the property boundary between the two states. One of the most notable occurred along the state borders near Charlotte. There were several surveys of the state line performed in the eighteenth century. However, as disputes arose and instrumentation and techniques continued to improve, the need to repeat the survey continued to arise. Finally, in 1815 a comprehensive survey was completed that defined the state line all the way to the Chattooga River. That boundary is still in question today.

You will most certainly cross the state line during this hike, but where you actually cross that boundary . . . well, that's another matter.

History comes alive in the reconstructed Webb Grist Mill (hike 28).

The hikes to the south of Charlotte are found mostly around the town of Fort Mill in South Carolina. Fort Mill is a quaint town with a rich history that dates back to several significant events during the Revolutionary and Civil Wars. Fort Mill's historic sites, farms, and modern facilities such as schools and a recreational complex are now connected by a web of greenway trails.

Anne Springs Close Greenway is a terrific addition to this South Carolina town and the greater Charlotte area. The greenway system has trails for mountain bikers and horseback riders, but every dirt path that is part of the greenway is open to hikers. This guidebook includes a variety of trails that explore Anne Springs Close Greenway. The History Walk is a great trail for hikers of all ages, and it includes highlights such as the Graham Cabin, the restored childhood home of evangelist Billy Graham's grandfather. The greenway's Webb Grist Mill Trail explores a reconstructed grist mill that dates to the same era as the Graham Cabin. If you want a more scenic nature tour, consider hiking the Lake Haigler Trail and look for geese on the banks of the lake before weaving in and out of the sweet-smelling peach orchards at the south end of the property. Or if you are in need of a longer hike, then venture to the Leroy Springs Recreational Complex and explore the wooded South Loop.

Another terrific place to hike, south of Charlotte, is at Cane Creek Park near the town of Waxhaw. The park offers a great network of trails and lots of activities to enjoy after the hike, including several options on or in the water at Cane Creek Lake. Waxhaw, like Fort Mill, is another terrific small historic town that is worth visiting before or after the hike. You can even visit the Museum of the Waxhaws to learn more about the area and US President Andrew Jackson, who was born in this region.

A small boat dock stretches into Cane Creek Lake near the end of hike 30.

Anne Springs Close Greenway: Lake Haigler

This trail starts at the Anne Springs Close Nature Center and follows the historic Nation Ford Road past Rush Pavilion to Lake Haigler. The route then does a semicircle around the scenic lake. At the halfway point you will veer south on the Blue Star Trail and travel a narrow trail through an upland hardwood forest. This out-and-back portion of the hike exits the trees at the peach grove fields located at the southwest corner of the property. From here the path backtracks to Lake Haigler, at which point you will contour the remainder of the shoreline before returning to the trailhead on Nation Ford Road.

Start: Anne Springs Close Nature Center

Distance: 4.4-mile balloon

Hiking time: About 2 to 2.5 hours

Difficulty: Moderate

Trail surface: Forested trail and dirt roads

Best season(s): Spring, when the peach trees are blooming

Other trail users: Equestrians

Canine compatibility: Leashed dogs permitted

Land status: Private greenway

Fees and permits: Trail-use fee, deposit at trailhead kiosk

Schedule: Open 7 a.m. to sunset

Maps: USGS Fort Mill; Anne Springs Close Greenway Map available at the trailhead kiosk and at the nature center

Trail contacts: Anne Springs Close Greenway, PO Box 1209, Fort Mill, SC 29716; (803) 548-7252; www.leroysprings.com/default.asp?lsc=239

Finding the trailhead: From downtown Charlotte follow I-77 South into South Carolina. At exit 88 turn left (east) onto Gold Hill Road. In 0.3 mile the road will turn into Springfield Parkway. Continue straight on Springfield Parkway for 1.3 miles to the intersection with the US 21 bypass. Turn right (south) on the bypass. Drive 1.0 mile and the entrance to Anne Springs Close Greenway will be on your left. Park at the trailhead kiosk to the south of the Nature Center. GPS: N35 02.253' / W80 56.477'

> *The Native American population in this area suffered tremendously from the diseases brought across the ocean by the European settlers. Lake Haigler was named for a great Catawba chief that once lived in the region.*

THE HIKE

The trailhead for this hike is located directly beside the Anne Springs Close Nature Center. Visiting the facility is a great way to start your hike, and if the building is still open when you finish, you can go back and ask the attendant any questions that may have arisen during your trek. Be sure to pick up a trail map at the nature center or trailhead kiosk as it includes an informative nature walk around Lake Haigler.

The trail starts by following the Blue Star Trail along the Nation Ford Road to Rush Pavilion. This wide dirt path seems pretty ordinary today, but it actually holds an important place in American history. The Nation Ford Road was part of the Great Philadelphia Wagon Road that stretched from Pennsylvania to Georgia. It was built in the early 1800s and served pedestrians, equestrians, and horse-drawn carriages. In fact, there are still some places where you can see evidence of overuse or erosion from wagon wheels!

When the Nation Ford Road arrives at Rush Pavilion, you will skirt the beautiful open-air building and walk through an open field down to the banks of Lake

A barren winter peach tree.

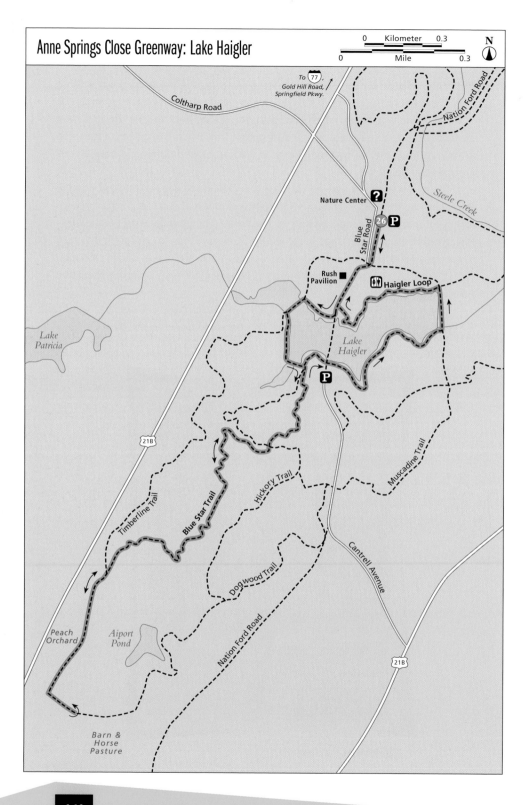

Anne Springs Close Greenway: Lake Haigler

Coltharp Road

To 77,
Gold Hill Road,
Springfield Pkwy.

Nation Ford Road

Steele Creek

Nature Center

Blue Star Road

26 P

Rush Pavilion

Haigler Loop

Lake Patricia

Lake Haigler

P

21B

Muscadine Trail

Timberline Trail

Blue Star Trail

Hickory Trail

Dogwood Trail

Cantrell Avenue

Nation Ford Road

21B

Peach Orchard

Aiport Pond

Barn & Horse Pasture

0   Kilometer   0.3

0   Mile   0.3

N

Haigler. At the shoreline of the lake, turn left and locate the Blue Star Trail, which follows the shoreline closely. The route now contours the ins and outs of the lake.

After hiking 0.5 mile you will cross to the west shore of Lake Haigler on a land bridge. Because this crossing is surrounded by water, it can become exceptionally muddy after a heavy rain. But that doesn't bother the equestrian riders, who also use this small portion of trail to cross the lake.

Past the bridge you will veer left and travel the east shore of a small duck pond. Past the pond turn right to remain on the Blue Star Trail. The path now travels away from the lake and into the forest. The trail is faint and sometimes hard to decipher. Thankfully, there is only one major intersection and if you stay straight when the thin path crosses the Hickory Trail roadbed, you should be able to stay on course. Beyond the Hickory Trail junction, you will pass two small seeping streams before exiting the woods at a peach grove.

The peach grove is gorgeous, especially in early spring when flowers fill the branches and again two months later when the sweet-smelling fruit weighs the limbs to the ground. At the same time that the path leaves the forest, it also intersects the Timberline Trail. The two paths join together and follow the western edge of the forest. Instead of looking for a defined path, think of this section as more of a corridor that exists between the woods and the peach fields.

The Blue Star Trail terminates at the southwest corner of the greenway property. Turn left on the Dogwood Trail to explore the southern portion of the peach orchard. When you arrive at the barn and horse pasture, turn around and retrace your steps to Lake Haigler.

When you return to the banks of Lake Haigler, turn right and follow the shoreline around the east half of the lake. At mile 3.8 look for a waterfall where a small outlet leaves the body of water. Continue to the north shore of the lake. Be sure to turn left and hug the shoreline at mile 3.8, where several paths diverge.

At the open field that leads to the Rush Pavilion, turn left and hike uphill to rejoin the Nation Ford Road and return to the nature center.

MILES AND DIRECTIONS

0.0 Start at the nature center parking area and hike south on a dirt road that acts as a corridor between the forest and the peach grove. This is the Nation Ford Road/Blue Star Trail.

0.2 Arrive at Rush Pavilion. Continue through the open field south of Rush Pavilion to the banks of Lake Haigler.

0.3 Turn right on the Blue Star Trail.

0.5 Follow the Blue Star Trail on a land bridge across Lake Haigler.

0.8 Just past the duck pond and Hickory Trail, turn right to stay on the Blue Star Trail. It now becomes a narrow path that winds through the woods.

0.9 Intersect the Hickory Trail and continue straight.

1.1 Cross a small stream.

1.5 Cross another seasonal stream.

1.8 Exit the woods into a peach grove. Hug the forest boundary to stay on the route.

2.0 Turn left (east) on the unmarked Dogwood Trail. Stay between the woods and the farmland to explore the final peach grove.

2.2 Turn around at the barn entrance and horse pasture. Retrace your steps to Lake Haigler. (***Side trip:*** If you want to take a different route back to the lake, you can also loop back using the Dogwood and Hickory Trails. Consult a park map.)

3.6 Arrive at Lake Haigler and turn right to continue contouring the shoreline.

3.8 Turn left and cross over the lake outlet.

3.9 At a junction with multiple trails, turn left (west) to stay near the lake.

4.1 When you arrive at the open field leading to Rush Pavilion, follow it north.

4.2 Pass Rush Pavilion and continue on the Nation Ford Road.

4.4 Return to the nature center parking lot and trailhead.

HIKE INFORMATION

Local information: Fort Mill Area Council, 101 S. White St., Fort Mill, SC 29715; (803) 547-5900; www.yorkcountychamber.com

Local events/attractions: Museum of York County, 4621 Mr. Gallant Rd., Rock Hill, SC 29732; (803) 329-2121; www.chmuseums.org. A natural history museum that is great for kids and adults alike.

Good eats: Longitude 81 Degrees, 971 Gold Hill Rd., Fort Mill, SC 29708; (803) 802-9981; www.longitude81degrees.com. You'll get wood-fired American fare with a Caribbean twist in an upscale environment here.

Organizations: Move Fort Mill Forward, 101 S. White St., Fort Mill, SC 29715; (803) 547-1007; www.movefortmillforward.com. Dedicated to revitalizing the town of Fort Mill.

Anne Springs Close Greenway: South Loop

The South Loop at Anne Springs Close Greenway could also be called the S loop. It is located in the southernmost potion of the greenway and it combines three trails: the Blue Star Trail, the School Loop, and the Sugar Loop. The trail is unique because it is bordered by busy roads, housing developments, shopping centers, and a school, yet it remains entirely in the forest and provides a true sense of isolation and nature. The path primarily follows shaded single-track trail. It contours the west bank of Steele Creek for a brief stretch before traveling east on the undulating hills of the Sugar Loop. At the end of the Sugar Loop, you will walk through the bridge that leads under Springfield Parkway and return to your car at the Leroy Springs Recreation Complex.

Start: Leroy Springs Recreation Complex

Distance: 6.0-mile loop

Hiking time: About 3 to 3.5 hours

Difficulty: Moderate

Trail surface: Forested trail

Best season(s): Year-round

Other trail users: Bikes

Canine compatibility: Leashed dogs permitted

Land status: Private greenway

Fees and permits: Trail-use fee, deposit at trailhead kiosk

Schedule: Open 7 a.m. to sunset

Maps: USGS Fort Mill; Anne Springs Close Greenway Map available at the trailhead kiosk and at the nature center

Trail contacts: Anne Springs Close Greenway, PO Box 1209, Fort Mill, SC 29716; (803) 548-7252; www.leroysprings.com/default.asp?lsc=239

Finding the trailhead: From downtown Charlotte follow I-77 South into South Carolina. At exit 88 turn left (east) onto Gold Hill Road. In 0.3 mile the road will turn into Springfield Parkway. Continue straight on Springfield Parkway for 3.1 miles to a T intersection at SC 160/Tom Hall Street. Turn right (south) on Tom Hall Street, then in another 0.2 mile, turn right (west) into Leroy Springs Recreation Complex. The trailhead kiosk is located behind the tennis courts and baseball fields to the north of the parking area. GPS: N35 00.637'/W80 55.284'

This hike offers a long wooded escape from a very urban setting. After starting next to the popular baseball fields and tennis courts at the Leroy Springs
Recreation Complex, the hike immediately dives into the woods. By following the pedestrian-only Blue Star Trail, the path winds through a forest filled with
beech, oak, and cedar trees. After briefly paralleling the recreation facility, the path
veers north and encounters a seeping stream that separates the hiker-friendly Blue
Star Trail from the School Loop West Trail, which is popular with mountain bikers.

You may be surprised to find such an expansive network of hiking, biking, and
riding trails so close to Fort Mill. The Anne Springs Close Greenway is comprised of
2,300 acres of former farmland that was owned by the Springs family for 200 years.
In 1995 the eight children of Bill Close and Anne Springs Close gave the property
to the community as a gift. That's some gift! It was named in honor of the children's
mother and as a tribute to her lifelong love of nature and recreation. Now the residents of Fort Mill, Charlotte, and everywhere else can travel to the greenway and
share in the stunning scenery and outdoor opportunities available here.

A wooden footbridge spans a seasonal seep.

After continuing along the Blue Star Trail, the path will skirt the edge of an open field before coming to a trail junction. The trail intersection occurs just before Steele Street, and by turning right on the School Loop West, the path remains well secluded within the woods. The path now travels up and down small hills before reaching the north tunnel bridge that allows hikers to pass under Springfield Parkway without having to navigate the traffic zooming overhead. At the tunnel exit the path continues on a pleasant wooded trail to reach the banks of Steele Creek. When you reach the water you can clearly make out the US 21 Business overpass located to your left. If you want to visit the nearby Webb Grist Mill, described in an alternate greenway hike, turn left to walk under the road and follow the north spur trail on the opposite side of the road. To remain on the South Loop, turn south and hike along the banks of the creek. This path and creek both serve as excellent resources for the students and teachers at Fort Mill Elementary and Middle Schools. The schools, located at the heart of the greenway's South Loop, allow classes direct access to the history and biology along the trail.

Eventually the trail crosses the creek on a suspension bridge, which is a huge favorite among the students. Past the bridge the trail veers right and then travels uphill to a nearby power box. A few feet beyond the fenced utility, the path intersects the Sugar Loop Trail. If you are feeling tired or weary at this point, continue straight on the School Loop East trail toward the recreation center. However, if you want to continue your hike on a really pleasant and remote extension, then turn left on the Sugar Loop. The trail travels well within the confines of the forest on rolling terrain. The route passes moss-covered rocks and several patches of lycopodium, a club moss that resembles small, green trees, line the path. Be careful about stooping and staring at the undergrowth for too long because mountain bikes often come careening around turns and speeding down hills on this trail.

When you return to the School Loop East, turn left to access the complex tunnel that travels under Springfield Parkway. The path now travels slightly uphill to return to your car (and civilization) at the trailhead parking lot.

MILES AND DIRECTIONS

0.0 Start at the Leroy Springs Recreation Complex and locate the wooden trailhead kiosk behind the baseball fields and tennis courts. Start your hike by turning east at the kiosk and following the Blue Star Trail.

0.3 The trail parallels the recreation complex before veering north into the woods. Bear right to avoid hiking on the web of mountain bike trails to the west.

0.5 Pass over a small seasonal stream.

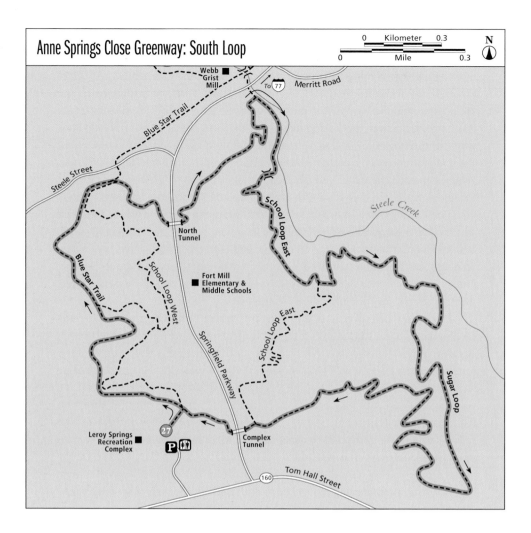

If you are interested in mountain-biking the trails at Anne Springs Close Greenway, consider learning the basics and going on group rides near Charlotte with the Tarheel Trailblazers (www.tarheeltrailblazers.com).

🌿 **Green Tip:**
Donate used gear to a nonprofit organization for kids.

1.0 Wind uphill on a gradual set of switchbacks. You will cross over several wooden footbridges that span small drainage ditches.

1.1 Cross a small stream.

1.5 Leave the Blue Star Trail, which exits the woods. Stay within the forest by turning right (east) on the School Loop West Trail.

2.1 At a trail junction veer left to remain on the School Loop West. Continue to follow signs toward the north tunnel.

2.3 Pass under Springfield Drive through the north tunnel. Continue the hike on the School Loop East Trail.

2.7 Arrive at the banks of Steele Creek and turn south. (***Side trip:*** If you want to take a short side trip to visit the Webb Grist Mill, turn left and hike north underneath Springfield Parkway.)

3.1 Cross a super-fun suspension bridge and veer left on the opposite shore to remain on the School Loop East.

3.6 When the trail exits the forest at a utility shed, it continues to the west and then arrives at a junction with the Sugar Loop Trail. Turn left (east) to travel the Sugar Loop.

5.7 The Sugar Loop reconnects with the School Loop East Trail. Turn left (west) and travel through the nearby Complex Tunnel that travels underneath Springfield Parkway.

6.0 Complete your hike at the Leroy Springs Recreation Center.

HIKE INFORMATION

Local information: Fort Mill Area Council, 101 S. White St., Fort Mill, SC 29715; (803) 547-5900; www.yorkcountychamber.com

Local events/attractions: The Fine Art and Master Craft Festival in Fort Mill takes place each fall. Get more information at Fort Mill Art on Main, 101 S. White St., Fort Mill, SC 29715; (803) 547-1007; www.movefortmillforward.com/FortMill ArtOnMain.asp

Good eats: Captain Steve's, 1975 Hwy. 21 Bypass, Fort Mill, SC 29715; (803) 547-2340; www.captainsteves.net. You're not too far away from Lake Wylie to enjoy some fish! A great place to pick up a takeout order on your way home.

Organizations: Move Fort Mill Forward, 101 S. White St., Fort Mill, SC 29715; (803) 547-1007; www.movefortmillforward.com. Dedicated to revitalizing the town of Fort Mill.

Anne Springs Close Greenway: Webb Grist Mill

This hike starts by heading north and looping around Lake Crandall, before veering southwest to meet the Norfolk Southern Railroad line and Steele Creek. The route then parallels the creek and crosses over several suspension bridges before arriving at the Webb Grist Mill. The modern structure is a reconstruction of the historic mill built in the 1770s that helped to give Fort Mill its name. From there the path continues along the creek to view an old millstone that has now been turned into a monument to commemorate the original grist mill. The trail then leaves the cool, shaded banks of Steele Creek and returns to the trailhead parking lot on the scenic but exposed Prairie Loop.

Start: Anne Springs Close Field Trail Barn Access
Distance: 3.9-mile loop
Hiking time: About 2 to 2.5 hours
Difficulty: Moderate
Trail surface: Forested trail and dirt roads
Best season(s): Fall, winter, spring
Other trail users: Equestrians and bikes
Canine compatibility: Leashed dogs permitted

Land status: Private greenway
Fees and permits: Trail-use fee, deposit at trailhead kiosk
Schedule: Open 7 a.m. to sunset
Maps: USGS Fort Mill; Anne Springs Close Greenway Map available at the trailhead kiosk
Trail contacts: Anne Springs Close Greenway, PO Box 1209, Fort Mill, SC 29716; (803) 548-7252; www.leroysprings.com/default.asp?lsc=239

Finding the trailhead: From downtown Charlotte follow take I-77 South into South Carolina. At exit 88 turn left (east) onto Gold Hill Road. In 0.3 mile the road will turn into Springfield Parkway. Continue straight on Springfield Parkway past Old Nation Road to the intersection with Field Trail Lane. Turn right (west) on Field Trail Lane and park at the red barn at the end of the road. GPS: N35 02.023' / W80 55.052'

> *If you are an educator or simply want to learn more about the Webb Grist Mill, there is a terrific link on the Anne Springs Greenway website for lesson plans involving the mill. For more info, check out www .leroysprings.com/default.asp?lsc=225.*

THE HIKE

To start this hike, begin at the red barn at the end of Field Trail Lane and hike east toward Springfield Parkway. When you reach the wooden information kiosk, turn left and hike north. The well-defined gravel trail will head to Lake Crandall, and you are welcome to travel this short out-and-back to visit the southern shore of the lake. However, the main route travels on the dirt roadbed on the west side of a pine stand that blocks the view of the nearby road.

Many hikers are used to seeing trail signs and blazes marking their paths. However, in this portion of the Anne Springs Close Greenway, trails should be thought of more like a corridor than a well-defined path. The corridor first travels on the greenway's Muscadine Trail, which is shared by both hikers and horseback riders. After passing the east shore of Lake Crandall, the path turns west and cuts in between Lake Crandall and Lake Frances before circling back toward the trailhead and veering southwest toward the Southern Railroad line. Note that once again, the trail leading toward the railroad tracks travels through open fields with multiple paths. Continue as straight as possible on a red dirt road, but don't worry

This millstone may have been used in the Webb Grist Mill in the early nineteenth century.

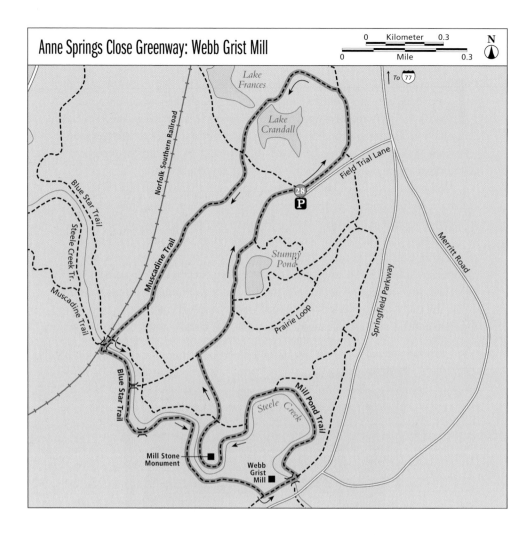

about veering off on an adjoining trail—it happens! And fortunately most of the trails in this section eventually reconnect.

At the Norfolk Southern Railway, the hike joins the Blue Star Trail and becomes more defined. The staggering Norfolk Southern Railway is situated high above the trail on a bridge. This railroad was initially built in the early 1900s as the South Carolina Railroad. The Springs family even helped to fund the initial venture, especially since it helped them ship their textiles and farm products to the market in Charleston. No longer in operation, the overgrown tracks still serve as a reminder the prosperous King Cotton reign in Fort Mill. The railroad has seen many upgrades and improvements and continues to be a very active railway.

Once you join the Blue Star Trail, you will parallel Steele Creek. The path crosses the creek twice on two different suspension bridges. And for a hiker, suspension bridges offer more sway, swing, and fun than ordinary bridges.

Just before the Blue Star Trail reaches Steele Street, the path reaches the headrace corridor. A sign at the narrow channel indicates that when the mill operator released water from Mill Pond, this ditch then directed a 4-inch stream of water toward the large waterwheel that powered the mill. Turn right at the headrace and hike toward Steele Street. Just before the road, turn left and hike east to join the bike-friendly Mill Pond Trail, where an adjacent spur leads to the restored 1770s Webb Grist Mill. This mill was one of the first of its kind in this area and for more than 100 years it was used to process corn and grain for Fort Mill residents. The mill was so significant to daily life in Fort Mill that it impacted the official name of the town, when it changed from its original title of Little York. The Springs family bought the mill in 1813 and it was used by area farmers to grind corn to cornmeal and wheat to flour.

Past the mill the trail continues along the banks of Steele Creek. The route encounters one more remnant of the Webb Grist Mill, an old millstone believed to have been part of the original mill operation. It has been mounted above a commemorative plaque. There are also remnants of the dam that fed the mill about 20 yards downstream from the monument.

Continuing past the millstone, the trail joins the Prairie Loop on its journey back to the trailhead. The path now leaves the shade of the forest and travels through open fields that lead back to the trailhead. The exposed dirt road that leads back to your car can be sweltering in the midday summer sun, so try to time this part of the hike for the morning or early evening. Conclude your trek at the red barn where you first started your journey.

MILES AND DIRECTIONS

0.0   From the red barn, hike east along Field Trail Lane.

0.1   At the wooden trail kiosk, turn left (north) on an old dirt roadbed and follow the pine stand that parallels the road. Do not follow the gravel road that leads to Lake Crandall, unless you specifically want to visit the nearby water and fishing pier.

0.3   A small spur trail continues north, but you will continue on the wide dirt road that veers west between Lake Crandall and Lake Frances.

0.8   At a four-way X intersection, continue diagonally to the southwest.

1.4   Reach the Norfolk Southern Railway and turn left (south) on the Blue Star Trail. Continue to veer left to avoid a stray spur trail.

1.6   Stay near the creek and cross over the suspension bridge.

1.8   On the west side of Steele Creek, continue to veer left to stay near the water and cross over the second suspension bridge. It will feel like you are backtracking, but turn left (south) after crossing the second bridge.

2.1 Meet the headrace that once channeled water to the grist mill. Turn right and travel toward Steele Street.

2.2 At a T intersection, turn right (east) and then take another immediate right (north) to meet the Webb Grist Mill.

2.3 You've reached the Webb Grist Mill! Take your time to explore the mill and then backtrack to the main path.

2.4 Turn left (east) on the main trail and cross over Steele Creek on a bridge, then take an immediate right on the Mill Pond Trail.

2.9 Veer left (west) at a trail junction to stay near the creek. You'll encounter a millstone-turned-monument that commemorates the original grist mill.

3.2 Continue straight and join the Prairie Loop.

3.4 The trail encounters several spur paths to the right. Continue to veer left (north) and stay on a straight course toward the trailhead.

3.9 End your hike when the Prairie Loop arrives at the red barn.

HIKE INFORMATION

Local information: Fort Mill Area Council, 101 S. White St., Fort Mill, SC 29715; (803) 547-5900; www.yorkcountychamber.com

Local events/attractions: The Fort Mill Fall Festival, 101 S. White St., Fort Mill, SC 29715; (803) 547-1007; www.movefortmillforward.com/FortMillFallFestival.asp This Halloween festival is a lot of fun when combined with a haunted hike!

Good eats: Six Pence Pub, 993 Markey St., Fort Mill, SC 29708; (803) 802-5885; www.sixpencepub.com. Everyone knows that good pub food and drinks taste great after a hike.

Organizations: Move Fort Mill Forward, 101 S. White St., Fort Mill, SC 29715; (803) 547-1007; www.movefortmillforward.com. Dedicated to revitalizing the town of Fort Mill.

Green Tip:
Borrow, rent, or share gear.

Anne Springs Close Greenway: History Walk

This path travels past several historic sites on its journey to the Anne Springs Close Nature Center. By starting at the Dairy Barn trailhead, the route first visits Coltharp Cabin, a small wooden farmhouse dating back to 1800. The trail then crosses the historic Nation Ford Road and enters the courtyard of Graham Cabin. This two-story cabin, built in 1780, was the childhood home of famous evangelist Billy Graham's grandfather. Past Coltharp Cabin, the trail delves into the forest and follows the curvaceous Steele Creek to a trail junction, where a springy suspension bridge leads across the water. Past the bridge you will travel a gentle uphill through a mixed hardwood forest to arrive at the Anne Springs Close Nature Center. When you are done visiting the Nature Center, you will then be able to backtrack to the trailhead on the historic Nation Ford Road.

Start: Anne Springs Close Dairy Barn trailhead

Distance: 1.6-mile figure eight

Hiking time: About 1 to 1.5 hours

Difficulty: Easy

Trail surface: Forested trail, a paved pathway, and dirt roads

Best season(s): Fall, winter, spring

Other trail users: Equestrians

Canine compatibility: Leashed dogs permitted

Land status: Private greenway

Fees and permits: Trail-use fee, deposit at trailhead kiosk

Schedule: Open 7 a.m. to sunset

Maps: USGS Fort Mill; Anne Springs Close Greenway Map available at the trailhead kiosk and at the nature center

Trail contacts: Anne Springs Close Greenway, PO Box 1209, Fort Mill, SC 29716; (803) 548-7252; www.leroysprings.com/default.asp?lsc=239

Finding the trailhead: From downtown Charlotte follow take I-77 South into South Carolina. At exit 88 turn left (east) onto Gold Hill Road. In 0.3 mile the road will turn into Springfield Parkway. Continue straight on Springfield Parkway to the intersection with US 21 Business/Old Nation Road. Turn right (north) on Old Nation Road, then in another 0.2 mile turn right (east) onto Dairy Barn Lane. Follow Dairy Barn Lane past the greenway headquarters and white dairy barn to the trailhead parking lot and kiosk. GPS: N35 02.676'/W80 55.970'

THE HIKE

f you even need to trick someone into going for a hike, then this trail is a good place to try it. This easy 1.6-mile hike passes by historic buildings, grazing animals, a scenic stream, and a tree identification trail, and it crosses over a memorable suspension bridge on its way to visit a nature center! Something along this route will be sure to appeal to even the most reluctant hiker.

To begin the hike, start at the Dairy Barn trailhead, which is located just past the beautiful white dairy barn that sits on top of a hill at Anne Springs Close Greenway. This structure was built as a working barn in 1946, but has since been remodeled and is now primarily used for public gatherings and special events.

The route travels first on a paved handicapped-accessible path, past the restrooms, and up to the top of a nearby hill to visit Coltharp Cabin. This one-room nineteenth-century cabin would have been appropriate lodging for a farm caretaker, who was typically a single white male. The structure would not only serve as his lodging, but also as an office and place to conduct business. This small cabin is perched in a great place to oversee the surrounding crops and cattle.

> 🌰 **Green Tip:**
> *Cotton clothing has a smaller carbon footprint*
> *(when washed in cold water) than either polyester or wool.*

Coltharp Cabin overlooks neighboring farmland and Steele Creek.

Notice also that the roof of the house has an extra row of shingles extending from the top of the A-frame. These angled slats were designed to face the same direction as incoming storms, and thus protect the top binding or seam of the roof.

Past Coltharp Cabin, the hike continues downhill on the paved path to intersect the Nation Ford Road. This historic wagon road is listed on the National Register of Historic Places. It connected Philadelphia, Pennsylvania, with Augusta, Georgia, and was known as the first major interior road in the eastern United States. Travel north, past the Nation Ford Road, to access the historic farmhouse that lies just beyond the famous thoroughfare. This concludes the handicapped-accessible portion of the route.

The large two-story farmhouse is more of a representation of the house of an eighteenth-century farm owner. In fact, this building holds particular significance to the region because it was the childhood home of evangelist Billy Graham's grandfather. Billy Graham grew up near Charlotte and is world-renowned as a famous Christian evangelist, especially during the second half of the twentieth century.

To continue the hike past the Graham homestead, walk to the south end of the courtyard, where a bench is situated to overlook Steele Creek. Much like Graham's vocation, the next step will be one of faith, because when looking down at the creek, it is hard to make out a trail. Nonetheless, travel the short, steep slope down to the water and you will notice a faint path take form along the shoreline. Follow the narrow path along the banks of the creek until you come to an intersection with the Nation Ford Road and a fabulous suspension bridge. Beyond the historic significance and miles of recreational trails, Anne Springs Close is a terrific destination due to the multiple swinging, swaying, fun suspension bridges located on the property.

Cross over the low-hanging bridge to the opposite shore, then continue slightly uphill on the main road, labeled Blue Star Trail. Follow this path until it exits the woods at the Anne Springs Close Nature Center. The center is typically only open on weekends, holidays, and special occasions, but if you see that the door is open, be sure to visit the facility.

When you are ready to turn around and hike back to the trailhead, start by backtracking on the Blue Star Trail and cross the suspension bridge for a second time. At this point continue east on the main path, the Nation Ford Road, also labeled the Blue Star Trail. Stay between the forest that shades Steele Creek and the farmland to the right. When you reach the intersection with the handicapped-accessible paved pathway, continue straight on the dirt road. You will notice that several trees to the left of the trail are labeled. This provides a great opportunity to learn the different leaf and bark characteristics of the various area trees. And if you still want to know more, once you reach the trailhead and get in your car, stop by the Greenway Headquarters on your way out and pick up a pamphlet that provides additional information on the labeled trees.

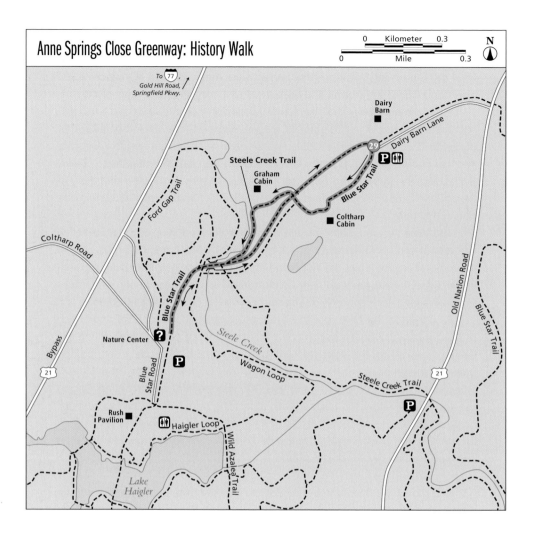

Anne Springs Close Greenway: History Walk

MILES AND DIRECTIONS

0.0 Start at the Dairy Barn trailhead. Follow the paved pathway west, past the restroom facilities and gradually uphill toward Coltharp Cabin.

0.2 Arrive at Coltharp Cabin. Explore the outside of the one-room cabin and then continue on the paved pathway.

0.3 Intersect the Nation Ford Road and continue straight toward the Graham Cabin courtyard.

0.4 Arrive at the Graham Cabin and find the next section of the hike to the west, along the banks of Steele Creek.

0.7 Leave the shaded bank of Steele Creek at an intersection with the Nation Ford Road and a long suspension bridge. Turn left (north) and hike over the bridge, then continue to hike south on the Blue Star Trail.

0.9 Arrive at the Anne Springs Close Greenway Nature Center. When you are ready to turn around, backtrack on the Blue Star Trail.

1.1 Cross the suspension bridge and continue on Nation Ford Road, which coincides with the Blue Star Trail.

1.6 Return to your car at the trailhead parking lot.

HIKE INFORMATION

Local information: Fort Mill Area Council, 101 S. White St., Fort Mill, SC 29715; (803) 547-5900; www.yorkcountychamber.com

Good eats: Jump N' Java Café, 1646 Hwy. 160 W., Fort Mill, SC 29708; (803) 547-1122. This place is perfect for a pre-hike pick-me-up!

Organizations: Move Fort Mill Forward, 101 S. White St., Fort Mill, SC 29715; (803) 547-1007; www.movefortmillforward.com. Dedicated to revitalizing the town of Fort Mill.

Fort Mill Art Guild, 1750 Hwy. 160 W., Suite 101-145, Fort Mill, SC 29708; (803) 548-3159; www.fortmillartguild.com. Fostering arts in the community of Fort Mill.

Discover More

Fort Mill is a fast-growing suburb of Charlotte. And even though Fort Mill falls in the shadows of the Queen City, it has a unique identity and captivating history of its own. The Catawba Indians have resided in present-day Fort Mill for thousands of years. In the 1750s the first Scotch-Irish settlers began inhabiting the region. However, it wasn't until after the Civil War, in 1873, that the town of Fort Mill was established. During "the war between the states," Fort Mill played a significant role as host to the last Confederate Government Cabinet Meeting. In fact, the president of the Confederacy, Jefferson Davis, spent three nights at the Springs' Plantation home located at the entrance of Dairy Barn Way—right next to modern-day Anne Springs Close Greenway. Fort Mill is also home to the US's only monument that specifically honors slaves who fought in the Confederate Army.

Cane Creek Park has a lot to offer. Located to the south of Charlotte in Waxhaw, the park has an extensive day-use area and a large campground that surround a 350-acre prized-bass lake. The property is connected by an extensive trail network. Some of the trails are for hikers only, while others are multiuse trails that are shared by hikers, mountain bikers, and horseback riders. This route explores several different trails in the day-use area. It first follows the Red Trail that weaves through the forest and traces the park's northern boundary. Then the path veers south to meet the banks of Cane Creek Lake. Once it arrives at the water, the hike travels the Orange Trail to encounter stunning views of Cane Creek Lake. Then the path joins the Yellow Trail to explore several of the park's recreational facilities, including a boating dock, picnic area, playground, and even a miniature golf course. These amenities are located very near the trailhead and can be enjoyed before or after the hike.

Start: Cane Creek Park Operation Center

Distance: 3.6-mile loop

Hiking time: About 1.5 to 2 hours

Difficulty: Easy; rolling hills and shoreline walking

Trail surface: Mostly dirt paths, a small section of paved trails

Best season(s): Year-round

Other trail users: Equestrians and mountain bikers

Canine compatibility: Leashed dogs permitted

Land status: County park

Fees and permits: A modest entrance fee is charged for pedestrians and vehicles

Schedule: Open during daylight hours. Specific hours vary throughout the year. Call (704) 843-3919 for current information.

Maps: USGS Unity; a trail map is available for a small fee at the park operation center. It is available for free download at the park's website.

Trail contacts: Cane Creek Park, 5213 Harkey Rd., Waxhaw 28173; (704) 843-3919; www.co.union .nc.us

Finding the trailhead: From Charlotte travel east on Andrew Jackson Highway (US 74) for approximately 23 miles. When you arrive at the outskirts of Monroe, take the US 601N/NC 200 S exit. In 0.25 mile turn right at Skyway Drive (NC 200 S). Drive for 1.3 miles and turn right (southwest) onto West Morrow Avenue, then continue on Lancaster Avenue (NC 200 S). After traveling 10.0 miles turn left at Tom Starnes Road (south). Take the first right onto Mary Elizabeth Church Road (southwest). After 0.8 mile take a slight left at Potter Road South (south), followed by a right (west) onto Harkey Road. Cane Creek Park is on your left in 1.2 miles. GPS: N34 50.555'/W80 41.130'

THE HIKE

Cane Creek Park is a terrific place to spend the morning, the day, or even the night. Located within an hour south of Charlotte, this county park has more than 1,000 acres of land and a 350-acre lake that are perfect for recreation and relaxation. Besides hiking, the park offers many sporting opportunities, rental boats, a picnic area, playground, ground campground, and incredible fishing. In fact, Cane Creek Lake is one of only three bass trophy lakes in North Carolina. If you have a family member who doesn't like to hike, he can sit by the shore and fish for bass, catfish, and bluegills while everyone else takes a walk.

One of the best aspects of hiking at Cane Creek Park is that after paying a modest entry fee, you are granted access to the trails and to all the other activities in the day-use area. There are some additional small fees for equipment rentals and/or a fishing license, but in general your whole family can spend the day hiking, playing, and basically feeling as if they are transported to a fabulous summer camp for a very low cost.

Cane Creek Park was created through the partnering and cooperation of Union County, the Union Conservation District, and the Soil Conservation Service. It opened its gates and its beautiful landscape to the public in 1978. To explore this beautiful park, start at the parking lot adjacent to the park operation center. When you first step out of your car, you will become excited about all the possibilities at Cane Creek Park. From the parking lot you can view a wooded playground and sparkling waterfront. Begin your hike by locating the restrooms to the west of the parking lot. If necessary, utilize this park facility before you leave, and then locate the Purple Trail that runs behind the building. Follow the Purple Trail north toward the main park road. Cross over the park road and join the Red Trail. Veer left on the Red Trail to travel this loop in a clockwise direction.

Once on the Red Trail, you will forget all about the busy activities that take place in the southern portion of the day-use area. A mixed hardwood forest, comprising pine and hardwood trees, surrounds the trail. The towering oak, maple, sourwood, and loblolly pine trees block out most of the ambient noise. The trail now follows a very peaceful and quiet route, paralleling Harkey Road to the south. However, unless the leaves are off the trees, you probably won't even know that the road is there.

After traveling 0.7 mile you will skirt several recreational fields to the south. Again, unless there is a very competitive game in progress, you probably won't even notice that the facilities are there. After hiking 1.0 mile you will arrive at an intersection with the Orange Trail. If you wish to shorten your hike by 2.0 miles and complete a much smaller loop, feel free to use this trail as a shortcut. Otherwise continue straight on the Red Trail.

In another 0.5 mile the trail will briefly leave the forest. You will be able to see Harkey Road to the north. You will also view a beautiful farm to the north of the trail. In the early spring the fields where the cattle and livestock graze will appear a light shade of purple due to no-till weeds and wildflowers. On a pretty day it is worth walking across the road to get a better view of the property.

Depending on which direction the wind is blowing, you may not only be able to view the farm, you might also smell it. Again, depending entirely on the conditions, the stench may go unnoticed or seem overbearing. If it does become overpowering, just try to think positive thoughts about how you are in fact in the country and no longer breathing the exhaust of downtown Charlotte.

A picnic pavilion overlooks Cane Creek Lake.

After passing through an open field of power lines, the trail veers south and loops around to meet the water. The next time you pass under the power lines, you will be able to see Cane Creek Lake. The water is beautiful, and it is impressive to see electrical towers built in the lake that carry the power lines to the opposite shore. From this point forward the route stays near the lake. When the trail intersects the Orange path for the second time, veer left to stay as close as possible to the water, and then again when you encounter the Yellow Trail.

Once you join the Yellow Trail, you will leave behind the serenity of the forest and enter a section of the park filled with laughter and activity. Take your time on the Yellow path to scope out the picnic area, horseshoe pit, swimming beach, and boating area. This will help you decide what you want to do next. When the dirt path transitions into pavement, you will follow it beside the park playground to the nearby parking lot to conclude your hike. Now, on to the next activity!

Discover More

Did you know that the nearby town of Waxhaw was named after the Waxhaws? The Waxhaws were a group of Native Americans that lived in this region, on the banks of Cane Creek. They were referred to as "flatheads" by the settlers. This name stemmed from the fact that Waxhaws placed small sandbags on the foreheads of their infants to create a flat face and wide-set eyes. President Andrew Jackson was also from the Waxhaw region. And there is an unending debate about which side of the North Carolina–South Carolina border he was born on. You can learn even more about this region at the Museum of the Waxhaws (www.museumofthewaxhaws.com).

MILES AND DIRECTIONS

0.0 To start the hike, park at the lot, on your right, immediately after passing the park operation center. From the parking lot, hike toward the restrooms that are located to the west and behind the park operation center.

0.1 Just behind the restrooms, to the west, you will encounter the Purple Trail. Turn right (north) and follow this trail across the paved park entrance. On the north side of the road, join the Red Trail and veer left (west) into the forest.

0.7 You may be able to catch glimpses of a soccer field and baseball diamond to the south of the trail.

Cane Creek Park

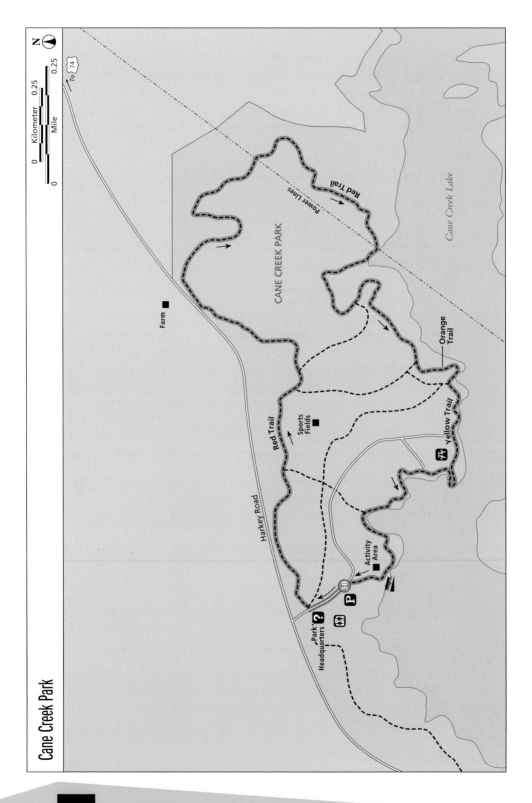

1.0 The hike will arrive at a junction with the Orange Trail and then, shortly thereafter, the Blue Trail. At both junctions continue straight (east) on the Red Trail.

1.4 The trail briefly exits the forest near Harkey Road. There is a beautiful farm located to the north of the road and within view of the trail.

1.8 The trail enters an open field and passes underneath a set of power lines. The route then returns to the forest and begins to veer toward the south.

2.2 Arrive at the banks of Cane Creek Lake and cross under the power lines for a second time. The path now continues west along the shoreline.

2.5 The Red Trail arrives at a junction with the Blue Trail. Veer left (south) to remain on the Blue Trail.

2.8 At the intersection with the Orange Trail, turn left (south) and join the Orange Trail to stay as close to the water as possible.

2.9 The Orange Trail and Red Trail reconnect. This time, turn left (west) to rejoin the Red Trail. Walk 200 yards on the Red Trail and then veer left (west) to join the Yellow Trail.

3.4 Follow the yellow path past the picnic area, beach, and miniature golf course. When you arrive at a short wooden pier across from a picnic pavilion, hike inland past the playground to the park operation center and parking area.

3.6 Conclude your hike at the parking lot behind the park operation center.

HIKE INFORMATION

Local information: Town of Waxhaw, Town Hall, PO Box 6, 317 N. Croome St., Waxhaw 28173; (704) 843-2195; www.waxhaw.com

Local events/attractions: Museum of the Waxhaws, 8215 Waxhaw Hwy., Waxhaw 28173; (704) 843-1832; www.museumofthewaxhaws.com. Come learn about the history of the Waxhaws as well as President Andrew Jackson.

Andrew Jackson State Park, 196 State Rd., S-29-184, Lancaster, SC 29720; (803) 285-3344; www.southcarolinaparks.com. Learn more about our nation's seventh president.

Good eats: Southsiders, 113 E. North Main St., Waxhaw 28173; (704) 243-1325. Great sandwiches and cold beer.

Organizations: Union County Community Arts Council, 120 N. Main St., Monroe 28112; (704) 283-2784; www.unionarts.org. Learn about the arts in Union County.

A wooden hut provides a hiding place where you can sit and look for birds at Sullivan Pond (hike 31).

Yes, you will have to drive a little farther to enjoy the trails found to the east of Charlotte. But the extra time and gas is well worth it. Most of the hikes in this region are located in the Uwharrie Mountains, but one short hike is located in Midland, halfway between Charlotte and Albemarle. Reed Gold Mine is a State Historic Site that offers a great place to stretch your legs, learn about the North Carolina Gold Rush, and pan for gold! The trails at the facility lead past buildings and tools used during the eighteenth century, including a historic stamp mill and engine house.

To the east of Reed Gold Mine, Morrow Mountain State Park can be found at the confluence of the Yadkin and Uwharrie Rivers. This park offers several mountains to climb, including Fall Mountain, Hattaway Mountain, Sugarloaf Mountain, and Morrow Mountain. Thankfully most of the climbs are gentle enough that you will still want to enjoy some of the other highlights at the state park, including river boating, picnicking, visiting the historic Kron House, or swimming in the large, enticing pool.

A little farther north, in the same watershed, is Lake Badin. There is a trail that starts at Kings Mountain Point and explores the ins and outs of the northeast corner of the lake. The hike is located in Uwharrie National Forest and offers a great place to look for waterfowl such as blue heron. The two established campgrounds near the trail allow you to extend your hike into an overnight.

Also located in Uwharrie National Forest is the Uwharrie Recreation Trail. The recreation trail explores more than 20 miles of the national forest. This book includes a route that travels north from the southern terminus. The green mountain laurel and clear streams in this portion of the forest will probably leave you wanting to explore the entire trail in the future.

Finally, south of the recreation trail and Uwharrie National Forest, visit the Pee Dee National Wildlife Refuge. As the only noncoastal national wildlife refuge in North Carolina, this property is home to hundreds of migrating waterfowl. The hike described in this book explores the wetlands at the refuge and includes a healthy portion of boardwalk that extends out over the water. You may also consider driving through the preserve after you hike to see if you can spot other wildlife, such a foxes, bobcats, and coyotes.

Spring flowers and old mining equipment greet visitors who come to Reed Gold Mine (hike 34).

Pee Dee National Wildlife Refuge

Exploring the Pee Dee National Wildlife Refuge is like going on safari. The trails and roads within the park reveal more wildlife than perhaps any other hike listed in this book. Not only are there deer, turkeys, foxes, and coyotes that roam the open farmland and dense forest at the refuge, but the lakes and wetland areas are home to a wide variety of migrating waterfowl. This hike explores the forest, fields, and wetlands on the property. The route starts by exploring Brown Creek Nature Trail, which winds beside the peaceful water of Brown Creek and through an open field of tall prairie grass. Next the hike travels to the nearby wetland area, where an extensive network of wooden boardwalks takes you out onto the water to look for birds. At the end of the boardwalk, the hike travels the Tall Pines Nature Trail through the forest. Then it loops back to the trailhead on a paved road that explores the outlying wetlands boundary. After the hike is finished, you will most likely want to spend some time driving through the refuge in search of additional wildlife sightings.

Start: The Pee Dee National Wildlife Refuge Nature Trails parking lot
Distance: 2.2-mile loop
Hiking time: About 1 to 1.5 hours
Difficulty: Easy
Trail surface: Single-track dirt trail, wooden boardwalk, and a paved refuge road
Best season(s): Winter, to view the migrating waterfowl
Other trail users: Cars can travel on the paved road.
Canine compatibility: Leashed dogs permitted

Land status: National wildlife refuge
Fees and permits: None
Schedule: Open 1 hour after sunrise to 1 hour before sunset
Maps: USGS Ansonville; Basic Pee Dee National Wildlife Refuge trail maps are available at the park headquarters
Trail contacts: Pee Dee National Wildlife Refuge, 5770 US Hwy. 52 N., Wadesboro 28170; (704) 694-6570; www.fws.gov/peedee

Finding the trailhead: From Charlotte take US 74 East toward Wadesboro. When you reach US 52, turn left and travel north. After driving 6.0 miles the Pee Dee National Wildlife Refuge will be on your right. Travel 0.25 mile past the restrooms and visitor information center at the entrance of the preserve to access the wetlands and nature trails parking area. GPS: N35 03.729' / W80 05.117'

THE HIKE

A s a national wildlife refuge, the Pee Dee preserve is governed by the Fish and Wildlife Service under the Department of the Interior. A wildlife refuge is different from other public lands, such as a national park, because its primary purpose is to conserve fish, wildlife, and plants. Wildlife refuges also have six public-use objectives: hunting, fishing, wildlife observation, nature photography, education, and interpretation.

The first national wildlife refuge was designated by President Theodore Roosevelt in 1903. Since then the network of preserves has grown to more than 553 government-supported refuges. There is a refuge in every state in the union, and North Carolina is home to ten. However, the Pee Dee National Wildlife Refuge is the only noncoastal refuge in the state of North Carolina. Its unique location helps to attract over 35,000 visitors annually.

Founded in 1963, the Pee Dee National Wildlife Refuge covers 8,500 acres of land, including upland pine forest, mixed pine and hardwood forest, wetlands, and farmland. The refuge also contains the largest bottomland hardwood forest

A wooden boardwalk stretches into the wetlands at Pee Dee National Wildlife Refuge.

in the piedmont region. With all of that property, you would think that the refuge might offer a large network of hiking trails. Unfortunately, the trails on the refuge are limited in number and distance, but hikers are allowed to walk on any of the refuge roads. But don't be disappointed, because many refuges do not have any hiking trails at all. Furthermore, Pee Dee National Wildlife Refuge allows hiking on all the gravel refuge roads throughout the park, and that means more than 30 miles of walking!

This hike combines two of the primary nature trails on the property with a paved refuge road. To begin the trek, start at the primary nature trail parking lot near Sullivan Pond. If you get out of your car and hear gunshots, do not be alarmed. Pee Dee National Wildlife Refuge is open for permitted hunting during designated hunting seasons. Initially it seems ironic that a refuge designated to protecting wildlife, would allow folks to come on the property and shoot animals. However, monitored hunting helps keep some animal species from becoming too populated and threatening the delicate balance of the food chain. Hunters are never allowed to target threatened or endangered wildlife—or hikers. And all of the paths and roads used on this hike are closed to hunters.

Start your hike by walking north, away from Sullivan Pond, and locate the Brown Creek Nature Trail sign. Follow the dirt path behind the sign into the forest. You will soon notice a trickling creek to your right. This is Brown Creek. The trail parallels the water for 0.3 mile before veering south and returning to the parking lot through an open field of tall grass. This grass is known as switch grass and is a remnant of the prairie piedmont grass, which is very similar to the tall grass found in western prairies.

Back at the parking lot, you will next hike south to the eastern shore of Sullivan Pond. On the bank of the pond sits a one-room wooden hut that is used to observe birds. Just to the east of the hut, there are steps leading down to a nearby wetland. Follow these steps downhill and to the connecting boardwalk. (The boardwalk may look wooden, but it actually is made of recycled plastic!) Continue straight on the boardwalk and venture out of the wooden platform into the flooded terrain. This is the perfect place to look for certain species of ducks including American shovelers, green-winged teals, black ducks, wood ducks, mallards, and northern pintails. The best time of the year to look for these migrating waterfowl in central North Carolina is November through February.

Continue to hike on the boardwalk and follow it off the open water and through a swampy forest filled with sycamore trees. Complete a loop on the board-walk and then retrace your steps to the wooden hut on the east bank of Sullivan Pond. Travel south past the hut to the edge of the forest. The Tall Pines Nature Trail soon takes shape. The trail travels an oval route through the surrounding forest. This hike does not explore the loop in its entirety, but instead veers left and follows the eastern portion of the trail, closest to the wetlands. (If you like, you can also veer right and explore the western half of the Tall Pines Nature Trail. Both paths lead to the paved refuge road where the hike continues.)

After traveling under the shade of the pine trees, the path exits the forest at a refuge road. Turn left and travel this paved path counterclockwise around the wetland area. This is another terrific section in which to look for nesting wood ducks, as well as songbirds resting in the trees. Wood ducks are the only native nesting waterfowl in the piedmont, and the wooden birdhouses on the lake are provided so that the wood ducks will be able to securely nest and raise their young.

At mile 1.8 you will come to an intersection with another refuge road. Turn left and follow the road west along the north boundary of the Sullivan Impoundment. The impoundment makes up a portion of the wetlands that is managed by the park. This area is flooded for part of the year and then allowed to drain during the summer months. This process encourages plants to grow in the moist soil that in turn produces food for the migrating waterfowl when they return to this region.

On the north side of the Sullivan Impoundment, the road parallels Brown Creek and follows the water upstream until it arrives back at the parking lot. Just because your hike is over doesn't mean you can't continue to enjoy your day at the Pee Dee Wildlife Refuge. Consider extending your visit by searching for wildlife from your car or by foot on one of the many refuge roads.

Discover More

The Pee Dee National Wildlife Refuge has a great website (www.fws.gov/northcarolina/kidlinks.html) that explains the significance of national wildlife refuges. It talks about some of the specific conservation projects taking place at the Pee Dee refuge. If you take kids with you on your hike to the preserve, be sure to let them check out some of the awesome kid links on the website, before of after the hike.

The Pee Dee National Wildlife Refuge website isn't just great for kids. It also contains many links and materials that will interest adults. For example, the website contains a link to some of the most recent wildlife pictures taken at the refuge. The wildlife photographer does a terrific job of beautifully capturing many of the different species that live in the park and visit it seasonally. Be sure to check out the "Photography Slideshow" at the Pee Dee National Wildlife Refuge website (www.fws.gov/peedee/).

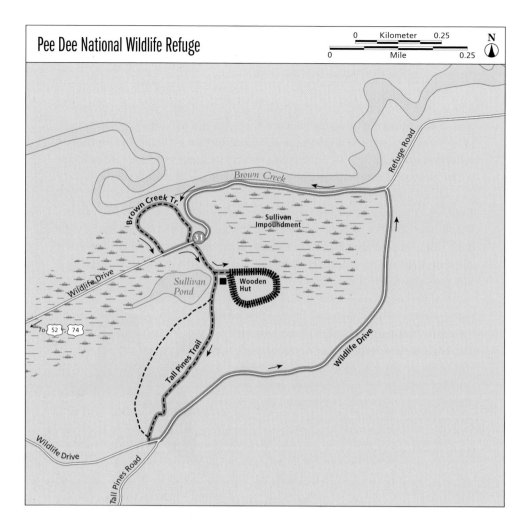

MILES AND DIRECTIONS

0.0 Start at the parking lot adjacent to Sullivan Pond. Hike north away from the pond. Cross the main park road and locate the Brown Creek Nature Trail sign. Follow the path behind the wooden sign.

0.3 The Brown Creek Nature Trail leaves the gurgling creek and travels inland through a field of tall prairie grass. Return to the parking lot, and then travel to the east shore of Sullivan Pond.

0.4 When you arrive at the wooden hut on the east bank of Sullivan Pond, take the set of steps east and downhill.

0.5 Continue straight (east) and follow the boardwalk, made of recycled plastic, into the wetland area.

0.7 When the boardwalk reenters the forest, turn right (north) and travel back to the wooden hut on the shore of Sullivan Pond.

0.8 Continue south past the hut and join the Tall Pines Nature Trail that leads into the forest.

0.9 The Tall Pines Nature Trail splits. Veer left to travel the route closest to the wetlands. (Do not take a sharp left-hand turn, which leads back to the nearby boardwalk.)

1.1 Exit the forest at a paved refuge road and turn left (east) to skirt the wetlands in a counterclockwise direction.

1.8 The road comes to a T intersection. Turn left (west) and continue on the paved refuge road. The Sullivan Impoundment will be on your left and Brown Creek will be on your right.

2.2 Conclude your hike at the nature trail parking lot.

HIKE INFORMATION

Local information: City of Wadesboro, 603 Woodland Dr., Wadesboro 28170; (704) 694-5171; www.cityofwadesboro.org

Local events/attractions: Fall Festival in Uptown Wadesboro, 107 E. Wade St., Wadesboro 28170; (704) 695-1644; www.uptownwadesboro.com. Celebrate fall in the quaint town of Wadesboro.

Good eats: The Malsgate, 121 E. Wade St., Wadesboro 28170; (704) 694-2206. Good sandwiches and fries for a hike at Pee Dee National Wildlife Refuge and a stroll through uptown Wadesboro.

Organizations: Anson County Arts Council, 110 S. Rutherford St., Wadesboro 28170; (704) 694-4950; www.ansoncountyartscouncil.org. Promoting arts and culture in Anson County.

> **Green Tip:**
> *Never let your dog chase wildlife.*

The Uwharrie Recreation Trail is a 20-mile National Recreation Trail that weaves its way north to south through the Uwharrie National Forest. It is the perfect trail to explore on a weekend backpacking trip. However, if you don't have two full days to hike, consider exploring this short out-and-back route at the southern terminus of the trail. The hike starts near the intersection of NC 24/27 and River Road, but after 0.25 mile of hiking, you will leave the roar of the highway behind you. The trail then surrounds you with a thicket of green mountain laurel trees and travels beside the gurgling Wood Run Creek. Eventually the path crosses over the creek and travels steadily uphill to explore the nearby ridge and surrounding mountains of Uwharrie National Forest. After gaining substantial elevation, the suggested day route departs the national recreation trail and follows a short spur to a lovely picnic spot at Wood Run Camp. Enjoy a rest at the sunny clearing before retracing your steps back to the trailhead.

Start: Uwharrie National Recreation Trail southern terminus
Distance: 4.6-mile out and back
Hiking time: About 2.5 to 3 hours
Difficulty: Moderate
Trail surface: Single-track dirt trail
Best season(s): Year-round
Other trail users: Mountain bikes are allowed on a small portion of this hike
Canine compatibility: Leashed dogs permitted

Land status: National forest
Fees and permits: None
Schedule: Open year-round
Maps: USGS Morrow Mountain; Uwharrie National Recreation trail map available at the Uwharrie National Forest headquarters
Trail contacts: Uwharrie Ranger District, 789 NC 24/27, East Troy 27371; (910) 576-6391; www.fs.usda.gov/nfsnc

Finding the trailhead: From Charlotte drive east on NC 24/27. After traveling approximately 40 miles, you will cross Lake Tillery. Past Lake Tillery continue to an intersection with River Road. Continue straight (east) at the River Road intersection, remaining on NC 24/27. Travel another 0.5 mile and then turn left (north) into the Uwharrie National Recreation Trail parking lot and trailhead. The trail begins on the west side of the parking lot and is blazed with white rectangles. GPS: N35 18.656'/W80 02.609'

THE HIKE

You have to travel a little farther to the east of Charlotte to find great hiking, compared to the many options that lie just to the west of the city. However, a trip out to the Uwharrie National Forest is well worth the drive, and once you arrive, you will find an endless array of recreation options and hiking trails.

At just over 50,000 acres, the Uwharrie tract was purchased by the US government in 1931. It wasn't until thirty years later that President John F. Kennedy designated the site a national forest. The forest offers a wealth of timber and clean water. For a recreationalist it also offers bridle and off-road-vehicle trails, hunting and fishing opportunities, biking, and, of course, hiking!

Among all of the hiking and multiuse trails inside Uwharrie National Forest, the Uwharrie National Recreation Trail is one of the most scenic, and it is also the longest. Spanning 20 miles from north to south, the trail travels through some of the most remote and picturesque parts of the national forest.

The Wood Run Creek crossing provides a fun place to rock-hop across the water.

Construction started on the Uwharrie National Recreation Trail in the early 1970s and was completed ten years later. The trail building was completed primarily by Boy Scout troops, and several senior scouts earned the rank of Eagle Scout by working on the trail. Joe Moffit was the scoutmaster in charge of the project. He grew up hunting and trapping in the Uwharrie wilderness during the Great Depression.

This particular hike explores the southern portion of the recreation trail and will probably leave you wanting to come back and backpack the entire trail or at least piece it together in sections. To begin the hike, locate the white blazes at the northwest corner of the parking lot. It is important that you double check and make sure that the path you are hiking has white markers, otherwise you might be on the yellow-blazed Dutchman's Creek Trail, which extends 10 miles into the forest.

If you cross under a set of power lines and arrive at a small creek bed within the first half mile, you can be sure that you are on the right trail. When you arrive at the headwaters of Wood Run Creek, you will notice the remains of several fire rings and backcountry campsites near the water. Unless otherwise marked, camping is allowed anywhere inside the national forest. However, if you do decide to spend the night, make sure you remember to follow leave-no-trace ethics—you may notice that several former campers were not so courteous.

The trail now parallels the creek for the next mile. At times you will not be able to see the trickling creek because of the thick mountain laurel that borders the trail. Starting in late April this beautiful evergreen plant will show off an impressive array of pink and white blooms. Inside the green tunnel the path travels over a collection of short rolling hills near the water, before arriving back at the shoreline.

At mile 1.3 you will cross over Wood Run Creek. There is no bridge so you will need to either rock-hop or wade across the creek. Typically, unless the region has seen very heavy and consistent rain, you should be able to cross without getting your feet wet.

Past the creek the trail travels a steady uphill on very rocky terrain. The trail on the east side of Wood Run Creek looks different than the green mountain laurel tunnels that you just walked through. Take several breaks to catch your breath and observe the jagged rock collections that line the trail. Eventually the route retains more of a forest feel and continues to travel slightly uphill.

Often hikers are surprised to find so much elevation to the east of Charlotte. And it may surprise you to learn that the Uwharrie Mountains were once over 20,000 feet high. These once-active volcanoes have been whittled away by erosion so now all measure under 1,000 feet.

At an intersection with the Keyauwee Trail, turn right on the blue-blazed path and leave behind the National Recreation Trail. Travel this short spur trail for 0.25 mile to arrive at Wood Run Camp. This campsite contains grassy fields and a restroom facility that make it the perfect place to stop and picnic before retracing your steps to the Uwharrie National Recreation Trail and returning to the trailhead.

If you wish to turn this hike into a loop instead of completing the out-and-back, you can follow the dirt road that departs Wood Run Camp to the southwest and follow it back to the parking lot at NC 24/27.

Discover More

If you like the idea of the 20+-mile Uwharrie Recreation Trail, then perhaps you might consider an even longer hike in the future. There is a trail that spans all the way across the state of North Carolina called the Mountains-to-Sea Trail. Its western end is in the Smoky Mountain National Park and the eastern terminus is along North Carolina's Outer Banks. In total the path stretches over 1,000 miles. This trail is not yet entirely complete and it still has some sections where road walking is required. However, several people each year will hike the entire length of the trail. You can access the trail to the northwest of Charlotte at Pilot Mountain and Stone Mountain. To find out more about the trail, contact the Friends of the Mountains-to-Sea Trail, PO Box 10431, Raleigh 27605; (919) 698-9024; www.ncmst.org.

Fungus adorns the cut end of a fallen log.

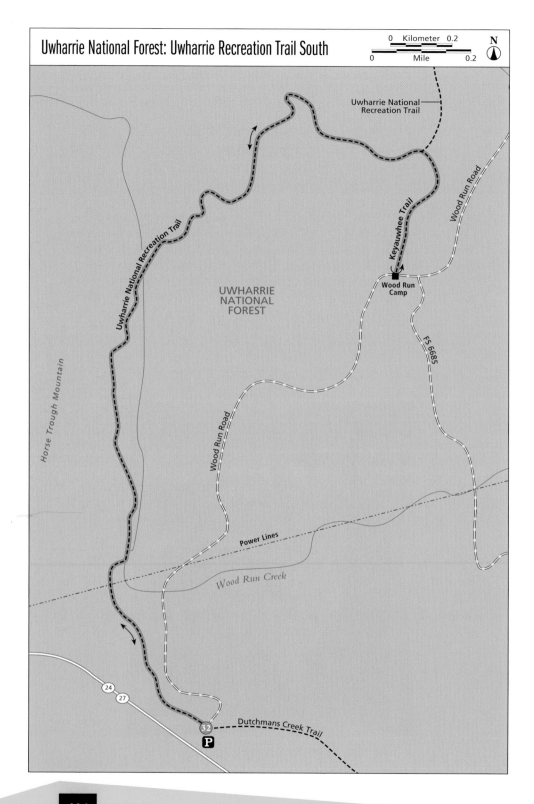

Uwharrie National Forest: Uwharrie Recreation Trail South

0 Kilometer 0.2

0 Mile 0.2

N

Uwharrie National
Recreation Trail

Wood Run Road

Keyauwhee Trail

Uwharrie National Recreation Trail

UWHARRIE
NATIONAL
FOREST

Wood Run
Camp

FS 6685

Horse Trough Mountain

Wood Run Road

Power Lines

Wood Run Creek

24
27

32

P

Dutchmans Creek Trail

0.0 Start at the parking lot off NC 24/27. Walk to the southwest corner of the parking lot and locate the white-blaze Uwharrie National Recreation Trail. Follow it northeast into the forest.

0.3 The trail will pass under a set of power lines and cross over a small seasonal stream before reentering the mixed pine and hardwood forest.

1.0 Step over another small seasonal stream that runs through the green mountain laurel thicket on either side of the trail.

1.3 Cross over Wood Run Creek by stepping on dry rocks or splashing through the water. Then start a challenging climb on the east shore of the creek.

1.4 Stay alert for the loose rocks at your feet and remember to look up and appreciate the intriguing rock formations and boulders that line the trail.

2.0 When you arrive at a trail intersection, leave the Uwharrie National Recreation Trail and turn right (south) onto the blue-blazed Keyauwee Trail. (**Note:** The Keyauwee Trail does allow mountain bikes, so don't be surprised if one comes speeding up behind you.)

2.3 Arrive at Wood Run Camp and enjoy a rest or a picnic under the—hopefully—sunny sky, before returning to the forest and retracing your steps on the Keyauwee Trail.

2.6 Remember to turn left (west) and rejoin the Uwharrie Trail. Then backtrack downhill to the banks of the Wood Run Creek.

4.6 Conclude your out-and-back hike at the Uwharrie National Recreation Trail parking lot and trailhead.

HIKE INFORMATION

Local information: Troy Town Hall, 315 N. Main St., Troy 27371; (910) 572-3661; www.troy.nc.us

Local events/attractions: Town Creek Indian Site, 509 Town Creek Mound Rd., Mount Gilead 27306; (910) 439-6802. Visit the sacred mound at a 1,000-year-old Native American village.

Good eats: BP Gas Station, 4021 NC Hwy. 109 N., Troy 27371; (910) 572-3474. Yes, it is a gas station, but it is a gas station with the world's best potato wedges.

Organizations: Montgomery Community Theater, PO Box 26, Troy 27371; (910) 576-2121; www.ncarts.org. Join this performing arts group and act out a day on the trail.

This beautiful loop in the Uwharrie National Forest is one of the farthest hikes away from Charlotte in this guidebook, but it is well worth the one-and-a-half-hour drive from the city to explore the undisturbed shoreline of Badin Lake. This route starts at the scenic Kings Mountain Point day-use area, and then immediately starts contouring the coves of Badin Lake. The single-track trail that winds along the water provides a great opportunity to look for blue herons. You may also be able to spot freshwater clams at the edge of the water. After hiking around a large peninsula, you will notice a few scattered houses on the east shore of Badin Lake, but then you will leave any sign of development behind as the trail travels inland to explore the forest. After passing through a mixed hardwood and pine forest, you will reemerge on the shore of the lake at the Arrowhead Campground. From here you will travel north through the Badin Lake Campground area to conclude your hike at Kings Mountain Point.

Start: Kings Mountain Point day-use area
Distance: 5.6-mile loop
Hiking time: About 3 to 4 hours
Difficulty: Moderate
Trail surface: Mostly dirt trail; paved paths near campgrounds
Best season(s): Year-round
Other trail users: None
Canine compatibility: Leashed dogs permitted

Land status: National forest
Fees and permits: None
Schedule: Open year-round
Maps: USGS Badin; Badin Lake trail map available at the Uwharrie National Forest headquarters
Trail contacts: Uwharrie Ranger District, 789 NC 24/27, East Troy 27371; (910) 576-6391; www.fs.usda.gov/nfsnc

Finding the trailhead: From Charlotte drive east on NC 49 North. After traveling approximately 40 miles, turn right (south) onto NC 109. Drive for 8.5 miles and then turn right (west) onto Mullinix Road. Stay on Mullinix Road for 1.5 miles to reach an intersection with McLeans Creek Road (FR 544). Turn right (west) on McLeans Creek Road and travel 1.6 miles to arrive at a junction with Badin Lake Road (FR 597A). Turn right (north) on Badin Lake Road. The road splits in 0.2 mile. Veer left (northwest) to stay on FR 597A. You will soon pass Group Camp Road (FR 6551) on your left. Continue straight for another 0.7 mile to arrive at Kings Mountain Point. The Badin Lake Trail travels across the neck of the point. Start your hike along the north shore, to the east of the fishing pier. GPS: N35 27.247' / W80 04.776'

THE HIKE

Lake Badin is a beautiful lake that spans more than 5,000 acres in the northwest corner of the Uwharrie National Forest. The large body of water was created in 1917 when the Narrows Dam was built near the town of Badin on the west shore of the lake. Because the body of water fills a valley in the Uwharrie Mountain chain, it is a relatively deep lake—measuring at just over 55 meters (180 feet). Amazingly, thanks to the presence of Uwharrie National Forest, a large percentage of the 115 miles of shoreline is undeveloped—unlike the busy banks of Lake Norman and Lake Wylie to the west of Charlotte.

There are many recreational opportunities and campsites to be found at Badin Lake. You may want to check out the two campgrounds that this trail passes through before planning your day hike. Both the Arrowhead and Badin Lake campgrounds are open year-round. If you decide to turn this day hike into a weekend outing, perhaps you will want to check out the nearby Uwharrie Recreation Trail South on your extended visit. That said, even if you don't leave the shore of Badin Lake, there are plenty of trails to keep you occupied.

The view from a small cove reveals the still waters of Badin Lake.

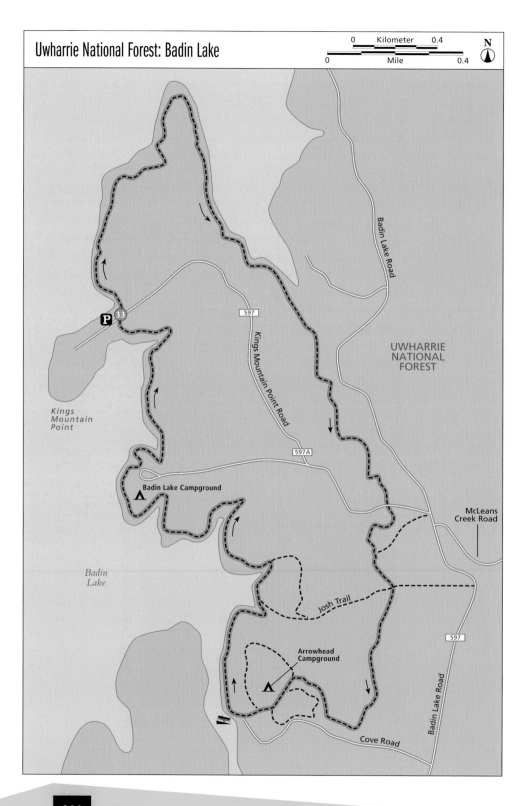

0   Kilometer   0.4

0   Mile   0.4

N

P 33

597

Kings Mountain Point Road

Badin Lake Road

UWHARRIE NATIONAL FOREST

Kings Mountain Point

597A

Badin Lake Campground

McLeans Creek Road

Badin Lake

Josh Trail

597

Arrowhead Campground

Badin Lake Road

Cove Road

The Badin Lake Loop is one of the most picturesque pedestrian-only routes in the national forest. To begin your hike, park at the Kings Mountain Point day-use area. You are probably scratching your head at this point thinking, Kings Mountain? Isn't that to the west of Charlotte? Yes, it is. We have covered a lot of Kings Mountains in this book, including Kings Mountain at Kings Mountain National Military Park, Kings Mountain State Park, Kings Pinnacle at Crowders Mountain State Park, and now Kings Mountain Point. But I guess since Charlotte is the Queen City, it makes sense that she is surrounded by kings.

From the day-use area, you will be able to locate the Badin Lake Loop running along the lakeshore and crossing the point at the east end of the parking area. Start your hike by walking north and traveling the path in a clockwise direction. As you head into the woods, you will be able to observe the Kings Mountain Point fishing pier jutting into the water on your left. The trail soon becomes very rocky—not with rough isolated rocks, but rather large smooth slabs of granite that delve into the lake. Be careful on this section as the rocks can become very slick after a rainstorm.

As you continue along the shoreline, you will notice several makeshift campsites near the water. Often there are rabbit trails at the campsite that make it hard to follow the true trail. But just remember, when in doubt, stay close to the water.

After hiking 1.0 mile you will make a 180-degree turn around the northernmost tip of a large peninsula. From here you will hike south along a quiet cove. On the opposite shore you will be able to see a few sparse lake houses. The trail continues to follow the water until it arrives at a small stream that trickles into the mighty lake. Here the path turns inland and spends 1.7 miles exploring the mixed pine and hardwood forest. The dense forest provides a great opportunity to spot wildlife. Deer, in particular, are very common in this part of the national forest.

Eventually the trail will arrive at a paved pathway. When this happens, you will know that you are getting close to Arrowhead Campground. Continue to follow the paved path past several campsites and into the heart of the campground. From here you will need to pay close attention and look for the trail to continue to the southwest of the campground restrooms. Once in the woods the trail again becomes a dirt path and leads to a nearby boat ramp, where the route resumes hiking along the shore of Badin Lake. Back along the lake, it is easy to spot Badin Lake

> **🍃 Green Tip:**
> *Wash dishes or clothes at least 200 feet from a river or lake. Bring the water to a spot with good drainage, and use only biodegradable soap in the smallest amount.*

Campground to the north. Although it seems as if it is relatively close, the multiple twists, turns, and small lake coves that line the path make the journey much longer than it appears.

When you arrive at Badin Lake Campground, stay near the water and skirt the campsites to your left. At this point in the hike, tempting campfire aromas may cause your stomach to growl. But if you continue pushing on along the water for another 0.5 mile, you will reach your car at Kings Mountain Point day-use area, where hopefully some tasty treats await you!

MILES AND DIRECTIONS

0.0 Begin your hike on the Badin Lake Loop at the northeast corner of the Kings Mountain Point parking area. Follow the path north along the Badin Lake shoreline.

0.3 The dirt path transitions into slick rock slabs. Be extra-cautious with your footing in this section, especially after (or during) a rainstorm.

1.0 You will arrive at the northernmost tip of a peninsula. Continue to follow the shore and hike south along the west boundary of a quiet cove.

2.0 Leave Badin Lake behind, and hike inland next to a small trickling creek.

2.3 Cross a dirt road (FR 597-A) and continue to follow the white-blazed Badin Lake Loop.

2.6 Arrive at an intersection with the green-blazed Josh Trail. The two routes are intertwined for the next 0.1 mile. Be sure to stay alert and follow the white blazes. The Josh Trail will eventually veer off to the right (west).

2.9 The trail crosses a second park road. Continue straight across the dirt road and hike back into the forest on the Badin Lake Loop.

3.2 The trail veers west and transitions into a paved pathway as it approaches Arrowhead Campground.

3.6 The hike exits the woods at the center of the Arrowhead Campground. Continue straight toward the restroom facilities. Just past the restrooms, after passing a second paved road on your right, the trail goes back into the forest and travels west and downhill to reach the lakeshore.

4.0 The dirt path resumes along the shore of the lake. Follow it north, away from the boat ramp and toward the shade of the forest.

33

5.2 Trace the meandering shoreline of Badin Lake to arrive at Badin Lake Campground. Continue beside the water to stay on the trail and avoid the campground. (***Note:*** After a heavy rain the trail between Arrowhead Campground and Badin Lake Campground may be slick and muddy.)

5.6 Conclude your hike at the Kings Mountain Point day-use area.

HIKE INFORMATION

Local information: Troy Town Hall, 315 N. Main St., Troy 27371; (910) 572-3661; www.troy.nc.us

Local events/attractions: See the crepe myrtle and pear trees in downtown Troy decorated for Christmas during the Holiday Lighting Ceremony. The event takes place each November. Call (704) 875-6541 or visit www.troy.nc.us for more information.

Good eats: BP Gas Station, 4021 NC Hwy. 109 N., Troy 27371; (910) 572-3474. Yes, it is a gas station. But it is a gas station with the world's best potato wedges.

Organizations: Montgomery Community Theater, PO Box 26, Troy 27371; (910) 576-2121; www.ncarts.org. Join this performing arts group and act out a day on the trail.

Want to extend your trip to Badin Lake and stay at one of the campgrounds along the scenic shoreline? For more information on Badin Lake Campground and Arrowhead Campground, visit the following links and search on the word "campground": www .fs.usda.gov or www.recreation.gov.

Reed Gold Mine State Historic Site: Reed Mine Hike

Reed Gold Mine is one of best places to take children hiking near Charlotte. Between gold panning, walking through an underground mine shaft, and visiting the Stamp Mill, you will forget that you are even exercising. This route starts at the Reed Gold Mine Visitor Center. If you choose to take the underground mine shaft tour, then it will also be the start of your hike. But don't worry if you are claustrophobic or don't have time for a tour, because you can also take an outdoor route up to the nearby mine shafts and engine house remains on the Upper Hill. Descending from the Upper Hill, the hike explores the restored Stamp Mill before traveling over the beautiful wooden boardwalks beside Little Meadow Creek. At the top of Lower Hill, you will pass by several of the remnants of the mining operation before heading to the panning operation and exploring the west side of the property to conclude the hike.

Start: Reed Gold Mine Visitor Center
Distance: 2.9-mile circuit
Hiking time: About 1.5 to 2 hours
Difficulty: Easy; rolling hills
Trail surface: Dirt trails, forested roadbeds, wooden boardwalks
Best season(s): Spring, summer, fall
Other trail users: None
Canine compatibility: Leashed dogs are allowed on the trails, but not inside the visitor center or in the underground mine.
Land status: State Historic Site

Fees and permits: No fees or permits required for hiking. There is a small charge to pan for gold.
Schedule: 9 a.m. to 5 p.m. Tues through Sat; gold panning is available Apr through Oct
Maps: USGS Locust; a trail map for the Upper and Lower Hills is available at the visitor center along with a self-guided tour
Trail contacts: Reed Gold Mine State Historic Site, 9621 Reed Mine Rd., Midland 28107; (704) 721-4653; www.nchistoricsites .org/reed

Finding the trailhead: From Charlotte drive east on Albemarle Road (NC 24/27). Enter into Cabarrus County. After continuing straight through a traffic light at the intersection with US 601, take the next left (north) onto Reed Mine Road. Drive 3.0 miles and the entrance of the mine will be on your right. GPS: N35 17.103'/W80 28.005'

This is a fabulous destination, family activity, and hike! Plus, the Reed Gold Mine has added an additional section of trails on the property, so your outing can last even longer.

Reed Gold Mine was home to the first significant gold discovery in the US. In 1799 John Reed farmed the land on either side of Little Meadow Creek. One day, when his young son Conrad was playing in the creek, he discovered a large shiny rock. Conrad brought the rock home to his parents and they used the ornamental stone as a doorstop for several years. In 1803 a jeweler from Fayetteville informed John Reed that the doorstop was in fact a gold. The jeweler offered to buy the 17-pound gold nugget and told Reed to name his price. Reed asked for a week's wages $3.50. The rock was really worth $3,600.

In light of the discovery of gold, people with gold fever flocked to Cabarrus County and began mining in the creeks, rivers, and on land. By 1949, most of the gold sources were depleted and many miners traveled west when the gold rush hit in California. The Reed Mine remained an active gold-mining site for more than one

The tall stone chimney still stands next to the remains of the engine house and boiler pit.

hundred years. A twenty-eight-pound gold nugget was found at the Reed Mine, which remains the largest nugget ever found east of the Mississippi River.

Today the legacy of the North Carolina Gold Rush and the dreams of so many miners are remembered at Reed Gold Mine. To start exploring the mine, stop in at the visitor center. There is a guided hike that tours an underground shaft. You may have to wait a few minutes for the tour to start but it is well worth it. When else can you say that part of your hike took place underground?

If it does not work to start your hike on the guided tour, exit the east side of the visitor center and follow a wooden boardwalk over Little Meadow Creek. When the boardwalk ends, follow the path uphill and veer left toward the Morgan Shaft headframe. As you walk you will be passing over several underground tunnels. The underground tour exits a shaft to the right of the trail, just before reaching the headframe. This angular piece of mining equipment once delivered supplies to the men working underground.

Continuing uphill from the shaft headframe, you will reach the excavated foundation of an engine house, boiler pit, and chimney. This was a more modern gold-culling facility that was built on the property in the second half of the nineteenth century. The tall brick chimney was integral in releasing steam that was used to give power to the refining mill. When you are ready to leave Upper Hill, continue on a gravel road downhill toward Little Meadow Creek. Before reaching the water, turn left and parallel the creek to the nearby Stamp Mill.

The Stamp Mill was used to process gold-laden rocks before the engine house was built. The reconstructed building at Reed Gold Mine is one of only six working stamp mills in the US. There are often seasonal employees stationed at the Stamp Mill to describe how water, mercury, fire, and steam were used to refine the dense rocks that contained veins of gold inside of them.

Beyond the Stamp Mill, the path continues near the water and soon encounters a set of wooden boardwalks. The heavy clomp of shoes on the boardwalk make for enjoyable walking, and the raised terrain provides terrific views of the creek.

When the trail veers to the left, you will climb a short hill and then continue to follow the path past several open mining shafts. Although these shafts are all fenced off, parents should still be cautious of their children's whereabouts. Do not

Do you live to the east of Charlotte? Do you want to start looking for gold on your property or at a creek that runs near your home? You can learn more about gold panning and even becoming a member of the Gold Prospectors Association of America by visiting www.goldprospectors.org.

allow any hiker, young or old, to play near the gaping holes in the ground. Past the open mine shaft the trail encounters a wooden shed that houses several old pieces of mining equipment. It also passes the remnants of one of the oldest and most beautiful trees that graced the Reed property. A wide tree stump is all that remains of the impressive Kelly Oak. Estimated to be 250 years old, it is intriguing to think of all the stories this one tree could have told us about this historic site. This dominating presence on the property was finally cut down, at the end of its life, in 2010.

When you leave the Kelly tree stump, return to Little Meadow Creek, cross the water, and turn left to explore the modern-day panning area. This is a really fun place to learn how to pan for gold and hopefully find a few shiny flakes while you are at it. Past the panning center is the newest trail at Reed Gold Mine. This wide dirt bed contours the west shore of the creek to an open field. Feel free to explore the field and enjoy the exposure to the sun, before returning through the forest to the visitor center and trailhead parking lot.

MILES AND DIRECTIONS

0.0 Start your hike at the visitor center. From there, choose your path. Either travel the underground mining tunnel with a tour guide, or exit the east side of the visitor center and follow the wooden boardwalk to the base of the Lower Hill.

0.3 Whether you went above ground or beneath it, hike north and uphill on a gravel path toward the Morgan Shaft headframe.

0.4 Past the headframe, continue to travel uphill on the gravel path and arrive at a wooden platform that overlooks the engine house foundation.

0.5 After circling around to the east side of the chimney, continue to hike southeast on the main trail artery past a spur trail to the Lower Hill. Before reaching Little Meadow Creek, turn left (south) on the Lower Hill Trail and follow signs toward the Stamp Mill.

0.7 Pass a trail to your left that leads to the Lower Hill. Continue straight (south) toward the Stamp Mill.

0.8 Arrive at the Stamp Mill. Take time to peak inside the building and talk to a staff member if one is on duty. Past the Stamp Mill continue to parallel the creek. The trail will travel over several wooden boardwalks in the next 0.25 mile.

1.0 The path climbs a small rise and turns toward the north. There are several open mill shafts and large round millstones near the trail.

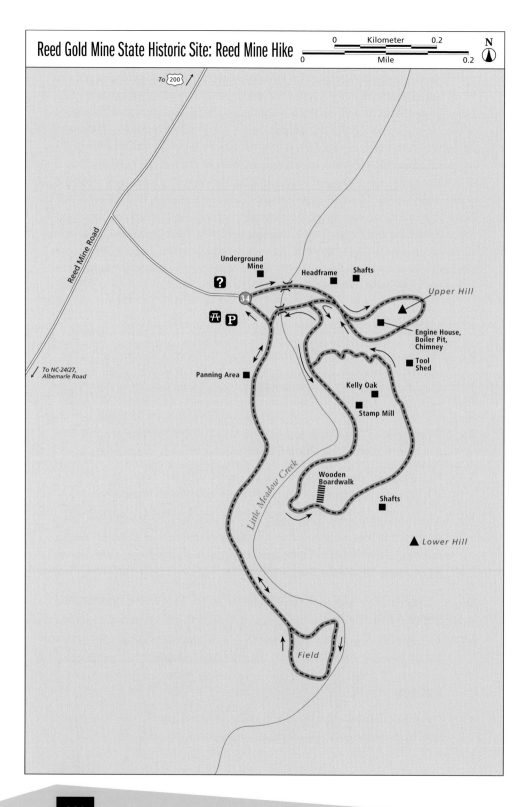

Reed Gold Mine State Historic Site: Reed Mine Hike

Kilometer
0   0.2

Mile
0   0.2

N

To 200

Reed Mine Road

To NC-24/27,
Albemarle Road

Underground
Mine

Headframe   Shafts

?

34

Upper Hill

Engine House,
Boiler Pit,
Chimney

Tool
Shed

Panning Area

Kelly Oak

Stamp Mill

Little Meadow Creek

Wooden
Boardwalk

Shafts

Lower Hill

Field

1.3 Arrive at a large open field on the crest of Lower Hill. There is a wooden toolshed on your right with old mining equipment, and the remains of Kelly Oak can be found on your left. Walk beside Kelly Oak and follow the winding downhill path behind the large wooden stump.

1.4 When you conclude the Lower Hill Loop, turn right (north) and travel over the wooden bridge that spans Little Meadow Creek.

1.5 Past the bridge turn left (south) to arrive at the Reed Gold Mine panning station. Take time to watch people panning—and take notes if you plan to do the same! When you are ready to continue hiking, head to the back southeast corner of the parking lot and look for a dirt roadbed that continues to the south.

2.0 The roadbed ends at an open field. Take your time to explore this exposed area. It is a 0.4-mile walk to travel the circumference of the field.

2.4 After traveling the perimeter of the field, retrace your steps on the roadbed back to the visitor center.

2.9 Conclude your hike at the visitor center—but not your day. Be sure to stick around and try your hand at gold panning or enjoy a picnic on the property before returning home.

HIKE INFORMATION

Local information: Town of Midland, 4293B Hwy. 24/27 E., PO Box 589, Midland 28107; (704) 888-2232; www.townofmidland.us

Local events/attractions: Concord Speedway, 7940 US Hwy. 601 S., Concord 28025. You're in racecar country, so make the most of it and check out a race!

Good eats: Pizza and Beyond, 251 Hwy. 24/27 W., Midland 28107; (704) 888-1992; www.pizzaandbeyond.blogspot.com. Enjoy a pizza on your way out of town, or place an order to go on your drive into town, and then enjoy a picnic a Reed Gold Mine.

Organizations: Arts Council Cabarrus, 65 Union St. S., Concord 28025; (704) 920-2787; www.cabarrusartscouncil.org. Get involved with the arts in Cabarrus County.

> 🌿 **Green Tip:**
> *Be green and stylish too—wear clothing made of organic cotton and other recycled products.*

Morrow Mountain State Park: Fall Mountain

This scenic loop at Morrow Mountain is one of the best hikes to the east of Charlotte. However, it has unfortunately been closed for over a year and a half because of damage to the boardwalks near the Yadkin River. There are plans to reopen this diverse route in the future. Be sure you call before visiting the park to check on the status of the trail. The loop starts near the banks of the Yadkin River and then does a quick "warm-up" hike on the Three Rivers Trail. When the path returns to the trailhead, it veers inland on the Fall Mountain Loop. The narrow dirt path travels through a beautiful mixed hardwood and pine forest and parallels a small stream before starting its gradual climb to the top of Fall Mountain. The ascent is challenging but manageable, and before you know it you'll be walking on a level ridgeline. At the north end of the ridge, the trail will loop back to the parking lot on a new and exciting reroute!

Start: Morrow Mountain boat launch parking lot
Distance: 5.0-mile figure eight (Approximate, as reroute will determine the exact distance.)
Hiking time: About 2.5 to 3 hours
Difficulty: Moderate
Trail surface: Mostly dirt trail (The reroute may include wooden boardwalks.)
Best season(s): Year-round
Other trail users: None
Canine compatibility: Leashed dogs permitted

Land status: State park
Fees and permits: None
Schedule: 8 a.m. to 6 p.m. Nov through Feb; 8 a.m. to 8 p.m. Mar, Apr, May, Sept, and Oct; 8 a.m. to 9 p.m. June through Aug
Maps: USGS Badin; basic Morrow Mountain State park map available at the park office
Trail contacts: Morrow Mountain State Park, 49104 Morrow Mountain Rd., Albemarle 28001; (704) 982-4402; www.ncparks.gov

Finding the trailhead: From Charlotte drive east on Albemarle Road (NC 24/27). After about 33 miles, you will pass through the city of Albemarle, then turn left (north) onto NC 740. Stay on NC 740 for 2.0 miles, then take a right (east) onto Morrow Mountain Road (NC 1798). Stay on Morrow Mountain Road for 3.5 miles to enter Morrow Mountain State Park. Once inside the park, follow the signs leading to the fishing and boating area on Lake Tillery. The road ends at a parking lot beside the lake. The trailhead is located in the southwest corner of the parking area. GPS: N35 22.879'/W80 03.735'

THE HIKE

As mentioned in the introduction, this hike has been closed to the public for some time. In 2010 the park experienced heavy rain and flooding along the banks of the Yadkin and Pee Dee Rivers. The high waters and subsequent washout caused major damage to the boating area at the park, and it also damaged the wooden boardwalks on the Fall Mountain trail. It is unknown when the trail will once again be open to the public, but there are plans to repair and reopen the path in the near future. Perhaps even by the time of printing, this path will be accessible to the public, but it is wise to call Morrow Mountain State Park and ask for a update before driving all the way from Charlotte to hike Fall Mountain. If you do arrive at the park and the trail is still closed, consider hiking the Hattaway Mountain Trail or the Sugarloaf-to-Morrow-Mountain hike. Do not try to stealth-hike the Fall Mountain Trail while it is closed!

The first portion of this hike has remained open to the public. The Three Rivers Trail explores the floodplain to the south of the boat launch and then climbs up a small rise to loop back to the trailhead. The path is scenic and full of wildflowers in the

Fall Dam releases water into the Yadkin River.

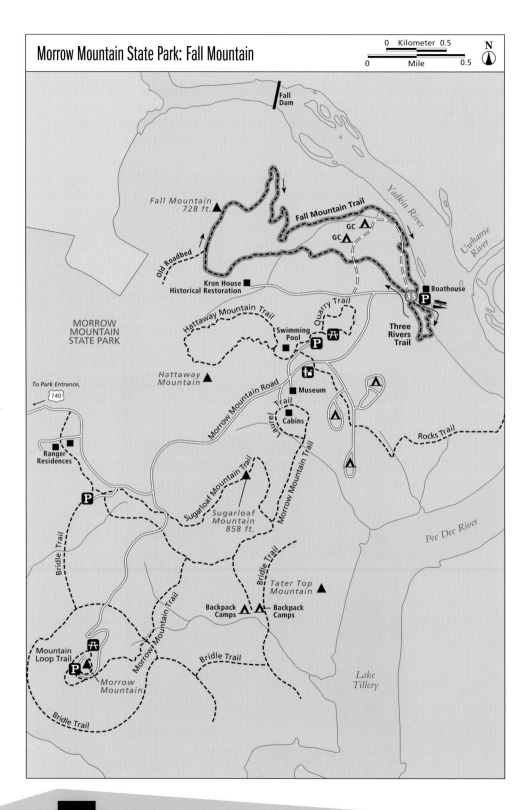

Morrow Mountain State Park: Fall Mountain

0 Kilometer 0.5
0 Mile 0.5

N

Fall Dam

Fall Mountain 728 ft.

Fall Mountain Trail

Yadkin River

GC

GC

Uwharrie River

Old Roadbed

Kron House Historical Restoration

Boathouse

Hattaway Mountain Trail

MORROW MOUNTAIN STATE PARK

Quarry Trail

Swimming Pool

Three Rivers Trail

To Park Entrance, 740

Hattaway Mountain

Morrow Mountain Road

Museum

Laurel Trail

Cabins

Rocks Trail

Ranger Residences

P

Sugarloaf Mountain Trail

Morrow Mountain Trail

Pee Dee River

Sugarloaf Mountain 858 ft.

Bridle Trail

Bridle Trail

Tater Top Mountain

Mountain Loop Trail

P

Morrow Mountain Trail

Backpack Camps

Backpack Camps

Lake Tillery

Morrow Mountain

Bridle Trail

Bridle Trail

spring. The first portion of the trail provides great views of the river to your left. This path, as well as the eastern portion of the Fall Mountain Trail, is situated in a unique location to view the Pee Dee River, Uwharrie River, and Yadkin River all at once. The Pee Dee River is formed by the confluence of the Yadkin and Uwharrie Rivers, and this meeting takes place directly across the river from the boat launch area.

At the conclusion of the Three Rivers Trail, turn left to join the Fall Mountain Trail. The path travels inland through a forest of oak, pine, beech, and holly trees. This portion of the state park is a great place to look for birds and wild animals. Morrow Mountain is a safe haven for local deer and turkey, and they are often seen on the trails, even during the day. Copious songbirds also make their home at the state park, where fallen trees amid the forest provide shelter for many different species including Carolina chickadees, wood thrushes, and brown thrashers.

After hiking 1.4 miles you will cross over a small stream and parallel the water uphill. Often the sound of croaking frogs can be heard near this water source, especially in the late winter and early spring when they are looking for mates. One interesting fact is that typically it is only the male frogs that fill the air with their chirping—to impress the ladies, of course.

Beyond the stream, the trail will pass beside a chain-link fence. At this point you are about half a mile north of the Kron House. There is no trail leading to the house, but you should consider taking some time after your hike to visit this 200-year-old homestead. Dr. Kron, a Prussian immigrant, is recognized as the first medical doctor in the region.

At mile 2.4 an old fire road joins the trail from the west, and the grade flattens out as the path now travels along the level ridge of Fall Mountain. In the winter this section of the hike will reveal views of Hattaway, Sugarloaf, and Morrow Mountains to the south.

At the north end of the ridge, the trail starts a steep, rocky descent that should be approached with caution. This section historically leads down to Fall Dam, however, the reroute might keep the new trail high above the floodplain. Whether or not you will still be able to see Fall Dam is unknown. But it is certain that you will enjoy a scenic and peaceful journey back to the trailhead parking lot, despite which direction the reroute travels. Oh, and be sure to keep your eyes peeled for white and gray gulls flying overhead. The nearby dam is one of their favorite hang-out spots.

MILES AND DIRECTIONS

0.0   The trailhead for the Fall Mountain Trail and the Three Rivers Trail is located at the southwest corner of the boat launch parking lot. Start your hike by following the Three Rivers Trail across the paved park road.

0.3 The Three Rivers Trail leaves the shore of the Pee Dee River and veers inland.

0.7 The Three Rivers Trail concludes by crossing over the paved park road a second time and reconnecting with the Fall Mountain Loop. Now turn left (west) and follow the Fall Mountain Loop through a forest filled with a mix of pine and hardwood trees.

1.4 Cross a small creek and veer left (west) to begin a gradual ascent to the top of Fall Mountain.

1.9 A chain-link fence near the trail signifies that you are half a mile north of the Kron House.

2.4 An old fire road joins the Fall Mountain Trail from the west. This marks the end of the steady ascent and the beginning of a relatively level ridgeline walk.

2.9 At the end of the ridge you will encounter the new reroute! Follow it closely, wherever it may lead.

5.0 Conclude your hike at the boat launch parking lot.

HIKE INFORMATION

Local information: Stanly County Convention and Visitor Bureau, 1000 N. First St., Suite 11, Albemarle 28001; (704) 986-2583; www.stanlycvb.com

Local events/attractions: Stanly County Museum, 245 E. Main St., Albemarle 28001; (704) 986-3777; www.stanlycountymuseum.com. "The land between the rivers" has been inhabited for more than 10,000 years. Learn about who was here before you at the museum.

Good eats: Boardroom Bar & Bistro, 135 W. Main St., Albemarle 28001; (704) 982-1908. Visit Boardroom Bar & Bistro on Facebook. It's open for lunch or dinner, with terrific Southern-style sandwiches.

> *The trailhead parking area for the Fall Mountain hike is also the parking area for the boat launch and boat-rental facility. Why not enjoy Morrow Mountain State Park, first on land and then on the water? Consider renting a canoe or rowboat at the boat dock and exploring the Yadkin, Pee Dee, and Uwharrie Rivers. The boat-rental area was affected by the washouts, so call ahead to be sure it's operational before you head out. Get more information at www.ncparks.gov/Visit/parks/momo/activities.php.*

Morrow Mountain State Park: Hattaway Mountain

This hike is short, diversified, and challenging—all in a good way. The route first explores the quarry trail near the picnic area at Morrow Mountain State Park. This argillite rock quarry is where members of the Civilian Conservation Corps harvested rock to build some of the buildings at Morrow Mountain State Park. Some of these structures are still used by the park and park visitors today. After exploring the jagged rock walls inside, the route then travels the steep slopes of Hattaway Mountain. This is a challenging ascent, the steepest in the park, but at just under half a mile, it does not last long. The flat ridge on top of Hattaway Mountain provides glimpses through the trees of neighboring Fall Mountain and Sugarloaf Mountain. The trail descends another very steep route off the west slope of the mountain. From there the hike will take you over the rolling terrain at the base of the mountain, before concluding at the Morrow Mountain State Park swimming pool.

Start: Morrow Mountain swimming pool and picnic area parking lot
Distance: 2.9-mile figure eight
Hiking time: About 1.5 to 2 hours
Difficulty: More difficult, steep ascent
Trail surface: Mostly single-track dirt trail, a brief paved portion connects the Quarry and Hattaway Mountain trails
Best season(s): Year-round
Other trail users: None
Canine compatibility: Leashed dogs permitted

Land status: State park
Fees and permits: None
Schedule: 8 a.m. to 6 p.m. Nov through Feb; 8 a.m. to 8 p.m. Mar, Apr, May, Sept, and Oct; 8 a.m. to 9 p.m. June through Aug
Maps: USGS Badin; basic Morrow Mountain State park map available at the park office
Trail contacts: Morrow Mountain State Park, 49104 Morrow Mountain Rd., Albemarle 28001; (704) 982-4402; www.ncparks.gov

Finding the trailhead: From Charlotte drive east on Albemarle Road (NC 24/27). After about 33 miles, pass through the city of Albemarle, then turn left (north) onto NC 740. Stay on NC 740 for 2.0 miles, then take a right (east) onto Morrow Mountain Road (NC 1798). Stay on Morrow Mountain Road for 3.5 miles to enter Morrow Mountain State Park. Once inside the park, follow the signs leading to the swimming pool and picnic area parking lot. The trailhead is located at the northeast corner of the parking area next to the picnic area. GPS: N35 22.630' / W80 04.280'

THE HIKE

This hike has a lot to offer. Although the total distance measures less than 3 miles, there is a good chance that you will spend the better part of your day exploring this section of the park—especially when the swimming pool is open! That's right, this hike starts and ends very close to the Morrow Mountain swimming pool. There are not many state parks that have swimming pools, and this one is large and refreshing, particularly on a hot summer day.

If you are hiking with children, or less motivated adults, it is best to reserve the swimming pool as an incentive for the end of the hike. There are a couple strenuous sections on this route where it will be good to have a reward in mind. However, not the first section. No, the first part of this hike travels a scenic and easy loop around the picnic area. You may wonder what is worth viewing along the outskirts of covered pavilions and picnic grills, but this trail visits one of the highlights of Morrow Mountain State Park—the historic quarry.

By starting at the picnic area at the northeast corner of the parking lot, you will follow the Quarry Trail in a clockwise direction. The path starts by traveling gently downhill beyond the picnic facilities and then curves to the east near a seasonal stream. Past the stream you will come to a small gully with exposed rock walls—this is the quarry.

The path travels through the historic argillite rock quarry.

There are several former rock quarries at Morrow Mountain State Park. Many of them, near the top of the mountains, were used by Native Americans. Archaeologists believe that indigenous people inhabited this land more than 12,000 years ago. In fact, it was one of the first regions of North Carolina to be occupied because of the temperate climate and lush river valley. The residents of the Uwharrie Mountains soon made use of rhyolite, a rock that naturally forms sharp pointed edges when chiseled.

This quarry, however, reveals argillite stone on either side of the trail. This rock could be harvested in bricklike rectangles and it was used by members of the CCC to build the first park buildings in the 1930s. There is a good chance that you will find intriguing smaller rocks on the ground, but remember leave-no-trace practices and state park rules both dictate that hikers are not allowed to take any stones or artifacts home as souvenirs.

Past the quarry the trail concludes its loop at the parking lot. Now, hike west across the parking lot to a set of steps that lead up to the nearby swimming pool. As tempting as the water may be, continue past the pool to join the Hattaway Mountain Trail. You will only be on the Hattaway Mountain Trail for a few minutes before it splits. Since the trail makes a loop, you can go in either direction to complete the hike, but it is recommended that you turn left and tackle the trail's steepest ascent while you still have relatively fresh legs. The trail now proceeds up, up, up to the ridgeline. There are a few short switchbacks to help you on your way, but even with the changes in direction, your calves will still start to burn. Thankfully, the ascent only lasts for 0.25 mile and then the trail once again levels out on top of the mountain. Breaks in the trees will reveal brief views from the ridge. You may be able to spot the river valley to your east, as well as several of the surrounding mountain peaks.

After 0.5 mile the trail once again encounters a steep grade, but at least this time you are going downhill. Take your time and be careful on the descent. Far more people get hurt going down a mountain than climbing uphill. Once you reach the base of Hattaway Mountain, you would think, or hope, that it would be a relatively flat hike back to the trailhead. However, the path now travels over several brief rises and dips before completing the loop at the east end of the mountain. From here, it is an easy hike out of the woods and past the swimming pool to conclude the route at the Morrow Mountain picnic grounds. Now it is time to reward yourself: You are in the perfect spot to spend the rest of the afternoon eating and swimming!

🌿 Green Tip:
Keep your dog on a leash at all times. Never let it approach other people or other pets unless invited to do so.

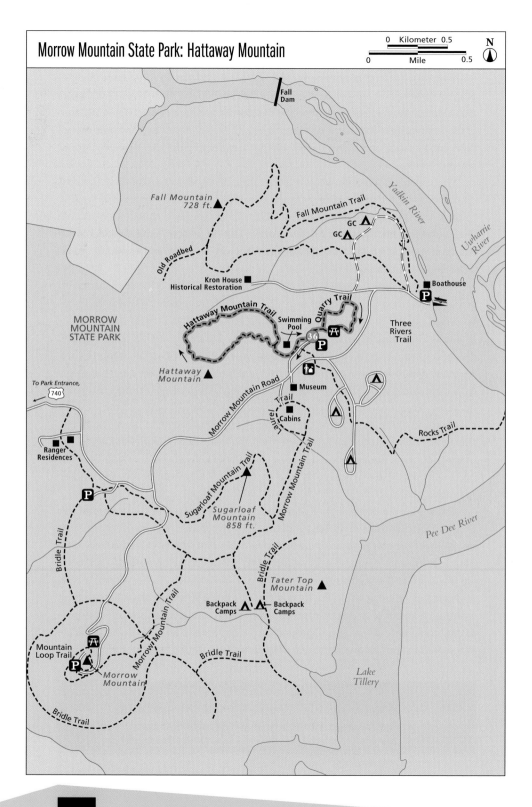

Morrow Mountain State Park: Hattaway Mountain

0   Kilometer 0.5

0   Mile   0.5

N

Fall
Dam

Yadkin River

Uwharrie River

Fall Mountain
728 ft.

Fall Mountain Trail

GC

GC

Old Roadbed

Kron House
Historical Restoration

Boathouse

P

MORROW
MOUNTAIN
STATE PARK

Hattaway Mountain Trail

Quarry Trail

Swimming
Pool

36

P

Three
Rivers
Trail

Hattaway
Mountain

To Park Entrance,
740

Morrow Mountain Road

Museum

Laurel Trail

Cabins

Rocks Trail

Ranger
Residences

Sugarloaf Mountain Trail

Sugarloaf
Mountain
858 ft.

Morrow Mountain Trail

P

Bridle Trail

Bridle Trail

Pee Dee River

Tater Top
Mountain

Morrow Mountain Trail

Backpack
Camps

Backpack
Camps

Mountain
Loop Trail

Bridle Trail

P

Morrow
Mountain

Bridle Trail

Lake
Tillery

0.0 To start this hike, park your car in the large parking lot that connects the Morrow Mountain picnic grounds with the swimming pool. From your car walk toward the picnic pavilions. At the edge of the parking lot, look to your left and locate the start of the Quarry Trail, marked with blue diamonds. Hike north and follow the dirt path into the woods to hike the trail in a clockwise direction.

0.3 Arrive at a small stream and veer right (east) to stay on the Quarry Trail.

0.4 The trail arrives at the argillite quarry. This is a bridge that explores the east side of the quarry, but it is not a continuation of the trail. In order to stay on the correct path, continue to hug the west side of the quarry.

0.6 Conclude the Quarry Trail at the restrooms adjacent to the picnic facilities. Now walk west across the wide parking lot.

0.7 Just to the west of the parking lot entrance there is a set of wooden steps that leads up to the swimming area. Follow these steps uphill and into the woods.

0.8 Hattaway Mountain towers above the swimming pool. Locate the Hattaway Mountain trail at the west end of the swimming complex and follow it into the woods.

0.9 The Hattaway Mountain Trail splits. Veer left (southwest) and travel uphill to complete the most challenging stretch of the loop trail.

1.2 Hooray! You made it to the top of the mountain. Now catch your breath and enjoy a casual jaunt on the level ridgeline.

1.7 The level ridge abruptly ends and then takes a nosedive toward the valley floor. Take your time and hike very carefully down the steep descent to prevent taking a nosedive of your own.

2.0 At the base of the mountain, the trail veers northeast and travels an undulating route.

2.6 The loop portion of the Hattaway Mountain Trail concludes. Veer left (east) to retrace your steps out of the woods and beside the swimming pool. Then follow the wooden steps back to the parking lot.

2.9 Conclude your hike at the Morrow Mountain picnic area. Then enjoy one of the many amenities that the state park has to offer, such as the swimming pool!

Local information: Stanly County Convention and Visitor Bureau, 1000 N. First St., Suite 11, Albemarle 28001; (704) 986-2583; www.stanlycvb.com

Local events/attractions: Badin Museum, 60 Falls Rd., Badin 28009; (704) 422-6900; http://badinmuseum.stevelee.name/. Its hours are limited, but when it is open, it is worth a visit.

Badin Firehouse Museum, 60 Falls Rd., Badin 28009; (704) 422-6900; http://badinmuseum.stevelee.name/firehouse. Like the Badin Historic Museum, this facility is only open to the public on Tuesday and Sunday, but it is always a crowd pleaser—especially with children.

Good eats: Harmancos, 1407 E. Main St., Albemarle 28001; (704) 982-5451; www.harmancos.com. There is something to suit every appetite at Harmancos.

Organizations: Stanly County Arts Council, 141 College Dr., Room 104 Snyder Building, Albemarle 28001; (704) 982-8118; www.co.stanly.nc.us. Promoting the arts in Stanly County.

The pool at Morrow Mountain State Park is open from June to Labor Day. A small fee is charged to access the swimming area. The entire facility is handicapped-accessible. The stone shower house located at the entrance of the pool was built in the 1930s by the Civilian Conservation Corp. For more information or to plan your trip, visit www.ncparks .gov/Visit/parks/momo/activities.php.

This route explores the southern portion of Morrow Mountain State Park. The expedition starts near the park entrance and follows a winding trail through the forest. After crossing a paved park road, this casual stroll transitions into a challenging hike that climbs to the summit of Sugarloaf Mountain and then descends into the valley before navigating the slopes of Morrow Mountain. Morrow Mountain is not only the tallest mountain in the park but—at 936 feet—it is also the tallest mountain in Stanly County. And while the trail travels to the roof of the state park, most of the views during the spring, summer, and fall will be at least partially obstructed by towering hardwood trees. There is, however, a beautiful observation hut and picnic facility on top of Morrow Mountain, which serves as a scenic reward after a long climb. After embracing the views of the Pee Dee River Valley and Uwharrie National Forest, the trail descends Morrow Mountain and returns to the base of Sugarloaf Mountain. From here the hike travels a peaceful woodland path that returns to the trailhead at the horse trailer parking lot.

Start: Morrow Mountain horse trailer parking lot

Distance: 5.8-mile balloon

Hiking time: About 3 to 4 hours

Difficulty: More difficult, substantial climbing

Trail surface: Single-track dirt trail

Best season(s): Fall, winter, spring

Other trail users: None

Canine compatibility: Leashed dogs permitted

Land status: State park

Fees and permits: None

Schedule: 8 a.m. to 6 p.m. Nov through Feb; 8 a.m. to 8 p.m. Mar, Apr, May, Sept, and Oct; 8 a.m. to 9 p.m. June through Aug

Maps: USGS Badin; basic Morrow Mountain State park map available at the park office

Trail contacts: Morrow Mountain State Park, 49104 Morrow Mountain Rd., Albemarle 28001; (704) 982-4402; www.ncparks.gov

Finding the trailhead: From Charlotte drive east on Albemarle Road (NC 24/77). After about 33 miles, pass through the city of Albemarle, then turn left (north) onto NC 740. Stay on NC 740 for 2.0 miles, then take a right (east) onto Morrow Mountain Road (NC 1798). Stay on Morrow Mountain Road for 3.5 miles to enter Morrow Mountain State Park. Once you arrive at the park, you will drive through the park gates and immediately pass an information hut on your right. Continue on the main park road and take your next right (south) to access the horse trailer parking lot. Park here and locate the trailhead near the entrance of the parking lot. GPS: N35 21.926' / W80 05.520'

THE HIKE

This hike combines the Sugarloaf Mountain and Morrow Mountain Trails to offer one of the longest treks in the park. It should also be noted, since this hike starts in the horse trailer parking lot, that all 16 miles of bridle paths at Morrow Mountain are also open to hiking. So once you have exhausted the pedestrian trails, feel free to explore the equestrian routes as well.

Beyond length, this trail also offers height. The route includes two challenging climbs to the top of Sugarloaf Mountain and Morrow Mountain. If you do not have the time or desire to climb both mountains, then feel free to bypass the Morrow Mountain spur and continue along the Sugarloaf Mountain Trail to enjoy a 2.8-mile outing.

The hike begins at the northeast corner of the horse trailer parking lot. Behind the trailhead a solitary dirt path leads you into the forest. Almost immediately this trail splits in two and begins the loop portion of the Sugarloaf Mountain Trail. Veer left and travel the route in a clockwise direction. At first the trail travels a moderately level route through a mixed hardwood and pine forest. There

The Sugarloaf Mountain Trail descends off of the east slope of the mountain.

are several roots and rocks scattered along the trail, including several beautiful white quartz rocks. These quartz serve as a reminder that America's first gold rush was located an hour away from Morrow Mountain in Cabarrus County. In 1799 when the gold rush started, these white rocks would have been mined and then scoured for gold veins.

After hiking 0.4 mile the path crosses a paved park road. Soon after passing over the road, the trail will begin its ascent up Sugarloaf Mountain. Although the climb to the summit of Sugarloaf Mountain is strenuous, it is not nearly as steep as the descent off the mountain's eastern slope. By taking your time and incorporating several rest breaks, you should be able to reach the top of Sugarloaf Mountain without too much difficulty. Once you reach the ridge, you will be able to spot intermittent views of the Pee Dee River and Morrow Mountain to the south.

Climbing down the backside of Sugarloaf Mountain, be extra-cautious and pay close attention to your foot placement. This trail has suffered slightly from erosion, and if you place your downhill foot too close to the trail's edge, the ground might slide out from under you. Once you have navigated the tricky terrain, you will arrive at the base of Sugarloaf, where a pleasant trail leads through a scenic forest filled with maple, sourwood, oak, and cedar trees. At mile 1.8 you will come to an intersection with a path that leads to a backcountry campsite. Shortly thereafter, when the trail reaches the top of a small rise, the Sugarloaf Trail will meet the Morrow Mountain Trail. Again, if you are feeling fatigued at this point, consider staying on the Sugarloaf Mountain Trail. Otherwise, turn left and begin your ascent up Morrow Mountain.

The trail doesn't start traveling uphill right away. Instead you will continue on a relatively level path that winds through the forest and then descends down to a trickling stream. After the stream the real climb begins and intensifies as you draw closer to the summit. When you arrive within a few hundred yards of the top of the mountain, the path joins the Mountain Loop Trail and levels out. This route circles the top of the mountain and provides several views of Uwharrie National Forest through the trees. When the trail crosses the parking lot directly below the summit, take the time to walk to the top of Morrow Mountain to visit the beautiful picnic facilities, informational plaques, and restrooms. At the summit you will learn that Morrow Mountain State Park was made possible through the generous land donation and vision of James McKnight Morrow. Before being named Morrow Mountain, this peak was known as Naked Mountain after a hurricane decimated the trees near the summit.

When you conclude the loop, backtrack along the Morrow Mountain Trail to reconnect with the Sugarloaf Mountain Trail. From this point, the path travels a shaded route through the forest and crosses over a seasonal stream before completing the Sugarloaf Mountain loop and concluding the hike at the horse trailer parking lot.

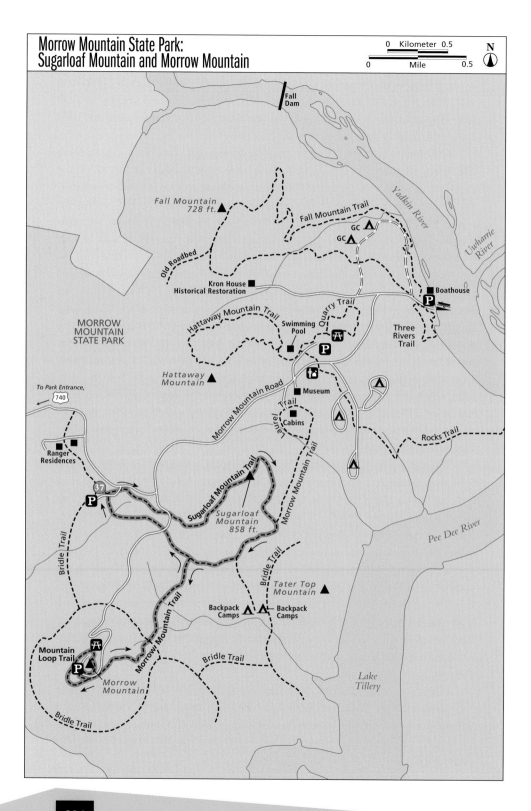

Morrow Mountain State Park: Sugarloaf Mountain and Morrow Mountain

0 Kilometer 0.5
0 Mile 0.5
N

Fall Dam

Fall Mountain
728 ft.

Fall Mountain Trail

Yadkin River

Uwharrie River

GC
GC

Old Roadbed

Kron House
Historical Restoration

Boathouse

MORROW
MOUNTAIN
STATE PARK

Hattaway Mountain Trail

Swimming Pool

Quarry Trail

Three Rivers Trail

Hattaway Mountain

Morrow Mountain Road

Museum

Laurel Trail

Cabins

Rocks Trail

To Park Entrance,
740

Ranger Residences

Sugarloaf Mountain Trail

Sugarloaf Mountain
858 ft.

Morrow Mountain Trail

Pee Dee River

Bridle Trail

Bridle Trail

Tater Top Mountain

Backpack Camps

Backpack Camps

Mountain Loop Trail

Morrow Mountain Trail

Bridle Trail

Lake Tillery

Morrow Mountain

Bridle Trail

0.0 The Sugarloaf trailhead is located very close to the entrance of the horse trailer parking lot, in the northeast corner. The trail is marked with orange diamonds. Follow the diamonds east into the forest.

0.1 The trail splits. Veer left (northeast) and travel the loop in a clockwise direction.

0.3 The path crosses a small stream on a wooden footbridge. The tread becomes increasingly rocky and includes white quartz rocks.

0.6 Cross a paved park road and continue to follow the orange diamonds. Expect the difficulty of the hike to increase as you begin your ascent up Sugarloaf Mountain.

0.7 The ascent becomes more gradual and a gentle slope continues to climb up the mountain. Scattered views become apparent through the trees.

1.0 The trail crests Sugarloaf Mountain and then begins a steep and challenging descent down the east slope of the mountain.

1.6 The path arrives at a junction with the blue-blazed Morrow Mountain Trail. The two paths converge. Continue on the joint Sugarloaf Mountain and Morrow Mountain Trail by veering to the right (south) and hiking down a small set of wooden steps.

1.8 Pass a spur trail on your left that leads to a backcountry campsite.

2.1 At the intersection with the Morrow Mountain Trail, leave the Sugarloaf Mountain Trail and turn left (south). Follow the blue triangles.

2.3 Cross a small stream and begin your ascent to the top of Morrow Mountain.

3.2 The difficult climbing ends at the intersection with the Mountain Loop Trail. Veer left (south) and follow the red squares as they contour around the mountain summit.

3.8 When the trail crosses the Morrow Mountain Parking Lot, leave the loop trail and take the opportunity to explore the mountain's summit. The peak of the mountain greets you with picnic tables, restrooms, information plaques, and terrific views.

4.0 Conclude the Mountain Loop Trail and continue straight (north) to retrace your steps down the mountain on the Morrow Mountain Trail.

37

5.1 At the intersection with the Sugarloaf Mountain Trail, turn left (west). The remainder of the hike travels moderate terrain through a predominantly hardwood forest.

5.2 Cross a paved park road, and continue hiking west on the Sugarloaf Mountain Trail.

5.7 Conclude the loop portion of the Sugarloaf Mountain Trail and turn left. Hike west to the nearby trailhead.

5.8 Conclude your hike at the horse trailer parking lot.

HIKE INFORMATION

Local information: Stanly County Convention and Visitor Bureau, 1000 N. First St., Suite 11, Albemarle 28001; (704) 986-2583; www.stanlycvb.com

Local events/attractions: Stanly County Museum, 245 E. Main St., Albemarle 28001; (704) 986-3777; www.stanlycountymuseum.com. "The land between the rivers" has been inhabited for over 10,000 years. Learn about who was here before you at the museum.

Good eats: Pontiac Pointe, 304 E. Main St., Albemarle 28001; (704) 984-6029; www.menu.pontiacpointe.com. If you go to Pontiac Pointe, you will find a large menu and maybe even some live music.

Organizations: Stanly County Arts Council, 141 College Dr., Room 104 Snyder Building, Albemarle 28001; (704) 982-8118; www.co.stanly.nc.us. Promoting the arts in Stanly County.

After finishing your hike, consider visiting the Kron House at Morrow Mountain. The nineteenth-century doctor after whom the house is named lived in the valley between Hattaway Mountain and Fall Mountain. He was the first doctor in the region. His reconstructed house, infirmary, and office are located at the original home site. Tours of the Kron House are available during special times of the year. Check the events link on the Morrow Mountain website for upcoming opportunities to visit the house.

North Region

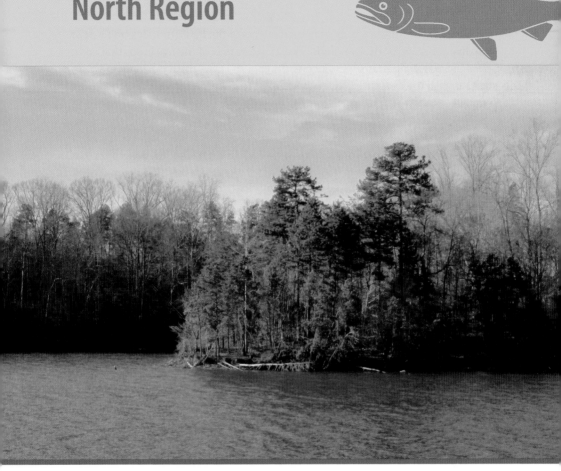

A view of Lake Norman from the Lake Shore Trail (hike 38).

The hikes to the north of Charlotte are found at Lake Norman State Park. The land for this large, gorgeous park was donated by Duke Power when the dam that created Lake Norman, otherwise known as "the inland lake," was built. The lake now provides hydroelectric energy to Gaston and Mecklenburg Counties and it is a popular recreation destination for boaters, anglers, skiers, and hikers.

There are many trails that weave through the large state park at the northeast corner of Lake Norman. One in particular, the Lake Shore Trail, hugs the water for most of the hike. The quiet coves along the trail are home to migrating waterfowl during the winter. And although the trail stays near the water, the tall hardwood and pine trees that line the path provide enough shade to keep you cool on a hot summer day.

The largest trail at Lake Norman State Park is the Itusi Trail. This trail is split into five separate loops. This guidebook explores four of the five loops that comprise the Itusi Trail. The newest loop is the Laurel Loop, which weaves a tight circuit through the forest that will delight hikers with its many twists and turns. The final hike in this guidebook explores a combination of the Hawk Loop, Norwood Creek Loop, and Hicks Creek Loop. Together they offer a variety of waterfront and woodland hiking.

If you travel up to Lake Norman State Park to go hiking, be sure to stop at the nearby town of Troutman for a bite to eat or to explore the quaint downtown.

A mountain biker navigates wide-open terrain on the Laurel Loop (hike 39).

Lake Norman State Park: Lake Shore Trail

Attention pedestrians: Lake Norman State Park reserved the most scenic route on the property just for hikers! Unlike the other multiuse trails at the park, this path is reserved for those traveling on two feet. The gorgeous loop contours the quiet undeveloped shoreline of northern Lake Norman. The path weaves in and out of protected coves, where nesting waterfowl can often be found. And because this route travels a peninsula with a small neck, almost the entire hike offers stunning views of the lake. Although the hike stays near the flat and tranquil water, the short but constant ups and downs on the trail make this hike feel more strenuous than you might expect. But if you take your time, a good attitude, a picnic, and perhaps your camera, this will soon become one of your favorite hikes near Charlotte.

Start: Lake Norman State Park Lakeshore trailhead
Distance: 5.2-mile loop
Hiking time: About 2 to 3 hours
Difficulty: Moderate; rolling hills
Trail surface: Forested and shoreline trail
Best season(s): Year-round
Other trail users: None
Canine compatibility: Leashed dogs permitted
Land status: State park
Fees and permits: No fees or permits required for day hiking
Schedule: 8 a.m. to 6 p.m. Nov through Feb; 8 a.m. to 8 p.m. Mar, Apr, Sept, Oct; 8 a.m. to 9 p.m. May through Aug. All trails close 30 minutes prior to park closing. Park and trails closed Christmas Day.
Maps: USGS Troutman; Lake Norman State Park map available at the park ranger station and at www.ncparks.gov/Visit/parks/lano/main.php
Trail contacts: Lake Norman State Park, 159 Inland Sea Lane, Troutman 28166; (704) 528-6350; www.ncparks.gov

Finding the trailhead: From Charlotte take I-77 North to exit 42. Turn left (west) off the interstate and travel US 21 to Troutman. When you arrive at downtown Troutman, take a left (south) onto Wagner Street. Follow Wagner Street (which changes to Perth Road at the town limits) for 1.6 miles and then veer right (west) onto State Park Road. Follow State Park Road for 3.6 miles to reach Lake Norman State Park. After you enter the park, continue on State Park Road toward the Cove Picnic Area. Before reaching the picnic area, turn left (west) onto Shortleaf Drive. The road bears right and reveals roadside parking. This is the trailhead for the Lakeshore Trail. After parking the car hike southeast to access the trail. GPS: N35 38.751'/W80 56.708' ake Norman is the largest man-made lake in North Carolina. Spanning more than 32,510 acres and housing 520 miles of shoreline, this massive body of water is nicknamed "the inland sea." And while much of the lakeshore is heavily developed, the northern coast remains scenic and undisturbed.

Duke Power started construction on the lake in 1959. Construction on the dam lasted more than four years and it took an additional two years to fill the entire lake. Amid the building process, Duke Power donated 1,328 acres of land, including 13 miles of pristine shoreline, to the state. The gift was designated to allow public access to the lake and preserve the natural beauty of the region. Originally named Duke Power State Park, the facility offers year-round recreational opportunities—not the least of which is hiking. Most of the trails at the park are shared between mountain bikers and hikers, but the southernmost peninsula near the boat launch and picnic area is reserved "solely" for bipeds.

A set of wooden bridges travels across steep ravines on the Lake Shore Trail.

The loop that explores this landscape is known as the Lake Shore Trail, and it begins at a small trailhead off Shortleaf Drive. The trail dives downhill and immediately veers east to contour the shoreline. The clear blue water of Lake Norman can be seen through the narrow strip of trees that separates the trail from the thin sandy beach. Frequent visitors to Lake Norman may be surprised to see the lake appear in different shades of blue throughout the year. Water usually appears blue because it reflects the color of the sky, but Lake Norman can also appear to have tints of red or green due to changing levels of sediment and algae within the water.

The trail soon comes to a trail junction with the red-blazed Short Turn Trail. This path is of little importance now, but in a few miles it may provide a shorter hike option to the weary hikers in your group. Continue to follow the white diamonds along the shore of the lake. The path now skirts the edge of the family campground and spends some time amid the forest to avoid the added mileage of two outstretching finger peninsulas that reach into the lake. Past this short inland stretch, the trail does not take any more mileage-saving turns. It is always intriguing, and sometimes exhausting, to think how much distance is added when you stay true to the shoreline as opposed to cutting straight across the neck of the landform to the opposing shore.

The path now continues to wind in and out of the silent coves of Lake Norman. If you walk softly, there is a good chance you will be able to spot wildlife along the edge of the water. Often nesting or migrating fowl can be found taking shelter near the shoreline. On a rare occasion freshwater otters can be spotted playing in the water. After hiking 2.7 miles you will once again intersect the Short Turn Trail. This red-blazed path might have more appeal at this point in the hike, and if you choose to turn left, you can conclude your hike in less than a mile. However, if you wish to continue on the Lake Shore Trail, then stay by the shoreline and follow the path until it crosses the road near the Lake Norman State Park boat launch.

Past the boat launch, the trail continues to hug the shoreline. At this point of the hike, the water that you are constantly enjoying to your right is actually the mouth of Hicks Creek, a tributary for Lake Norman. You may be able to notice the opposite shoreline drawing closer as you continue north. However, even though the waterway narrows, this area still looks very much a part of the larger lake. When you arrive at a spur trail that leads to the park's group campground, you will turn left and hike inland away from the water.

Inland is a relative term at this point in the hike, because after a short 0.2-mile walk, you will be back beside the water on the west side of the Lake Norman peninsula. The trail continues to trace the shoreline for another mile to return to the trailhead off Shortleaf Drive.

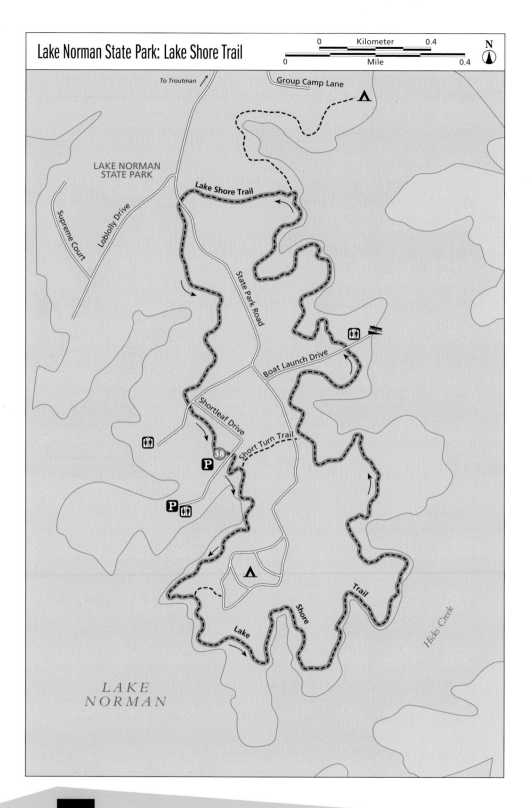

Lake Norman State Park: Lake Shore Trail

To Troutman

Group Camp Lane

LAKE NORMAN
STATE PARK

Supreme Court

Loblolly Drive

Lake Shore Trail

State Park Road

Boat Launch Drive

Shortleaf Drive

Short Turn Trail

38

Lake Shore Trail

LAKE
NORMAN

Hicks Creek

0.0 From the roadside parking lot off Shortleaf Drive, head east into the woods and follow the white diamonds that mark the Lake Shore Trail downhill and toward the water.

0.2 The path arrives at the lakeshore and continues to parallel the lake throughout several small coves.

0.5 Arrive at a junction with the Short Turn Trail. Continue straight (south) to bypass the red-blazed path.

0.8 The trail briefly leaves the water and travels inland through a mixed forest of pine, holly, and beech trees.

1.8 The trail passes over several wooden bridges that keep your feet dry and provide great views on the nearby inlet.

2.7 The trail arrives at its second intersection with the Short Turn Trail. If you wish to shorten your hike, then turn left on the Short Turn Trail and return to the trailhead. Otherwise, continue straight (north) on the Lake Shore Trail.

3.1 Cross a paved park road that leads to a boat ramp. Rejoin the shoreline on the opposite side of the road and continue to weave in and out of the lake coves.

4.0 After crossing over several wooden bridges, you will arrive at a trail junction. The spur trail that continues straight leads to a group campground, but you will turn left (west) and hike away from the water.

4.2 Rejoin the shore of Lake Norman on the west side of the park peninsula.

4.8 Cross one final paved park road and then continue to travel on an undulating path through the woods.

5.2 Conclude your hike at the Lake Shore trailhead at the Shortleaf Drive parking area.

> 🌿 **Green Tip:**
> *Especially for day hikes, use a camp stove for cooking so there's no need to make fire. Another alternative is to bring cold picnics so there is no need to cook.*

HIKE INFORMATION

Local information: Lake Norman Tourism Information: Visit Lake Norman, 199900 W. Catawba Ave., Suite 102, Cornelius 28031; (704) 987-3300; www .visitlakenorman.org

Local events/attractions: Iredell Museum of Arts, 134 Court St., Statesville 28677; (704) 873-4734; www.iredellmuseums.org

Preservation Statesville, 643 Walnut St., Statesville 28677; (704) 450-9828; www .preservationstatesville.org

Good eats: Pellegrino's Trattoria, 275 N. Main St., Troutman 28166; (704) 528-1204; www.pellegrinostrattoria.com. Located in historic downtown Troutman, this trattoria serves pizza and traditional Italian fare.

Organizations: Lake Norman Shag Club, www.lakenormanshagclub.com. Need some more exercise after the hike? Check out the nearby shag club. Events are held monthly at different locations around the lake.

Discover More

Do you enjoy hiking and want to consider participating in some group outings? Do you want to be a part of a group that values the trails and the outdoors as much as you do? Consider joining the Carolina Berg Wanderers. This Charlotte-based group was formed in the 1970s when several of the founding members where considering a hike in Germany. The word *berg* actually means mountain in German. Today, the group is still active and the activities include more than just hiking. The members of the Berg Wanderers plan hiking, biking, and paddling expeditions in the Charlotte area and beyond. The group also has a monthly indoor meeting that includes some "housekeeping" details and a guest speaker. To find out more about the Carolina Berg Wanders, visit www.carolinabergs.com.

Lake Norman State Park: Itusi Trail—Laurel Loop

The Laurel Loop is the newest path at Lake Norman State Park. The 4.7-mile route explores the eastern boundary of the property, just inside the park entrance. The trail is used by both mountain bikers and hikers. It travels mostly within the confines of a mixed upland forest comprising oak, beech, maple, and pine. However, the path does traverse some exposed terrain, which parallels a power-line boundary. The path also observes winter views of Lake Norman and crosses several small seasonal streams that lead to the nearby lakeshore. Even though a large portion of this route is circuitous, you will not feel as if you are simply weaving within the woods. Instead, the heavy tree cover and varying terrain leave you feeling immersed by the forest. This is a terrific hike if you want to feel lost in the forest and lost in your thoughts, while remaining on a very well-marked trail.

Start: Lake Norman State Park Itusi Trail parking lot

Distance: 4.7-mile loop

Hiking time: About 2 to 3 hours

Difficulty: Moderate; rolling hills

Trail surface: Forested and shoreline trail

Best season(s): Fall

Other trail users: Mountain bikes

Canine compatibility: Leashed dogs permitted

Land status: State park

Fees and permits: None for day hiking

Schedule: 8 a.m. to 6 p.m. Nov through Feb; 8 a.m. to 8 p.m. Mar, Apr, Sept, and Oct; 8 a.m. to 9 p.m. May through Aug. All trails close 30 minutes prior to park closing. Park and trail are closed on Christmas Day.

Maps: USGS Troutman; Lake Norman State Park map available at the park ranger station and at www.ncparks.gov/Visit/parks/lano/main.php

Trail contacts: Lake Norman State Park, 159 Inland Sea Lane, Troutman 28166; (704) 528-6350; www.ncparks.gov

Special considerations: The Itusi Trail is closed to all users when it is excessively wet, hazardous conditions exist, or if major maintenance needs to be completed. To check the trail status before traveling to the park, users should visit www.tarheeltrailblazers.com or call the park office. The Itusi Trail is primarily a mountain bike trail, so hikers and runners must travel in the opposite direction of the bikes, and they must also yield to bikers.

Finding the trailhead: From Charlotte take I-77 North to exit 42. Turn left (west) off the interstate and travel US 21 to Troutman. When you arrive at downtown Troutman, take a left (south) onto Wagner Street. Follow Wagner Street (which changes to Perth Road at the town limits) for 1.6 miles and then veer right (west) onto State Park Road. Follow State Park Road for 3.6 miles to reach Lake Norman State Park. After you enter the park, continue on State Park Road across a bridge and then turn left (west) into your first parking lot. The Laurel Loop trailhead is located near the parking lot entrance next to the Alder trailhead. GPS: N35 40.369'/W80 55.929'

THE HIKE

One of the many highlights of writing a hiking guidebook is being able to introduce a new hike to the public. If you have already heard of the Laurel Trail Lake in Norman State Park, you are doing a great job of staying current on regional trail news. If not, then join the rest of the community in checking out this terrific new route.

Part of the Itusi trail network at Lake Norman State Park, the Laurel Loop opened in 2010. Currently the route covers 4.7 miles of trail, but there are plans to extend the trail in the future to a projected distance of 8.0 miles. A large portion of the existing trail was constructed by mountain-biking clubs in the community, including the Tarheel Trailblazers and Dirt Divas. But like the rest of the Itusi Trail, this loop is for the use of both cyclists and pedestrians. And the terrific signs and trail regulations help every user enjoy their time on the path, regardless of how they decide to travel the terrain.

To begin the hike, start in the main Itusi parking lot and locate the Alder trailhead at the south end of the parking lot. The Laurel Loop starts just to the left of the Alder Trail, near the main park road. The first 0.25 mile of the route has traffic flowing in both directions. During this first stretch you should be attentive for hikers and mountain bikers coming in either direction.

Follow the path into the woods and gently downhill. You will soon arrive at Hicks Creek. Follow the wide channel of flowing water upstream to access the main park road. Cross Hicks Creek on the paved road. Then, on the other side of the bridge, look for the trail to continue on your right. Once you reenter the forest, the trail will split. Hikers will want to veer left and travel the trail clockwise. (**Note:** The park annually reverses the travel direction for bikers and hikers on January 1, so if the pedestrian signs dictate that you should hike counterclockwise, then do so! Unfortunately this means you will have to start at the end of the hike description and Miles and Directions section and work your way backwards.)

The first section across Hicks Creek travels slightly uphill through a forest of maple, oak, beech, and pine trees. You will notice that the trail offers lots of sharp turns and quick changes in direction. At times it almost feels as if the trail is traveling on a set of switchbacks built on level terrain. All these changes in direction add difficulty to the trail for the mountain bikers, and it also lengthens the overall distance of the hike, while staying in a relatively confined space.

After hiking 1.0 mile the trail exits the forest at a power-line corridor. Here the route turns right and travels south through the exposed strip of land. Helpful trail signs keep you aware of how far you have traveled on the Laurel Loop and also point you back into the woods after briefly hiking parallel to the power lines.

Back inside the confines of the forest, you may be able to spot several wildflowers bordering the trail, including butterfly weed and bluestar plants. A wildflower identification book is a helpful tool to carry on this hike or any other. However, such a resource can often turn a short hike into a day spent in the field.

A view of Hicks Creek from the Laurel loop at Lake Norman State Park.

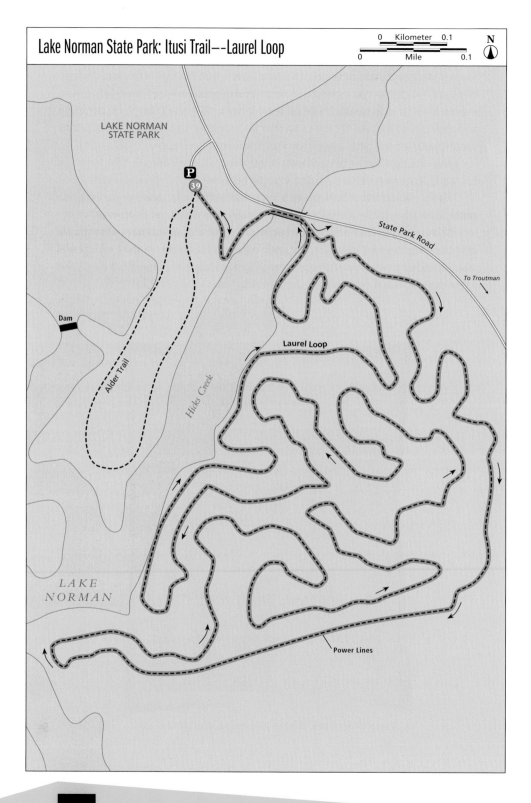

Lake Norman State Park: Itusi Trail--Laurel Loop

0   Kilometer   0.1
0   Mile   0.1

N

LAKE NORMAN
STATE PARK

P
39

State Park Road

To Troutman

Dam

Alder Trail

Hicks Creek

Laurel Loop

LAKE
NORMAN

Power Lines

Beyond the intricate beauty of nature that borders the trail, you will notice well-thought-out and -constructed attractions on the trail as well. Many of the ramps and rockwork found on the trail are designed to add technical obstacles for mountain bikers, but it keeps the trail interesting for hikers as well. At one point the trail even goes through a tree with two trunks that diverge near the ground. If you are interested in helping construct or maintain trails, ask at local parks how you can volunteer. Or get in touch with your local outdoor store or hiking club to see if you can participate in an upcoming trail crew activity.

As the Laurel Loop gently winds downhill, you will be able to glance intermittent views of the water to the south. Although the trail never provides unobstructed views of Hicks Creek, it does pass over several small tributaries that trickle into the much larger body of water. Toward the end of the hike, you will parallel the shoreline of the creek before completing the loop portion of the trail. At this point turn left and hike south on the main park road across the nearby bridge. Past the bridge the path delves back into the forest on your left, and you will be able to retrace your steps uphill to the nearby Itusi parking lot and trailhead.

MILES AND DIRECTIONS

0.0 Start at the Laurel Loop trailhead just to the east of the Alder Trail. Follow the path into the woods and gently downhill to the banks of Hicks Creek.

0.3 The trail exits the forest at the main park road. Turn right (south) and follow the paved road across a bridge.

0.4 Just past the bridge the trail resumes on your right and immediately splits in two. Veer left to travel the path in a clockwise direction. (**Note:** The park changes the direction for hikers and bikers each year. So you may need to hike this trail in reverse depending on the directional signs.)

1.0 The route leaves the forest and travels south, next to a long strip of power lines.

1.4 The trail reenters the forest and continues to travel a route filled with copious twists and turns.

3.5 Glimpses of Hicks Creek are available through the trees.

4.3 Conclude the loop portion of the hike and turn south to join the main park road and cross over the bridge once again.

4.4 Turn left past the bridge and follow the Laurel Trail uphill to the nearby parking lot.

4.7 Conclude your hike at the Itusi parking lot.

Local information: Lake Norman Tourism Information: Visit Lake Norman, 199900 W. Catawba Ave., Suite 102, Cornelius 28031; (704) 987-3300; www .visitlakenorman.org

Local events/attractions: Iredell Museum of Arts, 134 Court St., Statesville 28677; (704) 873-4734; www.iredellmuseums.org

Preservation Statesville, 643 Walnut St., Statesville 28677; (704) 450-9828; www.preservationstatesville.org

Good eats: Kat's Patch, 629 N. Main St., Troutman 28166; (704) 528-6669; www .katspatch.com. They have barbecue and burgers to satisfy any appetite.

Organizations: Lake Norman Ski Club, 643 Williamson Rd., Mooresville 28117; www.lakenormanskiclub.8m.com. Enjoy the lake on land and on the water!

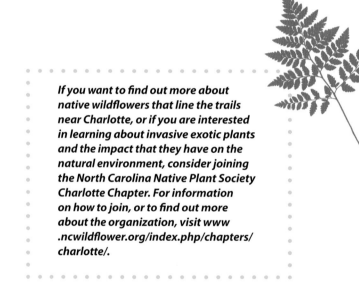

If you want to find out more about native wildflowers that line the trails near Charlotte, or if you are interested in learning about invasive exotic plants and the impact that they have on the natural environment, consider joining the North Carolina Native Plant Society Charlotte Chapter. For information on how to join, or to find out more about the organization, visit www .ncwildflower.org/index.php/chapters/ charlotte/.

🌿 Green Tip:
If you're toting food, leave the packaging at home. Repack your provisions in ziplock bags that you can reuse and that can double as garbage bags on the way out of the woods.

This route explores some of the most popular mountain biking/hiking trails at Lake Norman State Park. But don't worry! Hikers are welcome, and a very well-regulated trail system helps everyone to enjoy the trail equally. The Itusi Trail is moderately graded and offers pleasant hiking and varied scenery. This route travels into the forest on the Hawk Loop and then veers west to explore the Norwood Creek Loop. From there the trail cuts inland and travels around the outskirts of the Hawk Loop. The hike concludes by offering an optional 1.0-mile excursion to the northeast boundary of the park on the Hicks Creek Loop. This last portion of the hike also reveals glimpses of Lake Norman and the wetlands surrounding the nearby Hicks Creek. To conclude the hike, the trail returns to the Hawk Loop and travels through a predominantly hardwood forest back across the state park road to complete the loop at the Itusi trailhead. This hike has many shorter options for those unwilling to hike the entire 6.6-mile circuit.

Start: Lake Norman State Park Lakeshore trailhead
Distance: 6.6-mile loop
Hiking time: About 3 to 4 hours
Difficulty: Moderate; rolling hills
Trail surface: Forested and shoreline trail
Best season(s): Year-round
Other trail users: Mountain bikes
Canine compatibility: Leashed dogs permitted
Land status: State park
Fees and permits: No fees or permits required for day hiking
Schedule: 8 a.m. to 6 p.m. Nov through Feb; 8 a.m. to 8 p.m. Mar, Apr, Sept, and Oct; 8 a.m. to 9 p.m. May through Aug. All trails close 30 minutes prior to park closing. Park and trails are closed Christmas Day.

Maps: USGS Troutman; Lake Norman State Park map available at the park ranger station and at www.ncparks.gov/Visit/parks/lano/main.php
Trail contacts: Lake Norman State Park, 159 Inland Sea Lane, Troutman 28166; (704) 528-6350; www.ncparks.gov
Special considerations: The Itusi Trail is closed to all users when it is excessively wet, hazardous conditions exist, or if major maintenance needs to be completed. To check the trail status before traveling to the park, users should visit www.tarheeltrailblazers.com or call the park office.

THE HIKE

As hikers, we are sometimes hesitant to share the trail with mountain bikers, especially when it means never knowing who is going to whiz around a turn and run you over. And it is especially aggravating to have to constantly step off the path for bikers, when the rule of the trail gives hikers the right of way. However, Lake Norman State Park does an amazing job of regulating multiuse trails. It is one place where hikers and bikers travel harmoniously through the woods.

Hikers have to let go of their egos a little bit, as the Itusi trails specify that pedestrians must yield to cyclists. But let's be honest: Stepping to the side of the trail for two seconds every now and then isn't the end of the world—and it is a lot less tense than the usual on-trail game of chicken. Plus, in return for this unselfish act, the bikers typically slow down and offer their thanks.

Furthermore, Lake Norman State Park requires that hikers and bikers travel in opposite directions—so simple, but so brilliant! This way, you never have to worry about bikes racing up behind you and scaring you half to death. Trail runners? Yes. Bikers? No!

And in case you ever get turned around or confused, there are helpful trail markers every 0.5 mile that remind hikers and bikers how far they have come and in which direction they need to go. And if you need any more incentive to like the bikers at Lake Norman State Park, then consider that it was the Charlotte-area mountain-bike clubs that helped design and develop the Itusi Trail network.

Itusi means *hawk* in the Catawba language. It is only appropriate that Lake Norman State Park title their largest trail with a Catawba name. The Catawba, which translates to *river people,* were the primary residents of this area until diseases brought to America by the European settlers decimated them. When Lake Norman was formed, it flooded a large area of land that was once home to the Catawba people.

The Itusi Trail encompasses all multiuse trails at Lake Norman State Park. In total more than 18 miles are already included in the network, with plans to expand in the future. This route follows three of the main loops within that system. The hike starts at the north end of the Itusi Trail parking area. Every other year hikers will travel this loop clockwise, and that means veering left at the trailhead information board. (**Note:** The park annually reverses the travel direction for bikers and hikers on January 1, so if the pedestrian signs dictate that you should hike counterclockwise, do so! Unfortunately this means you will have to start at the end of the hike description and Miles and Directions section and work your way backward.)

The hike follows a well-defined path through a mixed forest of tall hardwoods and coniferous pine trees. After hiking nearly 0.75 mile, the path arrives at a trail junction. Turn left to explore the Norwood Creek Loop. This path starts by crossing a small stream on a wooden bridge and then continues to travel clockwise along the banks of Norwood Creek. This corridor beside the water is a good place to keep an eye out for lizards and frogs that prefer the waterfront property. When the path leaves the creek side, it travels gently uphill and through a forest dotted with sourwood, sycamore, and cedar trees.

The Itusi Trails are well marked in both directions for hikers and mountain bikers.

Lake Norman State Park: Itusi Trail—Hawk Loop, Norwood Creek Loop, and Hicks Creek Loop

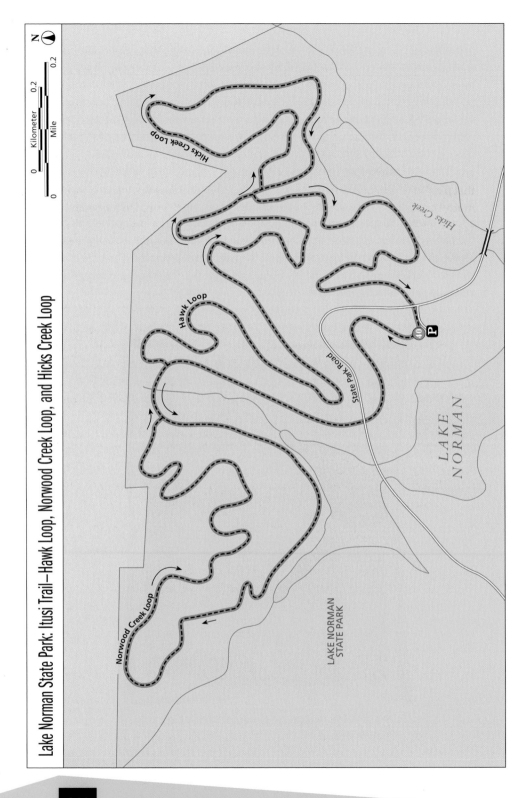

When you conclude the Norwood Creek Loop, backtrack to the main path and turn left on the primary Hawk Loop. The Hawk Loop is a great place to look for soaring birds, particularly when you come out of the forest at a power-line field, where you may be able to spot a turkey vulture overhead. Depending on how you feel at this point, hopefully he isn't directly overhead.

Continue on the Hawk Loop until you reach a junction with the Hicks Creek Loop. Leave the main trail and follow the Hicks Creek Loop inland and uphill, before tracing it gently down to the north shore of Hicks Creek. There is a small stream that parallels the trail back to the Hawk Loop, but don't confuse this with the much, much larger Hicks Creek, which is slightly visible through the trees to the south.

When you return to the Hawk Loop, continue to follow the winding path through the woods. The trail will briefly parallel the park road before crossing the paved street and leading you back to the Itusi trailhead.

MILES AND DIRECTIONS

0.0   Locate the Itusi trailhead at the northwest corner of the parking lot. Find the directional signs and follow the hiker symbol into the woods. (**Note:** The park changes the direction for hikers and bikers each year. So you may need to hike this trail in reverse depending on the directional signs. For the purpose of this guidebook, the Miles and Directions follow a clockwise direction.)

0.7   The Hawk Loop arrives at a junction with the Norwood Creek Loop. Turn left (west) to follow the Norwood Creek Trail.

0.8   Travel over a wooden bridge and up a small hill to where the Norwood Creek Trail splits. Turn left (south) to travel the loop in a clockwise direction.

3.0   Complete the Norwood Creek Loop and turn left (east) to return to the Hawk Loop.

4.8   The trail comes to an intersection with the Hicks Creek Loop. Turn left (east) and continue to veer left to travel the trail in a—you guessed it—clockwise direction.

5.8   At the conclusion of the Hicks Creek Loop, turn left (south) to continue on the Hawk Trail.

6.5   Be careful as you cross the main park road.

6.6   Conclude your hike at the Itusi trailhead and primary hiking/biking parking lot.

HIKE INFORMATION

Local information: Lake Norman Tourism Information: Visit Lake Norman, 199900 W. Catawba Ave., Suite 102, Cornelius 28031; (704) 987-3300; www .visitlakenorman.org

Local events/attractions: Iredell Museum of Arts, 134 Court St., Statesville 28677; (704) 873-4734; www.iredellmuseums.org

Preservation Statesville, 643 Walnut St., Statesville 28677; (704) 450-9828; www.preservationstatesville.org

Good eats: Red Light Café, 104 N. Main St., Troutman 28166; (704) 528-5000. A great place to stop and eat breakfast before your hike.

Organizations: Lake Norman Yacht Club, 297 Yacht Rd., Mooresville 28117; (866) 457-2582; www.lakenormanyachtclub.com. I don't have a yacht or sailboat, but maybe you do!

> *Want to get involved in building trails like you see in the Itusi network? Check with a local outfitter or at your local park to find out how you can help.*

Fungus grows on a fallen log near the trail.

Clubs and Trail Groups

Organized group hikes in the Charlotte region are provided by Charlotte Outdoor Adventures (CHOA) and the Carolina Berg Wanderers. Both clubs require membership and club fees.

Charlotte Outdoor Adventures, PO Box 10293, Charlotte 28212; (704) 906-5479; www.choa.com
Carolina Berg Wanderers, www.carolinabergs.com, bergpres@gmail.com

---

HELP US KEEP THIS GUIDE UP TO DATE

Every effort has been made by the author and editors to make this guide as accurate and useful as possible. However, many things can change after a guide is published—trails are rerouted, regulations change, techniques evolve, facilities come under new management, and so on.

We would appreciate hearing from you concerning your experiences with this guide and how you feel it could be improved and kept up to date. While we may not be able to respond to all comments and suggestions, we'll take them to heart, and we'll also make certain to share them with the author. Please send your comments and suggestions to the following address:

GPP
Reader Response/Editorial Department
PO Box 480
Guilford, CT 06437

Or you may e-mail us at: editorial@globepequot.com

Thanks for your input, and happy trails!

Hike Index

About the Author

Jennifer Pharr Davis grew up in the North Carolina mountains, where she developed a love for hiking at a young age. When she was twenty-one, Jennifer hiked the entire Appalachian Trail as a solo female, and as a result she fell in love with long-distance backpacking. Since then Jennifer has hiked more than 9,000 miles of trails in North America including the Pacific Crest Trail, Vermont's Long Trail, and two through-hikes on the Appalachian Trail. She has hiked and traveled on six continents, with some of the highlights including Mount Kilimanjaro, the Inca Trail to Machu Picchu, and the 600-mile Bibbulmun Track in Australia. At press time Jennifer holds endurance records on three long-distance trails, and in 2011 she grabbed the speed record for the Appalachian Trail, hiking the full 2,181 miles in 46.5 days while averaging 47 miles a day. Jennifer resides in Asheville, North Carolina, with her husband, Brew Davis, and is the owner and founder of Blue Ridge Hiking Co.

American Hiking Society

Because you
hike.
We're with you
every step of the way

As a national voice for hikers, **American Hiking Society** works every day:

- Building and maintaining hiking trails
- Educating and supporting hikers by providing information and resources
- Supporting hiking and trail organizations nationwide
- Speaking for hikers in the halls of Congress and with federal land managers

Whether you're a casual hiker or a seasoned backpacker, become a member of American Hiking Society and join the national hiking community! You'll enjoy great member benefits and help preserve the nation's hiking trails, so tomorrow's hike is even better than today's. We invite you to join us now!

**American
Hiking
Society**